D1707319

New Trends in Macroeconomics

Claude Diebolt
Catherine Kyrtsou
Editors
in collaboration with Olivier Darné

New Trends
in Macroeconomics

With 44 Figures
and 38 Tables

 Springer

Dr. Claude Diebolt
Directeur de Recherche au CNRS
University of Strasbourg I
BETA/CNRS, Faculty of Economics
61 Avenue de la Forêt Noire
67085 Strasbourg Cedex
France
E-mail: cdiebolt@cournot.u-strasbg.fr

Dr. Catherine Kyrtsou
University of Macedonia
Department of Economics
Egnatia Street 156
54006 Thessaloniki
Greece
E-mail: ckyrtsou@uom.gr

Cataloging-in-Publication Data
Library of Congress Control Number: 2005929196

ISBN-10 3-540-21448-8   Springer Berlin Heidelberg New York
ISBN-13 978-3-540-21448-9   Springer Berlin Heidelberg New York

Springer is a part of Springer Science+Business Media
springeronline.com

© Springer-Verlag Berlin Heidelberg 2005
Printed in Germany

Cover design: Erich Kirchner
Production: Helmut Petri
Printing: Strauss Offsetdruck

SPIN 11617327   Printed on acid-free paper – 43/3111 – 5 4 3 2 1

Acknowledgments

First of all, we want to acknowledge the contributions of the authors. Their support was invaluable.

Special thanks go to Olivier Darné who kept the manuscript on the rails. We thank him for his care and persistence.

We wish also to give thanks to Amélie Charles for helpful assistance.

At the Springer Verlag, Dr. Martina Bihn guided us skillfully through the dark, displaying insight into what the book should look like. We thank her, for her encouragement and constant support.

We are also grateful to Professor Theodore Palivos for his great interest in this work.

Finally, we would like to thank our families, whose support is so essential.

Preface

That macroeconomic theory and macroeconometrics are, in the near future and more than ever, indispensable tools in the study of economics is no longer a very controversial statement. It is now generally agreed that economic theory, combined with historical, statistical and mathematical methods are necessary at the theoretical level, to formulate problems precisely, to draw conclusions from postulates and to gain insight into workings of complicated processes, and at the applied level, to measure variables, to estimate parameters and to organise the elaborate calculations involved in reaching empirical results. This book is an illustration of the Editors belief in this principle. It offers new insights in macroeconomic analysis. It deals with both theory and empirical results related to the dynamics within the structure of macroeconomic variables as well as between them. More precisely five axes are distinguished. There are theoretical and applied works with developments on (1) mechanisms of economic dynamics, (2) structures of macroeconomic variables, and (3) relationships between macroeconomic time series. The book also presents methodologies where (4) linear testing is improved and (5) new non-linear techniques are applied.
Turning to the individual contributions now.

Bénassy's chapter studies the propagation of macroeconomic shocks using a dynamic model with wage and price staggering. He finds evidence in favour of a persistent response of both output and inflation to monetary shocks.

Karagiannis, Palivos and Papageorgiou present an one-sector growth model where the technology is described by a Variable Elasticity of Substitution production function. It is shown that this model can exhibit unbounded endogenous growth despite the absence of exogenous technical change and the presence of non-reproducible factors, such as labour.

Stengos and Liang study the effect of financial development on growth using an additive Instrumental Variable-augmented Partially Linear Regression model. They conclude that financial development affects growth in a positive but non-linear way employing a Liquid Liabilities index and in an almost linear way when a Private Credit index is taken into account. Nevertheless, the effect becomes ambiguous in the case of a Commercial Central Bank index.

The transition from theoretical evidence to empirical testing is well done by Hendry. Hendry's chapter is focused in the gap that exists between macroeconomic theory models and applied econometric findings. He describes some of the sources of these gaps and suggests possible solutions.

In the Gogas and Serletis chapter the revenue-smoothing hypothesis is tested using annual data for the US over the period form 1934-1994. Although Mankiw (1987) and Poterba and Rotemberg (1990) works found evidence supporting the previous hypothesis in the US, the obtained results by Gogas and Serletis do not support the theory of optimal seigniorage.

The performance of structural VAR models to capture structures produced by two stochastic dynamic general equilibrium models is the main point of study in the Canova and Pires Pina's chapter. More specifically, their criticism is to a particular type of identification restrictions routinely used in applied work. To avoid eventual biases they propose an alternative identification technique.

Paya and Peel examine the Keynes-Einzig conjecture by using monthly data for six currencies against the US Dollar for the period 1921-1936. Empirical findings suggest that excess returns are predictable, and that deviations form covered interest parity (CIP) are large and systematic. Evidence of non-linear adjustment of CIP is also provided.

In a fractional cointegration framework given in Davidson's chapter, it is investigated the relationship between government popularity and economic performance in the UK. The tests reveal little or no evidence of a link between the political and economic cycles. This conclusion reinforces the idea that political cycles are generated by the internal dynamics of the opinion formation process.

As it has been underlined by Hendry, the gap between macroeconomic theory models and applied econometric findings arises because much of the observed macroeconomic data variability is due to various non-stationarities. These sources of non-stationarity, deriving from the technical progress, new legislation, institutional change, financial innovation and political factors, induce both evolution and structural breaks which change the distributional properties of the data.

Darné and Diebolt, in their chapter, propose a more technical approach to deal with non-stationarity in macroeconomic series. They give a selective survey on different non-stationarity tests and discuss some problems with these tests and some solutions and alternatives that have been suggested. They also present the relation between non-stationarity and some economic theory.

The importance of seasonality and non-stationarity for the forecasting accuracy is emerged in the Kouassi and Labys's chapter. This is illustrated in the context of structural time series models. The major result of their work is that the recognition of the presence of seasonal unit-roots can have important implications for forecasting and modelling.

The Kyrtsou and Volrow's chapter concludes this collective volume. The authors suggest the use of a new methodology, well known in physical sciences, for the identification of complex underlying dynamics in economic series. This method is the Recurrence Quantification Analysis. The empirical results of the chapter provide evidence for the existence of highly complex deterministic dynamics in the US macroeconomic and financial series. The possibility to obtain such features in real economic series, that we would not be able to find using only traditional linear techniques, makes the new world of non-linear complex dynamics very attractive. Further research on the impact of the application of these new tools to macroeconomic data is certainly needed.

From the mechanisms of propagation of macroeconomic shocks to growth and monetary theories, macroeconometrics and complex dynamics, we hope to provide a complete overview on the recent developments and "New Trends in Macroeconomics". It is now time to let the authors speak for themselves!

Strasbourg, France   *Claude Diebolt*
April 2005   *Catherine Kyrtsou*

Contents

List of Contributors

Jean-Pascal Bénassy
CEPREMAP-ENS, 48 Boulevard
Jourdan, 75014 Paris, France.
jean-pascal.benassy@cepremap.
cnrs.fr

Fabio Canova
IGIER-Universitá Bocconi, via
Salasco 5, 20136 Milano, Italia.
fabio.canova@uni-bocconi.it

James Davidson
University of Exeter, School of Business
and Economics, Streatham Court,
Rennes Drive, Exeter EX4 4PU, UK.
james.davidson@exeter.ac.uk

Olivier Darné
CERESUR, University of La Réunion,
Faculty of Law and Economics, 15
Avenue René Cassin, BP 7151, 97715
Saint Denis Mess cedex 9, France.
olivier.darne@univ-reunion.fr

Claude Diebolt
BETA-CNRS, University Louis Pasteur
of Strasbourg, Faculty of Economics
and Management, 61 avenue de la Forêt
Noire, 67085 Strasbourg Cedex, France.
cdiebolt@cournot.u-strasbg.fr

Periklis Gogas
Department of Economics, University
of Abertay-Dundee, North College
Campus and A. Michailides S.A.,
Agricultural Industries, Thessaloniki,
56430, Greece.
perrygogas@usa.net

David F. Hendry
Economics Department, Oxford
University, Manor Road Building,
Manor Road, Oxford, OX1 3UQ, UK.
david.hendry@nuffield.ox.ac.uk

Giannis Karagiannis
University of Macedonia, Department
of International & European Economic
& Political Studies, 156 Egnatia Street,
GR-540 06 Thessaloniki, Greece.
karagian@uom.gr

Eugene Kouassi
University of Abidjan - Cocody,
Department of Economics, P.O. Box V,
Abidjan 43, Ivory Coast.
Eugene_kouassi@hotmail.com

Catherine Kyrtsou
University of Macedonia, Department
of Economics Egnatia str., 156 54006,
Thessaloniki, Greece.
ckyrtsou@uom.gr

Walter C. Labys
West Virginia University, Regional
Research Institute, Natural Resource
Economics Program, 2034 Agricultural
Sciences Building, PO Box 6108,
Morgantown, WV. 26506-6108.
wlabys@wvu.edu

Zhihong Liang
Department of Economics, University
of Guelph, Guelph, Ontario N1G 2W1,
Canada.
zliang@uoguelph.ca

Theodore Palivos
University of Macedonia, Department of
Economics, 156 Egnatia Street, GR-540
06 Thessaloniki, Greece.
tpalivos@uom.gr

Chris Papageorgiou
Louisiana State University, Department
of Economics, Baton Rouge, LA 70803,
USA.
cpapa@lsu.edu

Ivan Paya
University of Alicante, Departamento
Fundamentos Analisis Economico,
E-03080 Alicante, Spain.
ivanpaya@merlin.fae.ua.es

David A. Peel
Lancaster University, Management
School, Lancaster LA1 4YX, UK.
d.peel@lancaster.ac.uk

Joaquim Pires Pina
University Nova of Lisbon, Faculty of
Economics, Campus de Campolide,
1099-032 Lisboa, Portugal.
jagl@fct.unl.pt

Apostolos Serletis
University of Calgary, Department of
Economics, Calgary, Alberta, T2N 1N4,
Canada.
serletis@ucalgary.ca

Thanasis Stengos
Department of Economics, University
of Guelph, Guelph, Ontario N1G 2W1,
Canada.
tstengos@uoguelph.ca

Costas E. Vorlow
Durham Business School, University of
Durham, Mill Hill Lane, Durham DH1
3LB, UK.
K.E.Vorloou@durham.ac.uk

The Propagation of Macroeconomic Shocks: A Dynamic Model with Contracts and Imperfect Competition

Jean-Pascal Bénassy

CNRS and CEPREMAP-ENS, 48 Boulevard Jourdan, 75014 Paris, France.
jean-pascal.benassy@cepremap.cnrs.fr

Summary. In order to study rigorously the propagation of macroeconomic shocks, we construct a dynamic model with wage and price staggering, where wage and price contracts are set by fully maximizing agents in a framework of imperfect competition. We derive the optimal values for wage and price contracts and compute closed form solutions to the resulting dynamics. We show that wage and price contracts of reasonable durations can create persistence and a hump in the response of both output and inflation to monetary shocks.

Key words: Persistence, Staggered wages, Staggered prices, Imperfect competition.

JEL codes: E32, E52

1 Introduction

The purpose of this article is to construct a dynamic general equilibrium model including staggered wage and price contracts, as well as imperfect competition. We will study with it the issue of the propagation of macroeconomic shocks, and notably whether one can obtain a response to monetary shocks similar to that observed in reality. On the empirical side, a number of recent studies have shown that both output and inflation display a persistent response to monetary shocks. Moreover this response seems to be humpshaped, first increasing, then decreasing (see, for example, Cogley and Nason [9]; Christiano, Eichenbaum and Evans [8]). On the other hand RBC type models have often had problems creating such a response to monetary shocks. Recently wage and price contracts[1] have been introduced in that line of models, in order notably to make the corresponding economies more responsive to monetary shocks, and a debate has developed as to whether such modeling would allow to obtain a persistent and hump shaped response to these shocks. Surprisingly

---

[1] In line with the initial works by Gray [12], Fischer [11], Phelps and Taylor [16], Phelps [15], Taylor [17, 18] and Calvo [6].

the answers are widely divergent. For example, Chari, Kehoe and McGrattan [5] conclude that there will be no persistence with reasonable values of the parameters, while Collard and Ertz [10] obtain a hump-shaped and persistent response with one or two years wage contracts[2]. The objective of this article is to investigate the matter analytically, which seems particularly useful in view of the conflicting answers indicated above. For that purpose we shall build a rigorous dynamic stochastic general equilibrium model with *both* price and wage contracts[3], solve it analytically and express the dynamics of output and inflation as a function of the fundamental underlying parameters. The reason why we study wage and price contracts together, and not in isolation, is that this appears to be instrumental in obtaining a hump-shaped response in both output and inflation, as we shall see below. We shall see that a persistent and humpshaped response of both output and inflation to monetary shocks can be obtained with reasonable parameters.

2 The Model

2.1 Markets and Agents

The economy studied is a monetary economy with markets for goods, at the (average) price P_t and markets for labor, at the (average) wage W_t. The goods and labor markets function under a system of imperfectly competitive labor contracts, which will be detailed below. There are firms and households. Let us begin with the production side. The output index Y_t is an aggregate of a continuum of output types, indexed by $i \in [0,1]$:

$$LogY_t = \int_0^1 LogY_{it} di \tag{1}$$

Each index Y_{it} is itself the aggregate of another infinity of output types indexed by k:

$$Y_{it} = \left(\int_0^1 Y_{ikt}^\theta dk \right)^{1/\theta} \tag{2}$$

One should think of the index i as representing sectors, while the index k refers to firms in these sectors. Quite naturally the substitutability is higher within sectors than across sectors. The representative firm has a Cobb-Douglas technology[4]:

$$Y_{ikt} = Z_t N_{ikt}^\alpha \tag{3}$$

---

[2]Other contributions along the same lines are found, for example, in Ambler, Guay and Phaneuf [1], Andersen [2], Ascari [3], Jeanne [13] and Yun [19].

[3]Microfounded dynamic models with one rigidity and analytical solutions are found in Jeanne [13] for price contracts, and in Ascari [3] and Bénassy [4, 5] for wage contracts. Andersen [2] compares the two types of contracts.

[4]Although capital could be introduced explicitly (cf. for example Bénassy [4]), we omit it here because it complicates substantially the exposition, and does not add much to the dynamics because of the low actual depreciation rate.

The representative household (we omit the index k at this stage, since the situation of all households in a sector i is fully symmetrical) works N_{it}, consumes C_{it} and ends the period with a quantity of money M_{it}. He maximizes the expected value of his discounted utility, with the following intertemporal utility:

$$U = \sum_t \beta^t \left[LogC_{it} + \omega Log \frac{M_{it}}{P_t} - V(N_{it}) \right] \tag{4}$$

where V is a convex function. At the beginning of period t there is a stochastic multiplicative monetary shock as in Lucas (1972): money holdings carried from the previous period M_{it-1} are multiplied by the same factor μ_t for all agents, so that the representative household starts period t with money holdings $\mu_t M_{it-1}$. His budget constraint in t is thus:

$$C_{it} + \frac{M_{it}}{P_t} = \frac{W_{it}}{P_t} N_{it} + \frac{\mu_t M_{it-1}}{P_t} + \Pi_{it} \tag{5}$$

where Π_{it} is the profits in sector i, which are distributed to the households who work in this sector.

2.2 Wage and Price Contracts

We will now describe the wage and price contracts, which are taken from Bénassy [4, 5], themselves inspired by Calvo [6]. Consider first the wage contracts. As in Calvo [6], in each period there is a random draw for all wage contracts, after which any particular contract continues unchanged (with probability γ), or is terminated (with probability $1 - \gamma$). In this last case a new contract wage is decided in each firm by the households working in that firm, on the basis of all information currently available. In period s a wage contract is negotiated for each period $t \geq s$. This new contract is denoted X_{st}. The difference with Calvo [6] is that he assumed X_{st} to be the same for all $t \geq s$, whereas we assume that the X_{st} can be different whatever $t \geq s$. Price contracts are modelled in a similar manner. If wages are not renegotiated, then the price mechanism is completely symmetrical to the wage mechanism: price contracts continue with probability ϕ, and are terminated with probability $1 - \phi$. If, however, wages in one particular firm are renegotiated, then prices in this firm are also automatically renegotiated. These possibilities, and their probabilities, are summarized in Figure 1. The basic idea underlying this formalization is that, if a firm is faced with a change in its cost structure because of wage renegotiation, then it will always want to change its price, which seems a reasonable assumption. We thus see that, taking into account both possibilities, the probability for a price contract to continue unchanged is $\gamma\phi$, and the probability to be renegotiated $1 - \gamma\phi$. We denote by Q_{st} the price contract signed in period s to be in effect in period $t \geq s$.

Fig. 1

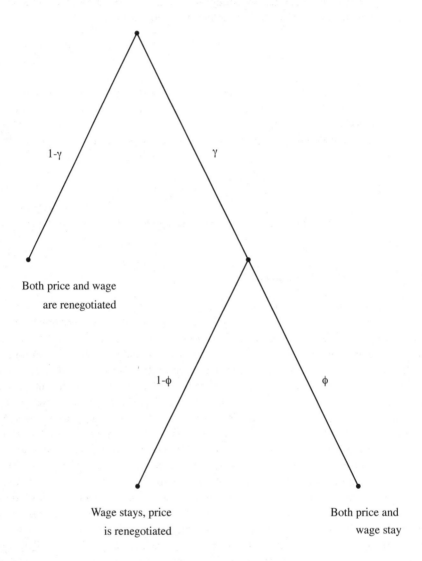

1-γ

γ

Both price and wage
are renegotiated

1-φ

φ

Wage stays, price
is renegotiated

Both price and
wage stay

We still have to specify more precisely how wage and price renegotiations are related across firms and sectors. We shall assume that all firms in the same sector *i* renegotiate their wages or prices at exactly the same time, which means that the random draws are actually organized sector by sector. These random draws are independent across sectors.

3 The Walrasian Regime

We shall now compute as a benchmark the Walrasian equilibrium of this economy. In that case there is a unique price P_t and wage W_t, which clear the goods and labor markets. The real wage is equal to the marginal productivity of labor:

$$\frac{W_t}{P_t} = \alpha \frac{Y_t}{N_t} \tag{6}$$

The households maximize the expected value of their utility (4) subject to the budget constraints (5). The Lagrangean of this maximization program is:

$$\sum \beta^t \left[LogC_t + \omega Log\frac{M_t}{P_t} - V(N_t) \right]$$

$$+ \sum \beta^t \lambda_t \left[\frac{W_t N_t}{P_t} + \frac{\mu_t M_{t-1}}{P_t} + \Pi_t - C_t - \frac{M_t}{P_t} \right] \tag{7}$$

and the first order conditions:

$$\lambda_t = \frac{1}{C_t} \tag{8}$$

$$\frac{\lambda_t}{P_t} = \frac{\omega}{M_t} + \beta E_t \left(\frac{\lambda_{t+1}\mu_{t+1}}{P_{t+1}} \right) \tag{9}$$

$$V'(N_t) = \frac{\lambda_t W_t}{P_t} \tag{10}$$

Using (8) and the fact that $\mu_{t+1} = M_{t+1}/M_t$, equation (9) is rewritten:

$$\frac{M_t}{P_t C_t} = \omega + \beta E_t \left(\frac{M_{t+1}}{P_{t+1}C_{t+1}} \right) \tag{11}$$

which solves as:

$$\frac{M_t}{P_t C_t} = \frac{\omega}{1-\beta} \tag{12}$$

Combining (6), (8) and (10), we see that Walrasian employment is constant and equal to N, given by:

$$NV'(N) = \alpha \tag{13}$$

In what follows we shall work with the following disutility for labor:

$$V(N_t) = \xi \frac{N_t^\nu}{\nu} \tag{14}$$

in which case equation (13) yields:

$$N = \left(\frac{\alpha}{\xi} \right)^{1/\nu} \tag{15}$$

and the Walrasian wage W_t^* and price P_t^* are equal to:

$$W_t^* = \frac{\alpha(1-\beta)}{\omega} \left(\frac{\xi}{\alpha}\right)^{1/\nu} M_t \tag{16}$$

$$P_t^* = \frac{1-\beta}{\omega} \left(\frac{\xi}{\alpha}\right)^{\alpha/\nu} \frac{M_t}{Z_t} \tag{17}$$

4 The Demand for Goods and Labor

We shall now study our model under wage and price contracts. It is assumed that households, possibly through trade-unions, decide on the level of wages, and supply the amount of labor demanded by firms at these wages. Similarly firms set prices and supply the amount of goods demanded. An important element for the determination of wage and price contracts is of course the demand for goods and labor, so we begin with that.

4.1 The Demand for Goods

At any time there may be a multiplicity of prices. This variety of prices can be due to two causes: first, there may be staggered prices, and thus there are different prices because price contracts have been signed at different points in time. Secondly, even if prices are fully flexible in each period, the workers in different firms may have different wage contracts, so that prices will differ even if all other economic conditions are the same. Consider first the firms producing final output. They competitively maximize profits, i.e. they solve the following program:

$$\text{Max } P_t Y_t - \int_0^1 P_{it} Y_{it} di \qquad \text{s.t.} \qquad \int_0^1 Log Y_{it} di = Log Y_t$$

whose solution is:

$$Y_{it} = \frac{P_t Y_t}{P_{it}} \tag{18}$$

$$Log P_t = \int_0^1 Log P_{it} di \tag{19}$$

Now firms in a sector i will similarly maximize profits, i.e. they solve:

$$\text{Max } P_{it} Y_{it} - \int_0^1 P_{ikt} Y_{ikt} dk \qquad \text{s.t.} \qquad \left(\int_0^1 Y_{ikt}^\theta dk\right)^{1/\theta} = Y_{it}$$

whose solution is:

$$Y_{ikt} = Y_{it} \left(\frac{P_{ikt}}{P_{it}}\right)^{-1/(1-\theta)} \tag{20}$$

$$P_{it} = \left(\int_0^1 P_{ikt}^{-\theta/(1-\theta)} dk \right)^{-(1-\theta)/\theta} \tag{21}$$

Putting together equations (18) and (20) we obtain the expression of the demand for goods:

$$Y_{ikt} = \frac{P_t Y_t}{P_{it}} \left(\frac{P_{ikt}}{P_{it}} \right)^{-1/(1-\theta)} \tag{22}$$

An important thing to remember for what follows is that, in view of equation (18), all sectors have exactly the same value of sales:

$$P_{it} Y_{it} = P_t Y_t \qquad \forall i \tag{23}$$

This will also imply that all households, whatever the sector they work in, have the same income, and consequently the same consumption and money holdings.

4.2 The Demand for Labor

Since firms supply the quantity of goods demanded (22), the demand for labor is simply obtained by combining (3) and (22), which yields:

$$N_{ikt} = \left(\frac{P_t Y_t}{Z_t P_{it}} \right)^{1/\alpha} \left(\frac{P_{ikt}}{P_{it}} \right)^{-1/\alpha(1-\theta)} \tag{24}$$

5 Price Contracts

We now turn to the derivation of optimal price contracts. They are characterized through the following proposition:

Proposition 1: *Assume that in period τ the wage in firm (i,k) is $W_{ik\tau}$. Then the price contract $Q_{ik\tau t}$ signed in period τ for a period $t \geq \tau$ is given by:*

$$\left(\frac{Q_{ik\tau t}}{Q_{i\tau t}} \right)^{(1-\alpha\theta)/\alpha(1-\theta)} = \frac{W_{ik\tau}}{\alpha\theta} \left(\frac{1-\beta}{\omega} \right)^{(1-\alpha)/\alpha} \left(\frac{1}{Q_{i\tau t}} \right)^{1/\alpha} \Omega_{\tau t} \tag{25}$$

with:

$$Q_{i\tau t} = \left(\int_0^1 Q_{ik\tau t}^{-\theta/(1-\theta)} dk \right)^{-(1-\theta)/\theta} \tag{26}$$

$$\Omega_{\tau t} = E_\tau \left[M_t^{(1-\alpha)/\alpha} Z_t^{-1/\alpha} \right] \tag{27}$$

Proof: Appendix 1.

Now we shall see below, within the proof of proposition 3 (Appendix 2), that all firms in the same sector i will actually have the same wage, and therefore, in view of (25), the same price. We shall now derive the value of this common price contract through the following proposition:

Proposition 2: *Assume that in period τ the common wage in sector i is $W_{i\tau}$. Then the price contracts $Q_{i\tau t}$ signed in period τ for period $t \geq \tau$ by all firms in sector i are given by:*

$$Q_{i\tau t}^{1/\alpha} = \frac{1}{\alpha\theta} \left(\frac{1-\beta}{\omega} \right)^{(1-\alpha)/\alpha} W_{i\tau} \Omega_{\tau t} \qquad (28)$$

where $\Omega_{\tau t}$ has been defined in formula (27).

Proof: Replace in formula (25) $W_{ik\tau}$ by $W_{i\tau}$ and $Q_{ik\tau t}$ by $Q_{i\tau t}$ \qquad\qquad Q.E.D.

6 Wage Contracts

We shall now compute the wage contracts signed in a period s for a period $t \geq s$. As will appear in the proof of proposition 3 (Appendix 2), these contracts will be the same for all firms and sectors, and we shall accordingly denote them as X_{st}. Before moving to a precise proposition, let us define some probabilities. If the wage contract X_{st} is still in effect at time t, it will be associated with prices which may have been set in any period τ, $s \leq \tau \leq t$. In view of the "survival rate" ϕ of price contracts, the probabilities $\pi_{\tau t}$ that the price was set in period τ are computed as:

$$\pi_{\tau t} = \phi^{t-s} \quad \tau = s \qquad \pi_{\tau t} = (1-\phi)\phi^{t-\tau} \quad s < \tau \leq t \qquad (29)$$

Proposition 3: *The wage contract X_{st} signed in s for period $t \geq s$ is given by:*

$$X_{st}^{\nu} = \frac{\xi}{\alpha^2\theta^2} \left[\frac{\alpha\theta(1-\beta)}{\omega} \right]^{\nu} \sum_{s \leq \tau \leq t} \pi_{\tau t} E_s \left[\left(\frac{M_t}{Z_t} \right)^{\nu/\alpha} \left(\frac{1}{\Omega_{\tau t}} \right)^{\nu} \right] \qquad (30)$$

where $\Omega_{\tau t}$ is given by equation (27) and the probabilities $\pi_{\tau t}$ by equation (29).

Proof: Appendix 2.

7 Macroeconomic Dynamics

We shall now compute the dynamics of the system under the following traditional processes for money and technology shocks[5]:

---

[5] Lowercase letters denote the logarithms of the corresponding uppercase letters.

$$m_t - m_{t-1} = \frac{u_t}{1 - \rho L} \tag{31}$$

$$z_t = \frac{\varepsilon_t}{1 - \varphi L} \tag{32}$$

7.1 The Dynamics of Output and Inflation

We shall first characterize the dynamic evolution of output and inflation through the following proposition:

Proposition 4: *Under the monetary and technology processes* (31) *and* (32) *the dynamic evolutions of output and inflation are given by:*

$$y_t = z_t - \frac{\gamma \phi \varepsilon_t}{1 - \gamma \phi \varphi L} + \frac{\alpha \gamma u_t}{(1 - \gamma L)(1 - \gamma \rho L)} + \frac{(1 - \alpha) \gamma \phi u_t}{(1 - \gamma \phi L)(1 - \gamma \phi \rho L)} \tag{33}$$

$$\pi_t = p_t - p_{t-1} = \frac{u_t}{1 - \rho L} - \frac{(1 - \gamma \phi)(1 - L)\varepsilon_t}{(1 - \varphi L)(1 - \gamma \phi \varphi L)}$$

$$- \frac{\alpha \gamma (1 - L) u_t}{(1 - \gamma L)(1 - \gamma \rho L)} - \frac{(1 - \alpha) \gamma \phi (1 - L) u_t}{(1 - \gamma \phi L)(1 - \gamma \phi \rho L)} \tag{34}$$

Proof: Appendix 3.

With an explicit expression for the dynamics of output and inflation, we can potentially compute any measure of persistence. With five autoregressive roots for output and seven for inflation (formulas 33 and 34), a numerical discussion would quickly become very clumsy, so we shall rather discuss the issue of whether the response of output and inflation to monetary shocks displays a hump, since this has been the object of controversy and is easily assessed from our formulas.

7.2 Output Dynamics and the Hump

Let us start with the output dynamics in response to a monetary shock, and see under which conditions we shall obtain a humpshaped response. From formula (33) the first period impact of a money shock on output is:

$$\alpha \gamma + (1 - \alpha) \gamma \phi \tag{35}$$

and the second period one:

$$\alpha \gamma (\gamma + \gamma \rho) + (1 - \alpha) \gamma \phi (\gamma \phi + \gamma \phi \rho) \tag{36}$$

So there is a hump if:

$$\alpha\gamma + (1-\alpha)\gamma\phi < \alpha\gamma^2(1+\rho) + (1-\alpha)\gamma^2\phi^2(1+\rho) \qquad (37)$$

which can be rewritten as:

$$\gamma(1+\rho) > \frac{\alpha + (1-\alpha)\phi}{\alpha + (1-\alpha)\phi^2} \qquad (38)$$

The corresponding region in (ϕ,γ) space is shown in Figure 2 as the set above the heavy line.

Fig. 2

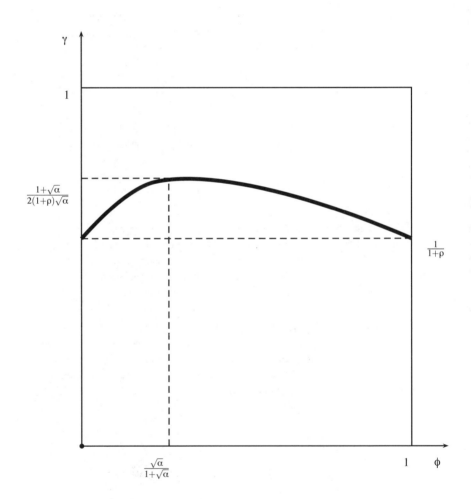

For given α the right hand side of formula (38) is maximal for $\phi = \sqrt{\alpha} / \left(1 + \sqrt{\alpha}\right)$ and then takes the value $\left(1 + \sqrt{\alpha}\right) / 2\sqrt{\alpha}$. This means that if:

$$\gamma > \frac{1 + \sqrt{\alpha}}{2 \left(1 + \rho\right) \sqrt{\alpha}} \tag{39}$$

then there will be a hump in output no matter what the degree of rigidity of prices. To get a numerical idea, we can consider the traditional values $\alpha = 2/3$, $\rho = 1/2$. Then we find that, if wage contracts are at least three quarters long on average, there will always be a hump in the response of output to monetary shocks.

7.3 Inflation Dynamics and the Hump

From formula (34) the first period impact on inflation is:

$$1 - \alpha\gamma - (1 - \alpha)\gamma\phi \tag{40}$$

and the second period one:

$$\rho - \alpha\gamma (\gamma + \gamma\rho - 1) - (1 - \alpha)\gamma\phi (\gamma\phi + \gamma\phi\rho - 1) \tag{41}$$

The condition for a hump in inflation is thus:

$$1 - \rho < \alpha\gamma (2 - \gamma - \gamma\rho) + (1 - \alpha)\gamma\phi (2 - \gamma\phi - \gamma\phi\rho) \tag{42}$$

The corresponding locus is represented in (ϕ, γ) space in Figure 3, together with the corresponding locus for the hump in output. The relevant region is to the right of the heavy line.

7.4 The Double Hump

The region with stripes in Figure 3 corresponds to the combinations of the (ϕ, γ) parameters such that the response of both output and inflation to monetary shocks displays a hump. To get a practical idea about this region, with the traditional values $\alpha = 2/3$, $\rho = 1/2$, if $\gamma > 3/4$ and $\phi > 1/3$, we will have a double hump. This corresponds to an average duration of contracts of 3 quarters for wages, and 1 month for prices, some very reasonable values indeed!

Fig. 3

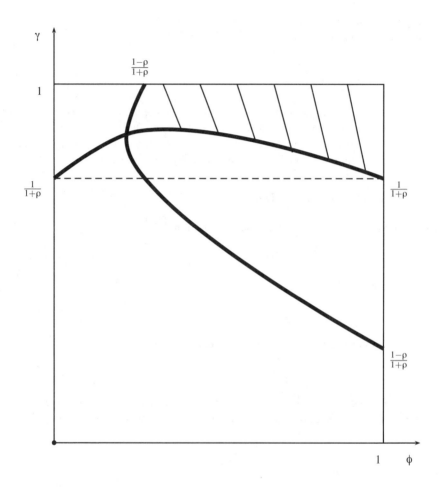

8 Conclusions

We constructed in this article a dynamic stochastic general equilibrium model where both wages and prices are staggered and set in a rigorous framework of monopolistic competition. We used a framework akin to that in Calvo (1983), so that the average duration of wage and price contracts can take any value between zero and infinity. We first derived the optimal prices and wages, then computed the resulting macroeconomic dynamics and obtained closed form solutions for the evolution of output and inflation. These formulas showed that it was possible to obtain a persistent response to monetary shocks. We investigated notably under which conditions a hump shaped response of output and inflation could be obtained, and we found that this would obtain for very reasonable durations.

Appendix 1

Proof of Proposition 1

Firm (i,k) maximizes its discounted expected real profits weighted by the marginal utility of goods (i.e. multiplied by $1/C_t$ since utility is logarithmic in consumption). We shall consider here only the terms corresponding to the price contracts signed at time τ and still in effect at time t. Since price contracts have a probability $\gamma\phi$ to survive each period, the contract signed in τ has a probability $\gamma^{t-\tau}\phi^{t-\tau}$ to be still in effect in period t, and the firm will thus maximize the following expected profit:

$$E_\tau \sum_{t=\tau}^{\infty} (\beta\gamma\phi)^{t-\tau} \frac{1}{P_t C_t} (P_{ikt} Y_{ikt} - W_{ik\tau} N_{ikt}) \tag{43}$$

subject to equation (22) giving the demand for goods :

$$Y_{ikt} = \frac{P_t Y_t}{P_{it}} \left(\frac{P_{ikt}}{P_{it}} \right)^{-1/(1-\theta)} \tag{44}$$

Note that in formula (43) we put $W_{ik\tau}$ as the relevant wage for all periods $t \geq \tau$. Indeed we consider only the price contracts that will still be in effect in period t. But, as we indicated above, if the wage changes, then the prices are automatically renegotiated, so that all price contracts that will remain must be based on the current wage $W_{ik\tau}$. Note also that, in the above formulas (43) and (44), we have to replace P_{ikt} by $Q_{ik\tau t}$ and P_{it} by $Q_{i\tau t}$ since these are the relevant prices for our maximization. Firms indexed by (i,k) maximize (43) subject to (44). Let us insert the value of Y_{ikt} (equation 44) into (43). Taking into account $Y_{ikt} = Z_t N_{ikt}^\alpha$, $C_t = Y_t$, $P_{ikt} = Q_{ik\tau t}$ and $P_{it} = Q_{i\tau t}$, the part of the maximand concerning $Q_{ik\tau t}$ is written, omitting irrelevant constant terms:

$$\left(\frac{Q_{ik\tau t}}{Q_{i\tau t}} \right)^{-\theta/(1-\theta)} - W_{ik\tau} \left(\frac{Q_{ik\tau t}}{Q_{i\tau t}} \right)^{-1/\alpha(1-\theta)} \left(\frac{1}{Q_{i\tau t}} \right)^{1/\alpha} E_\tau \left[\frac{1}{P_t Y_t} \left(\frac{P_t Y_t}{Z_t} \right)^{1/\alpha} \right] \tag{45}$$

The first order condition in $Q_{ik\tau t}$ is:

$$\left(\frac{Q_{ik\tau t}}{Q_{i\tau t}} \right)^{-1/(1-\theta)} = \frac{W_{ik\tau}}{\alpha\theta} \left(\frac{Q_{ik\tau t}}{Q_{i\tau t}} \right)^{-1/\alpha(1-\theta)-1} \left(\frac{1}{Q_{i\tau t}} \right)^{1/\alpha} E_\tau \left[\frac{1}{P_t Y_t} \left(\frac{P_t Y_t}{Z_t} \right)^{1/\alpha} \right] \tag{46}$$

In view of equation (12) this is rewritten:

$$\left(\frac{Q_{ik\tau t}}{Q_{i\tau t}}\right)^{(1-\alpha\theta)/\alpha(1-\theta)} = \frac{W_{ik\tau}}{\alpha\theta}\left(\frac{1-\beta}{\omega}\right)^{(1-\alpha)/\alpha}\left(\frac{1}{Q_{i\tau t}}\right)^{1/\alpha} E_\tau\left[\frac{1}{M_t}\left(\frac{M_t}{Z_t}\right)^{1/\alpha}\right]$$

(47)

which is equation (25).

Appendix 2

Proof of Proposition 3

Household (i,k) (i.e. a household working in firm k in sector i) maximizes his discounted expected utility. We will consider here only the terms corresponding to the wage contracts signed at time s and still in effect at time t, which we will denote as X_{ikst}. Since wage contracts have a probability γ to survive each period, the wage contract signed in s has a probability γ^{t-s} to be still in effect in period t, and the household (i,k) will thus maximize the following expected utility:

$$E_s \sum_{t \geq s} \beta^{t-s}\gamma^{t-s}\left[LogC_{ikt} + \omega Log\frac{M_{ikt}}{P_t} - \frac{\xi N_{ikt}^\nu}{\nu}\right]$$

(48)

subject to the budget constraints in each period:

$$C_{ikt} + \frac{M_{ikt}}{P_t} = \frac{X_{ikst}}{P_t}N_{ikt} + \frac{\mu_t M_{ikt-1}}{P_t} + \Pi_{it}$$

(49)

and the equations giving the demand for labor (24):

$$N_{ikt} = \left(\frac{P_t Y_t}{Z_t P_{it}}\right)^{1/\alpha}\left(\frac{P_{ikt}}{P_{it}}\right)^{-1/\alpha(1-\theta)}$$

(50)

We see that N_{ikt} depends on P_{ikt}, the price effective in period t , which itself depends on the period τ when it has been set. This period τ can be any period between s and t. So we index employment by τ as well, denoting it $N_{ik\tau t}$, and formula (50) is rewritten, for $s \leq \tau \leq t$:

$$N_{ik\tau t} = \left(\frac{P_t Y_t}{Z_t Q_{i\tau t}}\right)^{1/\alpha}\left(\frac{Q_{ik\tau t}}{Q_{i\tau t}}\right)^{-1/\alpha(1-\theta)}$$

(51)

Now the price $Q_{ik\tau t}$ set in period τ, $s \leq \tau \leq t$, is given by formula (25), where the relevant wage is X_{ikst}:

$$\left(\frac{Q_{ik\tau t}}{Q_{i\tau t}}\right)^{(1-\alpha\theta)/\alpha(1-\theta)} = \frac{X_{ikst}}{\alpha\theta}\left(\frac{1-\beta}{\omega}\right)^{(1-\alpha)/\alpha}\left(\frac{1}{Q_{i\tau t}}\right)^{1/\alpha}\Omega_{\tau t}$$

(52)

where $\Omega_{\tau t}$ is defined in equation (27). The employment corresponding to a price set in period τ is thus, combining equations (51) and (52):

$$N_{ik\tau t} = \left(\frac{P_t Y_t}{Z_t Q_{i\tau t}}\right)^{1/\alpha} \left[\frac{X_{ikst}}{\alpha\theta}\left(\frac{1-\beta}{\omega}\right)^{(1-\alpha)/\alpha}\left(\frac{1}{Q_{i\tau t}}\right)^{1/\alpha}\Omega_{\tau t}\right]^{-1/(1-\alpha\theta)} \tag{53}$$

So, to summarize, the household will maximize expected utility (48) subject to the budget constraints (49) and the fact that employment $N_{ik\tau t}$ is equal with probability $\pi_{\tau t}$ to the value in equation (53), where the probabilities $\pi_{\tau t}$ are given by formula (29) above. Inspecting this maximization problem we first see that all households with the same index i face exactly the same economic situation, so that in equilibrium:

$$X_{ikst} = X_{ist} \qquad \forall k \tag{54}$$

We have already seen that all households have the same income, and therefore the same consumption and money holdings:

$$C_{ikt} = C_t \qquad M_{ikt} = M_t \qquad \forall i,k \tag{55}$$

Households indexed by (i,k) maximize (48) subject to (49) and (53). Let us insert the value of $N_{ik\tau t}$ (equation 53), together with the relevant probabilities (29), into (48) and (49). Taking into account (55), the corresponding Lagrangean is written (we only keep the terms that we shall use):

$$E_s \sum_{s \leq \tau \leq t} \pi_{\tau t} \frac{\lambda_{ik\tau t}}{P_t} X_{ikst}^{-\alpha\theta/(1-\alpha\theta)} \left(\frac{P_t Y_t}{Z_t Q_{i\tau t}}\right)^{1/\alpha} \Phi_{i\tau t}^{1/(1-\alpha\theta)}$$

$$-E_s \sum_{s \leq \tau \leq t} \pi_{\tau t} \frac{\xi}{\nu} X_{ikst}^{-\nu/(1-\alpha\theta)} \left(\frac{P_t Y_t}{Z_t Q_{i\tau t}}\right)^{\nu/\alpha} \Phi_{i\tau t}^{\nu/(1-\alpha\theta)}$$

$$+E_s \sum_{s \leq \tau \leq t} \pi_{\tau t} \left(Log C_t - \lambda_{ik\tau t} C_t\right) \tag{56}$$

where:

$$\Phi_{i\tau t} = \alpha\theta \left(\frac{1-\beta}{\omega}\right)^{(\alpha-1)/\alpha} \frac{Q_{i\tau t}^{1/\alpha}}{\Omega_{\tau t}} \tag{57}$$

Maximization in C_t yields:

$$\lambda_{ik\tau t} = \frac{1}{C_t} \tag{58}$$

so that the term in X_{ikst} is:

$$X_{ikst}^{-\alpha\theta/(1-\alpha\theta)} E_s \sum_{s \leq \tau \leq t} \pi_{\tau t} \frac{1}{P_t C_t} \left(\frac{P_t Y_t}{Z_t Q_{i\tau t}}\right)^{1/\alpha} \Phi_{i\tau t}^{1/(1-\alpha\theta)}$$

$$-X_{ikst}^{-\nu/(1-\alpha\theta)} E_s \sum_{s \leq \tau \leq t} \pi_{\tau t} \frac{\xi}{\nu} \left(\frac{P_t Y_t}{Z_t Q_{i\tau t}}\right)^{\nu/\alpha} \Phi_{i\tau t}^{\nu/(1-\alpha\theta)} \tag{59}$$

The first order condition in X_{ikst} is:

$$\alpha\theta X_{ikst}^{-1/(1-\alpha\theta)} E_s \sum_{s\leq\tau\leq t} \pi_{\tau t} \frac{1}{P_t C_t} \left(\frac{P_t Y_t}{Z_t Q_{i\tau t}}\right)^{1/\alpha} \Phi_{i\tau t}^{1/(1-\alpha\theta)}$$

$$= \xi X_{ikst}^{-\nu/(1-\alpha\theta)-1} E_s \sum_{s\leq\tau\leq t} \pi_{\tau t} \left(\frac{P_t Y_t}{Z_t Q_{i\tau t}}\right)^{\nu/\alpha} \Phi_{i\tau t}^{\nu/(1-\alpha\theta)} \qquad (60)$$

We have already seen (equation 54) that X_{ikst} does not depend on the firm k, but only on the sector i, so that in formula (60) $X_{ikst} = X_{ist}$. This means also that in formula (25) giving firms' prices, wages are independent of k, and therefore so are prices. Proposition 2 gives the value of the price contract in that case. Since the relevant wage is X_{ist}, we replace $W_{i\tau}$ by X_{ist} in formula (28), and obtain the price in sector i:

$$Q_{i\tau t}^{1/\alpha} = \frac{X_{ist}\Omega_{\tau t}}{\alpha\theta} \left(\frac{1-\beta}{\omega}\right)^{(1-\alpha)/\alpha} \qquad (61)$$

Inserting (61) into formula (57) we first obtain $\Phi_{i\tau t} = X_{ist}$. Inserting this and (61) into the first order condition (60) we obtain:

$$X_{ist}^{\nu} \alpha^2\theta^2 \left(\frac{1-\beta}{\omega}\right)^{(\alpha-1)/\alpha} E_s \sum_{s\leq\tau\leq t} \pi_{\tau t} \left[\frac{1}{P_t C_t}\left(\frac{P_t Y_t}{Z_t}\right)^{1/\alpha}\frac{1}{\Omega_{\tau t}}\right]$$

$$= \xi \left[\alpha\theta\left(\frac{1-\beta}{\omega}\right)^{(\alpha-1)/\alpha}\right]^{\nu} E_s \sum_{s\leq\tau\leq t} \pi_{\tau t} \left[\left(\frac{P_t Y_t}{Z_t}\right)^{\nu/\alpha}\left(\frac{1}{\Omega_{\tau t}}\right)^{\nu}\right] \qquad (62)$$

and using equation (12):

$$X_{ist}^{\nu} \alpha^2\theta^2 E_s \sum_{s\leq\tau\leq t} \pi_{\tau t} \left[M_t^{(1-\alpha)/\alpha} Z_t^{-1/\alpha}\frac{1}{\Omega_{\tau t}}\right]$$

$$= \xi E_s \sum_{s\leq\tau\leq t} \pi_{\tau t} \left[\left(\frac{M_t}{Z_t}\right)^{\nu/\alpha}\left(\frac{1-\beta}{\omega}\right)^{\nu}\left(\frac{\alpha\theta}{\Omega_{\tau t}}\right)^{\nu}\right] \qquad (63)$$

Now the term on the left hand side simplifies:

$$E_s \sum_{s\leq\tau\leq t} \pi_{\tau t} \left[M_t^{(1-\alpha)/\alpha} Z_t^{-1/\alpha}\frac{1}{\Omega_{\tau t}}\right] = E_s \sum_{s\leq\tau\leq t} \pi_{\tau t} \left[\frac{M_t^{(1-\alpha)/\alpha} Z_t^{-1/\alpha}}{E_\tau M_t^{(1-\alpha)/\alpha} Z_t^{-1/\alpha}}\right]$$

$$= E_s \sum_{s\leq\tau\leq t} \pi_{\tau t} E_\tau \left[\frac{M_t^{(1-\alpha)/\alpha} Z_t^{-1/\alpha}}{E_\tau M_t^{(1-\alpha)/\alpha} Z_t^{-1/\alpha}}\right] = E_s \sum_{s\leq\tau\leq t} \pi_{\tau t} = 1 \qquad (64)$$

so that formula (63) is rewritten:

$$X_{ist}^{\nu} = \frac{\xi}{\alpha^2\theta^2} \left[\frac{\alpha\theta(1-\beta)}{\omega}\right]^{\nu} E_s \sum_{s\leq\tau\leq t} \pi_{\tau t} \left[\left(\frac{M_t}{Z_t}\right)^{\nu/\alpha}\left(\frac{1}{\Omega_{\tau t}}\right)^{\nu}\right] \qquad (65)$$

We see that X_{ist} does not depend on i, and we denote it as X_{st}. This yields formula (30).

Appendix 3

Proof of Proposition 4

We shall first derive the aggregate price. Loglinearizing equation (30) giving the new wage contracts X_{st}, and using equation (27), we find:

$$x_{st} = \frac{1}{\nu} \sum_{s \leq \tau \leq t} \pi_{\tau t} E_s \left[\frac{\nu}{\alpha} (m_t - z_t) - \nu E_\tau \left(\frac{1-\alpha}{\alpha} m_t - \frac{1}{\alpha} z_t \right) \right]$$

$$= \frac{1}{\nu} \sum_{s \leq \tau \leq t} \pi_{\tau t} E_s \left[\frac{\nu}{\alpha} (m_t - z_t) - \nu \left(\frac{1-\alpha}{\alpha} m_t - \frac{1}{\alpha} z_t \right) \right]$$

$$= \sum_{s \leq \tau \leq t} \pi_{\tau t} E_s m_t = E_s m_t = m_s + \frac{\rho (1 - \rho^{t-s}) u_s}{(1-\rho)(1-\rho L)} \qquad (66)$$

Now the price $q_{\tau t}$ set in period τ for period $t \geq \tau$, but on the basis of a wage x_{st} set in $s \leq \tau$, is, from equation (28):

$$q_{\tau t} = \alpha x_{st} + \alpha Log \Omega_{\tau t} = \alpha x_{st} + (1-\alpha) E_\tau m_t - E_\tau z_t \qquad (67)$$

To obtain the aggregate price in t, we first sum across τ, with probabilities $\pi_{\tau t}$:

$$\sum_{s \leq \tau \leq t} \pi_{\tau t} \left[\alpha x_{st} + (1-\alpha) E_\tau m_t - E_\tau z_t \right] \qquad (68)$$

and then, with probabilities $(1-\gamma)\gamma^{t-s}$ across periods s, so that:

$$p_t = \sum_{s \leq t} (1-\gamma)\gamma^{t-s} \sum_{s \leq \tau \leq t} \pi_{\tau t} \left[\alpha x_{st} + (1-\alpha) E_\tau m_t - E_\tau z_t \right] =$$

$$\alpha \sum_{s \leq t} (1-\gamma)\gamma^{t-s} x_{st} \sum_{s \leq \tau \leq t} \pi_{\tau t} + \sum_{s \leq t} (1-\gamma)\gamma^{t-s} \sum_{s \leq \tau \leq t} \pi_{\tau t} \left[(1-\alpha) E_\tau m_t - E_\tau z_t \right] \qquad (69)$$

The first term is equal to:

$$\alpha \sum_{s \leq t} (1-\gamma)\gamma^{t-s} x_{st} \sum_{s \leq \tau \leq t} \pi_{\tau t} = \alpha \sum_{s \leq t} (1-\gamma)\gamma^{t-s} E_s m_t = \alpha \sum_{j \geq 0} (1-\gamma)\gamma^j E_{t-j} m_t \qquad (70)$$

As for the second term:

$$\sum_{s \leq t} (1-\gamma)\gamma^{t-s} \sum_{s \leq \tau \leq t} \pi_{\tau t} \left[(1-\alpha) E_\tau m_t - E_\tau z_t \right]$$

$$= \sum_{\tau \leq t} \left[(1-\alpha) E_\tau m_t - E_\tau z_t \right] \sum_{s \leq \tau \leq t} (1-\gamma)\gamma^{t-s} \pi_{\tau t}$$

$$= \sum_{\tau \le t} \left[(1-\alpha) E_\tau m_t - E_\tau z_t \right] \left[(1-\gamma) \gamma^{t-\tau} \phi^{t-\tau} + (1-\phi) \phi^{t-\tau} \sum_{s<\tau} (1-\gamma) \gamma^{t-s} \right]$$

$$= \sum_{\tau \le t} (1-\gamma\phi) \phi^{t-\tau} \gamma^{t-\tau} E_\tau \left[(1-\alpha) m_t - z_t \right]$$

$$= \sum_{i \ge 0} (1-\gamma\phi) \gamma^i \phi^i E_{t-i} \left[(1-\alpha) m_t - z_t \right] \tag{71}$$

So, to summarize, the aggregate price is equal to:

$$p_t = \alpha \sum_{j \ge 0} (1-\gamma) \gamma^j E_{t-j} m_t + \sum_{i \ge 0} (1-\gamma\phi) \gamma^i \phi^i E_{t-i} \left[(1-\alpha) m_t - z_t \right] \tag{72}$$

Applying the formulas of lemma 1 in the appendix to the money and technology processes (31) and (32), we obtain:

$$p_t = m_t - \frac{\alpha\gamma u_t}{(1-\gamma L)(1-\gamma\rho L)} - \frac{(1-\alpha)\gamma\phi u_t}{(1-\gamma\phi L)(1-\gamma\phi\rho L)} - \frac{(1-\gamma\phi)\varepsilon_t}{(1-\phi L)(1-\gamma\phi\phi L)} \tag{73}$$

which, combined with $m_t = p_t + y_t$, yields (33) and (34).   Q.E.D.

Appendix 4

Lemma 1: *Assume the technological and monetary processes:*

$$z_t = \frac{\varepsilon_t}{1-\phi L} \tag{74}$$

$$m_t - m_{t-1} = \frac{u_t}{1-\rho L} \tag{75}$$

Then:

$$\sum_{j=0}^{\infty} \chi^j E_{t-j} z_t = \frac{\varepsilon_t}{(1-\phi L)(1-\chi\phi L)} \tag{76}$$

$$(1-\chi) \sum_{j=0}^{\infty} \chi^j E_{t-j} m_t = m_t - \frac{\chi u_t}{(1-\chi L)(1-\chi\rho L)} \tag{77}$$

Proof: Let us begin with the technology term:

$$\sum_{j=0}^{\infty} \chi^j E_{t-j} z_t = \sum_{j=0}^{\infty} \frac{\chi^j \phi^j \varepsilon_{t-j}}{1-\phi L} = \frac{\varepsilon_t}{(1-\phi L)(1-\chi\phi L)} \tag{78}$$

Let us now rewrite m_t and compute its expected value:

$$m_t = m_{t-j} + \frac{u_{t-j+1}}{1 - \rho L} + \ldots\ldots + \frac{u_t}{1 - \rho L} \tag{79}$$

$$E_{t-j} m_t = m_{t-j} + \frac{\rho u_{t-j}}{1 - \rho L} + \ldots\ldots + \frac{\rho^j u_{t-j}}{1 - \rho L} = m_{t-j} + \frac{\rho \left(1 - \rho^j\right) u_{t-j}}{(1 - \rho)(1 - \rho L)} \tag{80}$$

$$(1 - \chi) \sum_{j=0}^{\infty} \chi^j E_{t-j} m_t = (1 - \chi) \sum_{j=0}^{\infty} \chi^j \left[m_{t-j} + \frac{\rho \left(1 - \rho^j\right) u_{t-j}}{(1 - \rho)(1 - \rho L)} \right]$$

$$= (1 - \chi) \left[\sum_{j=0}^{\infty} \chi^j L^j m_t + \sum_{j=0}^{\infty} \frac{\rho \chi^j L^j u_t}{(1 - \rho)(1 - \rho L)} - \sum_{j=0}^{\infty} \frac{\rho \chi^j \rho^j L^j u_t}{(1 - \rho)(1 - \rho L)} \right]$$

$$= \frac{(1 - \chi) m_t}{1 - \chi L} + \frac{(1 - \chi) \rho u_t}{(1 - \rho)(1 - \chi L)(1 - \rho L)} - \frac{(1 - \chi) \rho u_t}{(1 - \rho)(1 - \chi \rho L)(1 - \rho L)}$$

$$= m_t - \frac{\chi u_t}{(1 - \chi L)(1 - \chi \rho L)} \tag{81}$$

Q.E.D.

References

1. Ambler S, Guay A, Phaneuf L (1997) Wage contracts and labor adjustment costs as internal propagation mechanisms. Manuscript, U.Q.A.M., Montréal
2. Andersen TM (1998) Persistency in sticky price models. European Economic Review 42: 593-603
3. Ascari G (2000) Optimising agents, staggered wages and persistence in the real effects of money shocks. The Economic Journal 110: 664-686
4. Bénassy J-P (2002) The macroeconomics of imperfect competition and nonclearing markets: A dynamic general equilibrium approach. Cambridge, M.I.T. Press
5. Bénassy J-P (2003) Staggered contracts and persistence: Microeconomic foundations and macroeconomic dynamics. Louvain Economic Review 69: 125-144
6. Calvo G (1983) Staggered prices in a utility-maximizing framework. Journal of Monetary Economics 12: 383-398
7. Chari VV, Kehoe PJ, McGrattan ER (2000) Sticky price models of the business cycle: Can the contract multiplier solve the persistence problem? Econometrica 68: 1151-1179
8. Christiano LJ, Eichenbaum M, Evans C (2001) Nominal rigidities and the dynamic effects of a shock to monetary policy. NBER, Cambridge, Massachusetts
9. Cogley T, Nason JM (1995) Output dynamics in real-business-cycle models. American Economic Review 85: 492-511.

10. Collard F, Ertz G (2000) Stochastic nominal wage contracts in a cash-in-advance model. Recherches Economiques de Louvain 66: 281-301
11. Fischer S (1977) Long term contracts, rational expectations and the optimal money supply rule. Journal of Political Economy 85: 191-205
12. Gray J-A (1976) Wage indexation: A macroeconomic approach. Journal of Monetary Economics 2: 221-235
13. Jeanne O (1998) Generating real persistent effects of monetary shocks: How much nominal rigidity do we really need? European Economic Review 42: 1009-1032
14. Lucas RE (1972) Expectations and the neutrality of money. Journal of Economic Theory 4: 103-124
15. Phelps ES (1978) Disinflation without recession: Adaptive guideposts and monetary policy. Weltwirtschaftliches Archiv 114: 783-809
16. Phelps ES, Taylor JB (1977) Stabilizing powers of monetary policy under rational expectations. Journal of Political Economy 85: 163-190
17. Taylor JB (1979) Staggered wage setting in a macro model. American Economic Review 69: 108-113
18. Taylor JB (1980) Aggregate dynamics and staggered contracts. Journal of Political Economy 88: 1-23
19. Yun T (1996) Nominal price rigidity, money supply endogeneity and business cycles. Journal of Monetary Economics 37: 345-370

Variable Elasticity of Substitution and Economic Growth: Theory and Evidence*

Giannis Karagiannis[1], Theodore Palivos[2], and Chris Papageorgiou[3]

[1] University of Macedonia, Department of International & European Economic & Political Studies, 156 Egnatia Street, GR-540 06 Thessaloniki, Greece. karagian@uom.gr
[2] University of Macedonia, Department of Economics, 156 Egnatia Street, GR-540 06 Thessaloniki, Greece. tpalivos@uom.gr
[3] Louisiana State University, Department of Economics, Baton Rouge, LA 70803, USA. cpapa@lsu.edu

Summary. We construct a one-sector growth model where the technology is described by a Variable Elasticity of Substitution (VES) production function. This framework allows the elasticity of factor substitution to interact with the level of economic development. First, we show that the model can exhibit unbounded endogenous growth despite the absence of exogenous technical change and the presence of non-reproducible factors. Second, we provide some empirical estimates of the elasticity of substitution, using a panel of 82 countries over a 28-year period, which admit the possibility of a VES aggregate production function with an elasticity of substitution that is greater than one and consequently of unbounded endogenous growth.

Key words: Elasticity of Substitution, Endogenous Growth, VES Production Functions

JEL Classification: O42

1 Introduction

The elasticity of factor substitution plays a crucial role in the theory of economic growth. Among others, it is one of the determinants of the level of economic growth; see, for example, de La Grandville [4] and Klump and de La Grandville [14]. It affects the speed of convergence towards the balanced growth path; see Klump and Preissler [15]. It can alter the behavior of the savings rate during the transition; see Smetters [31]. It influences the aggregate distribution of income; the seminal work on this topic is Hicks [9]. Finally, it may itself be a source of unbounded growth; see Solow [143] and Palivos and Karagiannis [26].

Most papers of economic growth that attempt to provide some quantitative properties of growth models rely on the Cobb-Douglas specification of the production

*Karagiannis and Palivos gratefully acknowledge financial support from the Greek Ministry of Education and the EU (Program PYTHAGORAS).

function, which, as it is well known, describes a process with an elasticity of factor substitution equal to one. Recently, several papers in the literature have investigated both theoretically and empirically the role played by the Constant Elasticity of Substitution (CES) production function, which allows the elasticity to take constant values that are either greater or lower than one. Examples include, among others, Klump and de La Grandville [14], Klump and Preissler [15], Miyagiwa and Papageorgiou [22], Duffy et al. [7] and Masanjala and Papageorgiou [20].

This paper extends this literature a step further by analyzing the role of a variable elasticity of substitution (VES) within a standard Solow-Swan growth model. Whereas the CES production function restricts the elasticity of substitution to be constant along an isoquant, this paper employs a specification, first introduced by Revankar [27], which allows the elasticity of substitution to interact with the level of economic development.

More specifically, a change in the economy's per capita capital affects the elasticity of substitution between capital and labor. This change feeds back into the economy influencing capital accumulation and output. It is shown that the model can exhibit unbounded endogenous growth despite the absence of exogenous technical change and the presence of non-reproducible factors, e.g., labor. Moreover, the paper uses a panel of 82 countries over a 28-year period to estimate an aggregate production function with variable elasticity of substitution. The estimation results provide first evidence in favor of a VES production function. In addition, the estimated elasticity of substitution in the sample is greater than one, which provides empirical support to the aforementioned theoretical result regarding unbounded endogenous growth.

The remainder of the paper is organized as follows. Section 2 analyzes the properties of Revankar's VES production function. Section 3 introduces this production function in an otherwise standard Solow-Swan model and derives necessary and sufficient conditions for unbounded endogenous growth. Section 4 offers a short review of the previous studies that have estimated VES functions. Section 5 discusses the data, the estimation techniques and the empirical results. Finally, Section 6 concludes the paper.

2 A VES Production Function

2.1 The Revankar VES Production Function

We use standard notation to denote a general production technology as $Y = F(K,L)$, where Y, K, and L stand for output, capital and labor, respectively. Following Revankar [27], we consider the following specification:[4]

$$Y = AK^{a\nu}[L + baK]^{(1-a)\nu}. \tag{1}$$

We mostly assume that the production function exhibits constant returns to scale, i.e., $\nu = 1$. This production function can be written in intensive form, $y = f(k)$ where $y \equiv Y/L$ and $k \equiv K/L$, as

---

[4] A very similar VES specification was developed by Sato and Hoffman [30].

$$y = Ak^a \left[1 + bak\right]^{1-a}. \tag{2}$$

It follows that

$$f'(k) = a\frac{y}{k} + a(1-a)b\frac{y}{1+abk}, \tag{3}$$

$$f''(k) = Aa(a-1)(1+abk)^{-a-1}k^{-1}. \tag{4}$$

Hence, this function satisfies standard properties of a production function, namely $f(k) > 0$, $f'(k) > 0$ and $f''(k) < 0 \; \forall k > 0$, as long as

$$A > 0, \quad 0 < a \leq 1, \quad b > -1 \quad and \quad k^{-1} \geq -b.$$

Note that if $b = 0$ then (2) reduces to the Cobb-Douglas case. On the other hand if $a = 1$ then it reduces to the Ak production function.

2.2 Some Properties of the VES

The limiting properties of (2) are:

$$\lim_{k \to 0} f(k) = 0, \quad \lim_{k \to \infty} f(k) = \infty \quad \text{if } b > 0 \tag{5}$$

$$\lim_{k \to -b^{-1}} f(k) = A(-b)^{-a}(1-a)^{1-a} > 0 \quad \text{if } b < 0$$

Furthermore, it follows from (3) that

$$\lim_{k \to 0} f'(k) = \infty, \quad \lim_{k \to \infty} f'(k) = A(ba)^{1-a} > 0 \quad \text{if } b > 0, \tag{6}$$

$$\lim_{k \to -b^{-1}} f'(k) = A\left[-b(1-a)\right]^{1-a} > 0 \quad \text{if } b < 0.$$

Thus, if $b > 0$ then one of the Inada conditions is violated; namely, the marginal product of capital is strictly bounded from below, which is equivalent to labor not being an essential factor of production, i.e., if $b > 0$, then $\lim_{L \to 0} F(K,L) = A(ba)^{1-a} > 0$. The labor share, s_L, implied by (2) is:

$$s_L = \frac{1-a}{1+bak}, \quad \text{where} \quad \lim_{k \to 0} s_L = 1-a, \tag{7}$$

$$\lim_{k \to \infty} s_L = 0 \text{ if } b > 0 \quad and \quad \lim_{k \to -b^{-1}} s_L = 1 \quad \text{if } b < 0.$$

On the other hand, the properties of the capital share, s_K, follow easily since $s_K = 1 - s_L = \frac{a+bak}{1+bak}$. For this production function, the elasticity of substitution between capital and labor $\sigma(x) = -\frac{f'(x)}{xf(x)}\frac{f(x)-xf'(x)}{f''(x)} > 0$ is

$$\sigma(k) = 1 + bk > 0. \tag{8}$$

Hence, $\sigma \gtrless 1$ if $b \gtrless 0$. Thus, the elasticity of substitution varies with the level of per capita capital, an index of economic development. Furthermore, σ plays an important role in the development process. To see why, note that (1) can be written as:

$$Y = AK^a L^{1-a} \left[1 + ba\frac{K}{L} \right]^{1-a},$$

or, using (8),

$$Y = AK^a L^{1-a} [1 - a + a\sigma(k)]^{1-a}. \tag{9}$$

Hence, the production process can be decomposed into a Cobb-Douglas part, $AK^a L^{1-a}$, and a part that depends on the (variable) elasticity of substitution, $[1 - a + a\sigma(k$
Once again, if $b = 0$ then $\sigma = 1$ and

$$Y = AK^a L^{1-a},$$

which is the Cobb-Douglas production function. In intensive form (1) is written as

$$y = Ak^a [1 - a + a\sigma(k)]^{1-a}. \tag{10}$$

Some of the properties of the VES are also shared by the CES. Exceptions include the elasticity of substitution which for the CES production function is constant along an isoquant, while for the VES considered here it is constant only along a ray through the origin (see equation 8). Also, factor shares behave slight differently, since for the CES $\lim_{k \to 0} s_L = 1$ if $\sigma > 1$ and $\lim_{k \to 0} s_L = 0$ if $\sigma < 1$.

3 VES in the Solow-Swan Growth Model

Next we introduce this VES specification in a standard Solow-Swan growth model (Solow [143]). The accumulation equation is

$$\frac{\dot{k}}{k} = s\frac{f(k)}{k} - n, \tag{11}$$

where s denotes the savings rate and n stands for the population growth rate. Using (10), we have

$$\frac{f(k)}{k} = Ak^{a-1} [1 - a + a\sigma(k)]^{1-a},$$

$$\lim_{k \to x} \frac{f(k)}{k} = \lim_{k \to x} f'(k), \qquad x = 0, \infty, b^{-1}$$

where $\lim_{k \to x} f'(k)$ is given by (6). Also,

$$\frac{\partial (f(k)/k)}{\partial k} = -A(1-a)k^{a-2} [1 + bak]^{-a} < 0.$$

Upon substitution, equation (11) becomes

$$\frac{\dot{k}}{k} = sAk^{a-1} [1 - a + a\sigma(k)]^{1-a} - n. \tag{12}$$

If $b > 0$ and hence $\sigma > 1$, the properties of the growth rate of per capita capital $\dot{k}/k$ are

$$\lim_{k \to 0} \frac{\dot{k}}{k} = \infty \qquad \text{and} \qquad \lim_{k \to \infty} \frac{\dot{k}}{k} = sA(ba)^{1-a} - n.$$

Thus, if $sA(ba)^{1-a} > n$, then the model exhibits unbounded endogenous growth; that is, there exists an asymptotic balanced growth path with positive per capita growth. This result is consistent with the findings of Jones and Manuelli [10, 11], who show that unbounded growth can occur despite the presence of non-reproducible factors, i.e., labor, and the absence of exogenous technical progress, as long as the marginal product of capital is strictly bounded from below. It is also consistent with the results in Palivos and Karagiannis [26], which shows that an elasticity of substitution that becomes asymptotically (as k grows) greater than one is necessary and sufficient for the existence of a lower bound on the marginal product of capital. Figure 1(a) illustrates the possibility of unbounded growth.

This possibility arises also with a CES production function as long as $\sigma > 1$. However, in this model the process is more explicit, since as it can be seen from (12) an increase in k affects the growth rate $\dot{k}/k$ through two channels. The first is through sAk^{a-1} for any given σ. This term is decreasing in k (the Cobb-Douglas part). The second is the change in σ, which is linear in k. So an increase in output raises σ, which raises output even further.

If $sA(ba)^{1-a} < n$, then the growth rate will eventually become zero. The economy will reach a steady state, which is given as the solution to the following equation (see Figure 1(b))

$$sA(k^*)^{a-1}[1 - a + a\sigma(k^*)]^{1-a} = n. \tag{13}$$

Consider next the case where $-1 < b < 0$ and $0 < k \leq -(1/b)$. In this case, if $sA[-b(1-a)]^{1-a} < n$, then there is again a unique steady state, given by (13) (see Figure 2(a)). On the other hand, if $-1 < b < 0$ and $sA[-b(1-a)]^{1-a} > n$, then the system will reach a corner solution, where $k = -1/b$ (Figure 2(b)).

4 Empirical Considerations of VES

The previous empirical studies using a VES production function (see Table 1) can be divided into two groups depending on whether they have used time-series or cross-section data.[5] The former group includes the studies of Sato and Hoffman [30], Lovell [16], Revankar [28], Lovell [18], Roskamp [29] and Bairam [1, 2]. Sato and Hoffman [30], using data from the private non-farm sector of the U.S. and Japan, concluded that "the overall impression is that the VES is more realistic than the CES," without however providing a formal statistical test. Revankar [28], on the other hand, using data for the private non-farm sector of the U.S., formally rejected the Cobb-Douglas form in favor of the VES, while Lovell [18] could not reject the CES specification in favor of the VES for the U.S. manufacturing sector as a whole.

Fig. 1. $b > 0$.

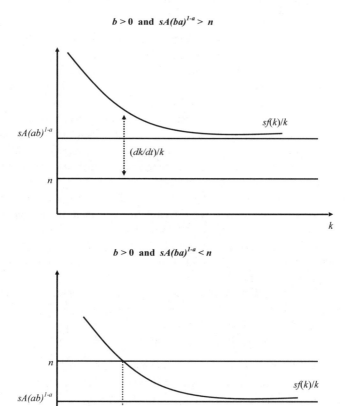

Fig. 2. $b < 0$.

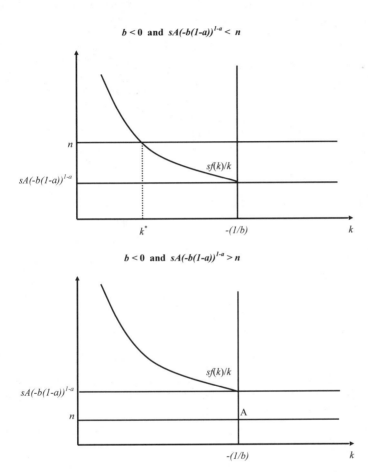

$b < 0$ and $sA(-b(1-a))^{1-a} < n$

$b < 0$ and $sA(-b(1-a))^{1-a} > n$

---

[5]Our (incomplete) review covers only production function that are linearly homogeneous.

Nevertheless, Lovell [16] rejected both the Cobb-Douglas and the CES specifications in favor of the VES for 16 two-digit U.S. manufacturing industries. Moreover, Bairam [1, 2] rejected the Cobb-Douglas in favor of the VES specification for the Japanese and Soviet economies. Roskamp [29], using data for manufacturing in Germany, provided estimates of the elasticity of substitution for 38 industries using both the CES and the VES, without formally testing for the most appropriate specification. With the exception of Roskamp [29], in 7 out of 38 industries, and of Bairam [1], these time-series studies estimated the elasticity of substitution to be less than one.

Study	Country	Period	Sector
Lu and Fletcher (1968)	U.S.	1957	Two-digit manufacturing
Sato and Hoffman (1968)	U.S.	1909-60	Private non-farm sector
	Japan	1930-60	Private non-farm sector
Lovell (1968)	U.S.	1949-63	Two-digit manufacturing
Diwan (1970)	U.S.	1955-57	Manufacturing firms
Revankar (1971a)	U.S.	1957	Two-digit manufacturing
Revankar (1971b)	U.S.	1929-53	Private non-farm sector
Lovell (1973a)	U.S.	1958	Two-digit manufacturing
Lovell (1973b)	U.S.	1947-68	Manufacturing
Meyer and Kadiyala (1974)	U.S.		Agriculture
Tsang and Yeung (1976)	U.S.	1957	Food & kindred products
Roskamp (1977)	Germany	1950-60	Manufacturing
Kazi (1980)	India	1973-75	Two- & three-digit manufacturing
Bairam (1989)	Japan	1878-1939	Economy
Bairam (1990)	U.S.S.R.	1950-75	Economy & manufacturing
Zellner and Ryu (1998)	U.S.	1957	Transportation equipment

Table 1. Previous Empirical Considerations of VES Production Functions.

The remaining studies reported in Table 1 fall in the group of cross-section studies. Lu and Fletcher [19] formally rejected the CES in favor of the VES specification in 7 to 9 (depending on various definitions of capital and labor inputs) out of the 17 two-digit manufacturing sectors included in their analysis. Similarly, Revankar [27] rejected the Cobb-Douglas in favor of the VES specification in 5 out of 12 two-digit U.S. manufacturing sectors. Lovell [17] rejected the Cobb-Douglas and the CES in favor of the VES specification in 3 out of 17 two-digit U.S. manufacturing sectors. Kazi [13] rejected in most cases the CES in favor of the VES specification. Furthermore, Diwan [5], using even more micro data for individual U.S. manufacturing firms, rejected both the Cobb-Douglas and the CES specifications in favor of the VES. A similar result was reached by Meyer and Kadiyala [21], who used agricultural experimental data. Finally, Tsang and Yeung [36] and Zellner and Ryu [37] provided estimates of both the CES and the VES for respectively the food and kindred products and transportation equipment industries in the U.S., but they did not formally tested for the more appropriate specification. With the exception of Lu and

Fletcher [19] and of Kazi [13], these cross-section studies gave estimates of the elasticity of substitution that were less than one.

5 Estimation of a VES Production Function

Whether or not the aggregate production technology is VES is an empirical question. We now turn our attention toward this estimation exercise. Our estimation of a VES specification for the aggregate production involves data on 82 countries for 28 years (1960-1987)[6]. We consider nonlinear least squares (NLLS) regressions to obtain our parameter estimates. We begin by briefly describing the data used in our estimation.

5.1 The Data

All of the raw data that we use are obtained from the World Bank's STARS database. In particular, GDP and the aggregate physical capital stock are converted into constant, end of period 1987 $U.S. The database also provides us with data on the number of individuals in the workforce between the ages of 15-64, as well as data on the mean years of schooling of members of the workforce. In addition to considering raw (unadjusted) labor, L, as an input in our VES specification, we also examined whether adjusting labor input for human capital accumulation affects our results. Here we follow Tallman and Wang [35] and adopt a simple proxy for human capital adjusted labor input. First, we define the stock of human capital in country i at time t, H_{it}, as $H_{it} = E_{it}$, where E_{it} denotes the mean years of schooling of the workforce (workers between the ages of 15-64 as in the measure of L) in country i at time t. The mean school years of education, E, is defined as the sum of the average number of years of primary, secondary and post-secondary education. Then we define *human capital adjusted labor supply* as $HL_{it} = H_{it} \times L_{it} = E_{it} \times L_{it}$. In estimating the VES specification for aggregate production, we will use both L and HL as measures of labor input. Further details concerning the construction of these data are provided in Duffy and Papageorgiou [6] and mean values of all relevant variables appear in the appendix.

5.2 Estimation Equation

Taking logs of both sides of (1) and assuming that technology grows exogenously at rate λ (i.e., $A = A_0 e^{\lambda t}$) yields our estimation equations:

$$\log Y_{it} = \log A_0 + \lambda t + a v \log K_{it} + \\ + (1-a)v \log[L_{it} + ba K_{it}] + \varepsilon_{it}, \tag{14}$$

---

[6]These data are from Duffy and Papageorgiou [6].

$$\log Y_{it} = \log A_0 + \lambda t + a \log K_{it} +$$
$$+ (1-a) \log [L_{it} + baK_{it}] + \varepsilon_{it}, \qquad (15)$$

where A_0 is initial technology, i is country index, t is time and ε is a random error. Note that in our estimations we consider both cases of non-constant ($v \neq 1$) and constant ($v = 1$) returns to scale. We estimated equations (14-15) by nonlinear least squares (NLLS) for the entire panel of 2,296 observations using our data on real GDP, physical capital and either raw labor supply, L, or human capital adjusted labor supply, HL, in place of L. The initial parameter choices for all of the NLLS estimation results reported in Table 2 were based on estimates we obtained from a preliminary OLS regression of $\log Y_{it}$ on a constant, $\log K_{it}$ and $\log L_{it}$ or $\log HL_{it}$. We also considered other initial parameter choices and obtained similar NLLS estimates.

The second column of Table 2 presents estimates for the unrestricted ($v \neq 1$) VES production function given by equation (14). All of the estimated coefficients are significantly different from zero at the 1 percent level and economically plausible, regardless of whether L or HL is used for labor input. Consistent with other studies using similar data, the time trend coefficient is negative and significant ($\lambda = -0.012, -0.014$) indicating that for the 82 countries of our sample, the log of real GDP has, on average, declined slightly over the period 1960-1987. The coefficients for a are 0.66781 and 0.70473 (and highly significant) for the models using raw and adjusted labor, respectively.

The key finding regarding our testable hypothesis is that the sign for the coefficient estimate b is found to be positive for both types of labor input and significant, thus providing first evidence of a VES aggregate production function. In particular, the estimated coefficient for b is 0.00050 for the unrestricted model using raw labor and 0.00141 for the same model using skilled labor. These estimates may at first seem too small but closer observation of their potential impact on the elasticity of substitution (i.e., $\sigma = 1 + bk$) suggests otherwise. Further, our results imply that the elasticity of substitution between capital and labor, σ, is in general greater than one. Given that the coefficient estimates for b are found to be different from zero, we can reject the Cobb-Douglas specification, for our 28 year and 82 country sample, over the more general VES specification.

Finally, for the unrestricted models the coefficient estimate for v is shown to be very close to unity ($v = 0.99779$). Thus, the constant-returns-to-scale (CRTS) restriction seems reasonable for the case where raw labor is used as input. Interestingly, the same is not true for the model using adjusted labor (HL) as the labor input since $v = 0.97126$ which is consistent with mild diminishing-returns-to-scale (DRTS). However, since the theory supposes that there are constant returns to scale in production, we also estimate the "restricted version" of the model above, using equation (15).

The results for the restricted ($v = 1$) VES production function are presented in the third column of Table 2. We see that while the magnitude of the NLLS estimates for all parameters in the restricted model differ slightly from those obtained using the unrestricted model, the signs and statistical significance of the coefficient estimates are largely unchanged by comparison. Once again the key parameter b is positive in

Labor (L)	Unrestricted ($v \neq 1$) NLLS	Restricted ($v = 1$) NLLS
a	0.66781***	0.67283***
	(0.06176)	(0.03770)
b	0.00050***	0.00046***
	(0.00018)	(0.00015)
λ	-0.01170***	-0.01177***
	(0.00093)	(0.00091)
A_0	24.753***	24.822***
	(1.8109)	(1.8028)
v	0.99779***	—
	(0.00501)	—
$-\ln L$	837.58	837.68
Adj. Labor (HL)		
a	0.70473***	0.73468***
	(0.06358)	(0.03775)
b	0.00141*	0.00070**
	(0.00083)	(0.00031)
λ	-0.01401***	-0.01549***
	(0.00098)	(0.00090)
A_0	29.336***	31.517***
	(1.9191)	(1.9013)
v	0.97126***	—
	(0.00488)	—
$-\ln L$	955.96	974.50
Obs.	2,296	2,296

Note: Standard errors are given in parentheses. *** Significantly different from 0 at the 1% level.
** Significantly different from 0 at the 5% level. * Significantly different from 0 at the 10% level.
Table 2. Nonlinear Regression Estimates.

sign and very significant when we use raw labor ($b = 0.00046$). However, when we restrict the model and use adjusted labor the coefficient estimate increases considerably ($b = 0.00070$) than that in the unrestricted model and becomes significant only at the 5 percent level. This result is not surprising because restricting the model with HL to obey CRTS results in compromising the accuracy of the coefficient estimate b.

Another interesting finding from our NLLS estimation concerns the implied country-specific labor and capital shares (s_L and s_K, respectively). In the special Cobb-Douglas case, the parameter b is equal to zero (see equation 15) and the terms $1 - a$ and a are readily interpreted as the labor and capital shares of output. However, under the VES specification, the labor share is given by $s_L = (1 - a)/(1 + bak)$ and the capital share by $s_K = (a + bak)/(1 + bak)$. Therefore both shares depend on the values of K, L, a and most importantly b. Since our estimated coefficients for b are positive and significantly different from zero, it follows that factor shares vary with a country's capital-labor ratio. This finding is important in light of Kaldor's [12] "stylized facts" about the shares of income accruing to capital and labor being relatively constant over time and countries. This view has been first challenged by the pioneer paper of Solow [33] and remains today an open research question (see, for example, Gollin [8] who finds that labor's share of national income across 31 countries is relatively constant). Our results certainly suggest that capital shares can vary considerably across countries and increase with the capital-labor ratio and therefore with economic development.

To summarize, the main finding from our nonlinear estimation exercises is that the coefficient estimates of b are found to be positive and significantly different from zero, implying a variable elasticity of substitution between capital and labor that is in general greater than unity. Of course, this is in contrast to the aggregate Cobb-Douglas production specification assumed by most theoretical and empirical studies.

6 Conclusions and Extensions

We have analyzed a one-sector growth model with a variable elasticity of substitution production function. First, we have shown that the model can exhibit unbounded endogenous growth despite the absence of exogenous technical change and the presence of non-reproducible factors, such as labor. Second, we have used a panel of 82 countries over a 28-year period to estimate an aggregate production function. Our empirical estimates of the elasticity of substitution support the possibility of unbounded endogenous growth.

In future work we plan to examine the robustness of our baseline OLS results when we correct for the fixed effects and endogeneity problems usually cited in the literature. Thus far, the aggregate input-output production relationship we have estimated using NLLS does not allow for the presence of *fixed effects* across countries. A "fixed-effects" specification would allow us to capture country-specific characteristics, e.g., geography, political factors or culture, that might affect aggregate output. Admitting the possibility of fixed effects implies that the error term in (14-15) can be written as $\varepsilon_{it} = \eta_i + \upsilon_{it}$, where η_i captures time-invariant fixed factors in country i. Given this specification, first differencing (14-15) gets rid of the fixed effect component in the error term, yielding the nonlinear equations:

$$
\log\left(\frac{Y_{it}}{Y_{i,t-1}}\right) = \lambda + a\upsilon\log\left(\frac{K_{it}}{K_{i,t-1}}\right) +
$$
$$
+ (1-a)\upsilon\log\left[\frac{L_{it} + baK_{it}}{L_{i,t-1} + baK_{i,t-1}}\right] + \upsilon_{it} - \upsilon_{i,t-1} \qquad (16)
$$

$$\log\left(\frac{Y_{it}}{Y_{i,t-1}}\right) = \lambda + a\log\left(\frac{K_{it}}{K_{i,t-1}}\right) +$$

$$+(1-a)\log\left[\frac{L_{it}+baK_{it}}{L_{i,t-1}+baK_{i,t-1}}\right]+\upsilon_{it}-\upsilon_{i,t-1}. \qquad (17)$$

While it is straightforward to estimate (16-17) using NLLS, the first-difference specification leads to another difficulty in that the lagged error term, $\upsilon_{i,t-1}$, is likely to be correlated with time t values of the explanatory variables, K_{it} and L_{it}. We plan to use a generalized method of moments (GMM) approach to estimate the parameters in (16-17), which is a more general estimation method than nonlinear two stage estimation in that the GMM approach allows for the possibility of both autocorrelation and heteroskedasticity in the disturbance term, $\upsilon_{it}-\upsilon_{i,t-1}$. Thus, it seems appropriate in the present context[7].

---

[7]The first paper that examined cross-country growth regressions adjusting for both the fixed-effects problem as well as for the endogeneity problem is Caselli et al. [3]. For further discussion on these issues the reader is referred to their paper.

Appendix

Country	Code	GDP (bill. US$)	Capital (bill. US$)	Labor (mill. age 15–64)	Education (avg yrs of edu.)
Algeria	DZA	38.7	142	7.87	2.51
Argentina	ARG	90	250	16	6.38
Australia	AUS	136	426	8.51	6.55
Austria	AUT	83.7	240	4.74	8.7
Bangladesh	BGD	11.3	22.4	38.3	2.56
Brazil	BRA	162	420	59	3.13
Belgium	BEL	104	274	6.24	7.87
Bolivia	BOL	3.62	13.3	2.59	4.29
Cameroon	CMR	6.4	9.75	4.03	1.68
Canada	CAN	260	600	14	8.98
Chile	CHL	13.8	35.5	5.9	6.06
China	CHN	103	309	513	3.36
Colombia	COL	21.5	48.2	13	3.54
Côte d'Ivoire	CIV	6.65	14	3.35	0.93
Costa Rica	CRI	2.87	10.9	1.04	6.14
Cyprus	CYP	1.91	6.15	0.38	6.91
Denmark	DEN	74.5	199	3.21	8.36
Ecuador	ECU	6.52	20.1	3.60	4.22
Egypt	EGY	17.2	25.5	19.9	3.59
El Salvador	SLV	3.71	6.19	1.96	3.54
Ethiopia	ETH	3.93	3.86	17.2	0.24
Finland	FIN	58.6	199	3.11	8.2
France	FRA	629	1620	33	8.01
Germany	DEU	831	2420	42	8.43
Ghana	GHA	4.27	8.77	4.97	2.98
Greece	GRC	31.5	82.1	5.90	7.76
Guatemala	GTM	5.08	10.1	3.04	2.72
Haiti	HTI	1.78	2.18	2.66	1.9
Honduras	HND	2.58	5.03	1.55	3.23
Iceland	ICE	3.08	7.96	0.129	7.58
Indonesia	IND	39	59.3	72.3	2.91
India	IND	155	365	343	2.37
Iran	IRN	109	183	17	2.02
Iraq	IRQ	49	71.6	5.62	2.33
Ireland	IRL	19.5	47.8	1.84	14.55
Israel	ISR	21.9	59.8	1.95	4.69
Italy	ITA	511	1480	36	6.96
Jamaica	JAM	2.71	13.3	1.04	6.89
Japan	JPN	1400	3600	74	10.67

Country	Code	GDP (bill. US$)	Capital (bill. US$)	Labor (mill. age 15–64)	Education (avg yrs of edu.)
Jordan	JOR	3.06	5.44	1.21	3.11
Kenya	KEN	4.36	19.2	6.53	2.48
Korea, Rep.	KOR	51.6	87.7	19.1	5.12
Madagascar	MDG	2.33	3.83	4.05	2.4
Malawi	MWI	0.77	2.03	2.68	3.34
Malaysia	MYS	16.3	34.5	6.54	4.32
Mali	MLI	1.36	3.34	3.04	0.49
Mauritius	MUS	1.02	3.63	0.5	5.41
Mexico	MEX	89.2	206	31	4.36
Morocco	MAR	11.1	25.1	8.7	1.33
Mozambique	MOZ	1.59	5.91	5.67	1.65
Myanmar (Burma)	MMR	6.95	12	16.7	1.68
Netherlands	NLD	159	483	8.59	8.1
New Zealand	NZL	26.8	77.5	1.8	7.06
Nigeria	NGA	22.4	68.8	37.6	1.34
Norway	NOR	51.9	204	2.48	8.87
Pakistan	PAK	16.7	31.8	36.3	1.49
Panama	PAN	3.14	7.04	0.92	5.66
Paraguay	PRY	2.12	4.12	1.41	5.42
Peru	PER	18.6	52.8	8.0	4.79
Philippines	PHI	23.5	49.5	22.5	6.14
Portugal	PRT	23.9	75.6	5.98	4.44
Rwanda	RWA	1.33	1.09	2.16	2.09
Senegal	SEN	3.32	6.55	2.61	0.98
Sierra Leone	SLE	0.44	0.83	1.59	1.21
Singapore	SGP	9.26	24.5	1.39	4.68
Spain	ESP	201	494	22	6.01
Sri Lanka	LKA	3.95	7.5	7.59	5.15
Sudan	SDN	12.4	13.8	8.44	0.88
Sweden	SWE	120	320	5.25	9.12
Switzerland	CHE	134	374	4.09	6.62
Tanzania	TZA	2.39	7.44	7.84	1.23
Thailand	THA	23.3	48.6	21.7	4.61
Tunisia	TUN	5.36	16.6	3.01	3.0
Turkey	TUR	37.1	93.2	21.9	3.11
Uganda	UGA	5.33	9.31	5.31	2.1
United Kingdom	GRB	510	1220	36	9.66
United States	USA	3100	8300	135	10.91
Uruguay	URY	5.96	18.4	1.77	6.07
Venezuela	VEN	37.2	116	6.71	4.28
Zaire	ZAR	6.2	8.1	11.9	2.57
Zambia	ZMB	1.76	11.9	2.42	2.55
Zimbabwe	ZWE	3.62	12.6	2.94	3.54

References

1. Bairam E (1989) Learning-by-doing, variable elasticity of substitution and economic growth in Japan, 1878-1939. Journal of Development Studies 25: 344-353
2. Bairam E (1990) Capital-labor substitution and slowdown in Soviet economic growth: A re-examination. Bulletin of Economic Research 42: 63-72.
3. Caselli F, Esquivel G, Lefort F (1996) Reopening the convergence debate: A new look at cross country growth empirics. Journal of Economic Growth 1: 363-389
4. de La Grandville O (1989) In quest of the Slutsky Diamond. American Economic Review 79: 468-481
5. Diwan RK (1970) About the growth path of firms. American Economic Review 60: 30-43
6. Duffy J, Papageorgiou C (2000) A cross-country empirical investigation of the aggregate production function specification. Journal of Economic Growth 5: 83-116
7. Duffy J, Papageorgiou C, Perez-Sebastian F (2004) Capital-skill Complementarity? evidence from a panel of countries. Review of Economics and Statistics 86: 327-344
8. Gollin D (2002) Getting income shares right. Journal of Political Economy 110: 458-474
9. Hicks JR (1932) Theory of wages. London: MacMillan
10. Jones LE, Manuelli RE (1990) A convex model of equilibrium growth: Theory and policy implications. Journal of Political Economy 98: 1008-1038
11. Jones LE, Manuelli RE (1997) Sources of growth. Journal of Economic Dynamics and Control 21: 75-114
12. Kaldor N (1961) Capital accumulation and economic growth. In Lutz FA, Hague DC (eds) The theory of capital, New York: St. Martin's Press
13. Kazi UA (1980) The variable elasticity of substitution production function: A case study from Indian manufacturing industries. Oxford Economic Papers 32: 163-175
14. Klump R, de La Grandville O (2000) Economic growth and the elasticity of substitution: Two theorems and some suggestions. American Economic Review 90: 282-291
15. Klump R, Preissler H (2000) CES production functions and economic growth. Scandinavian Journal of Economics 102: 41-56
16. Lovell CAK (1968) Capacity utilization and production function estimation in postwar American manufacturing. Quarterly Journal of Economics 82: 219-239
17. Lovell CAK (1973) CES and VES production functions in a cross-section context. Journal of Political Economy 81: 705-720
18. Lovell CAK (1973) Estimation and prediction with CES and VES production functions. International Economic Review 14: 676-692
19. Lu Y, Fletcher LB (1968) A generalization of the CES production function. Review of Economics and Statistics 50: 449-452
20. Masanjala WH, Papageorgiou C (2004) The Solow model with CES technology: Nonlinearities and parameter heterogeneity. Journal of Applied Econometrics 19: 171-201
21. Meyer RA, Kadiyala KR (1974) Linear and nonlinear estimation of production functions. Southern Economic Journal 40: 463-472
22. Miyagiwa K, Papageorgiou C (2003) Elasticity of substitution and growth: Normalized CES in the Diamond model. Economic Theory 21: 155-165
23. Nakatani I (1973) Production functions with variable elasticity of substitution: A comment. Review of Economics and Statistics 55: 394-396
24. Nehru V, Dhareshwar S (1993) A new database on physical capital stock: Sources, methodology and results. Revista de Análisis Económico 8: 37-59
25. Nehru V, Swanson E, Dubey A (1995) A new database on human capital stock in developing and industrial countries: Sources, methodology and results. Journal of Development Economics 46: 379-401

26. Palivos T, Karagiannis G (2004) The elasticity of substitution in convex models of endogenous growth. Unpublished Manuscript
27. Revankar NS (1971) A class of variable elasticity of substitution production functions. Econometrica 39: 61-71
28. Revankar NS (1971) Capital-labor substitution, technological change and economic growth: The U.S. experience, 1929-1953. Metroeconomica 23: 154-176
29. Roskamp KW (1977) Labor productivity and the elasticity of factor substitution in West Germany industries. Review of Economics and Statistics 59 366-371
30. Sato R, Hoffman F (1968) Production functions with variable elasticity of substitution: Some analysis and testing. Review of Economics and Statistics 50: 453-460
31. Smetters K (2003) The (interesting) dynamic properties of the neoclassical growth model with CES production. Review of Economic Dynamics 6: 697-707
32. Solow RM (1956) A contribution to the theory of economic growth. Quarterly Journal of Economics 70: 65-94
33. Solow RM (1958) A Skeptical note on the constancy of the relative shares. American Economic Review 48: 618-631
34. Summers R, Heston A (1991) The penn world tables (mark 5): An expanded set of international comparisons, 1950–1988. Quarterly Journal of Economics 106: 327-368
35. Tallman EW, Wang P (1994) Human capital and endogenous growth: Evidence from Japan. Journal of Monetary Economics 34: 101-124
36. Tsang HH, Yeung P (1976) A generalized model for the CES-VES family of production function. Metroeconomica 28: 107-118
37. Zellner A, Ryu H (1998) Alternative functional forms for production, cost and returns to scale functions. Journal of Applied Econometrics 13: 101-127

Financial Intermediation and Economic Growth: A Semiparametric Approach

Thanasis Stengos[1] and Zhihong Liang[2]

[1] Department of Economics, University of Guelph, Guelph, Ontario N1G 2W1, Canada.
tstengos@uoguelph.ca
[2] Department of Economics, University of Guelph, Guelph, Ontario N1G 2W1, Canada.
zliang@uoguelph.ca

Summary. In this paper we examine the effect of financial development on economic growth in an additive Instrumental Variable (IV)-augmented Partially Linear Regression (PLR) model using panel data of 66 countries for the period 1961-1995. Three common measures of financial development are used. Our results show that the effect of the exogenous component of a financial intermediary development index on economic growth depends greatly on the definition and measurement of that index. Financial development affects growth in a positive but non-linear way using a Liquid Liabilities index and in an almost linear way when using a Private Credit index. The effect becomes ambiguous when a Commercial-Central Bank index is used.

1 Introduction

The role of financial development on economic growth has been examined both theoretically and empirically in the recent literature. As summarized by Levine [11], financial intermediaries act as facilitators to (i) produce information ex-ante about possible investments and allocate capital accordingly (ii) monitor investments and exert corporate governance after providing finance (iii) facilitate the trading, diversification, and management of risk (iv) mobilize and pool savings and (v) ease the exchange of goods and services. Below we will provide a brief review of the recent theoretical and empirical literature on the subject.

The theoretical models focus on modeling the particular services provided by the financial sector and how these services influence resource allocation, productivity improvement and economic growth. Diamond [4] highlights the role of improving corporate governance of financial intermediary. In his model the intermediary mobilizes the savings of many individuals and lends these resources to firms. The financial intermediary has a gross cost advantage in monitoring and eliminates the free-rider problem since the intermediary does the monitoring for all the investors. Furthermore, as financial intermediaries and firms develop long-run relationships, the information acquisition costs can be further lowered. Bencivenga and Smith [2] emphasize the role of the financial intermediaries in diversifying the liquidity risk. In their endogenous growth model, agents have to leave a part of their assets as liquid assets, which is unproductive to meet their unforeseeable liquidity risk. Financial intermediaries which pooled savings together enable the economy to reduce the fraction of savings held in the form of unproductive liquid assets. Consequently, higher proportion of savings is shifted to productive asset, which in turn affects the equilibrium growth rate. Greenwood and Jovanovic [7] develop a model in which both financial development and economic growth are endogenously determined. Financial intermediaries collect and analyze information, improve capital allocation and promote growth. Concurrently, growth stimulates financial development because it allows for implementation of costly financial structures. King and Levine [10] construct a model in which the financial intermediary sector plays an active role in identifying, managing, and financing the most promising productivity-enhancing activities. In these ways, better financial systems stimulate economic growth by accelerating the rate of innovation.

The empirical studies examine the evidence regarding the possible contribution of the financial sector to economic growth. The advent of large macroeconomic data sets makes these empirical studies possible. The empirical work involves cross-country studies, panel studies, pure time-series investigations, and country case studies. One of the most influential studies on the subject is King and Levine [9]. They construct four different financial development indicators, and based on data covering a cross-section of 80 countries during the period 1960-1989, they report that higher levels of financial development are significantly and robustly correlated with faster current and future rates of economic growth, physical capital accumulation, and economic efficiency improvements. In addition, they conclude that the link between economic growth and financial development is not just a contemporaneous correlation. Instead, finance seems to lead economic growth in an important way. This work does not, however, confront the potential biases caused by simultaneity or omitted variables, including country-specific effects, as pointed out by Beck, Levine and Loayza [1].

Levine, Loayza, and Beck [12] use econometric techniques that directly confront the potential biases induced by simultaneity, omitted variables and unobserved country-specific effects to examine the role of financial development: a cross-sectional instrumental- variable (IV) estimator and Generalized Method of Moments (GMM) dynamic panel estimators. The cross-sectional and panel results confirm that the weakly exogenous components of financial intermediary development exert a statistically significant and positive influence on economic growth. The authors therefore conclude that the data suggest a strong, positive, link between financial intermediary development and economic growth.

However, the above studies all rely on the notion that the relationship between economic growth and financial intermediaries is linear. Some recent studies explore the possible non-linear relationship between financial development and economic growth. Economic theory exploring this aspect suggests that there is a nonlinear effect of financial intermediary development on economic growth. Khan [8] presents a non-linear relationship between financial and economic development. Financial institutions have generally a positive effect on growth whose magnitude varies positively with the level of economic growth. Deidda and Fattouh [3] present a simple model with risk averse agents and costly financial transactions such that the growth effect of financial development is ambiguous at low levels of development, while it becomes eventually positive as development proceeds. Running a threshold regression model they find that in low-income countries there is no significant relationship between financial development and growth, whereas in high income countries there is positive and strongly significant relationship. Similar work by Xu [20] using a VAR model finds that there is strong evidence that financial development is important to economic growth both in the short term and in the long term. For the low or lower-middle income countries in his sample financial development display negative effects on GDP growth and investment, while the reverse is true for the high income countries.

Rioja and Valev [16] argue that the relationship between financial development and growth varies according to the level of financial development of the country. They divide the countries into three groups according some threshold level of financial development. Using GMM dynamic panel techniques they find that financial development has a large, positive effect on growth in the middle and high regions, and negligible effects on economic growth in the low region.

The econometric techniques used in the literature involve GMM or IV estimation in order to tackle the issue of simultaneity, VAR causality tests in order to find the direction of causality between financial development and growth, or threshold regression model to uncover a possibly non-monotonic relationship. In this paper we adopt a new methodological approach to confront the above issues that is more flexible than what has been adopted so far in the literature. We use an IV augmented semiparametric partial linear regression (IV-PLR) model to investigate the possible effect of financial development on growth. Hence we tackle both the issues of simultaneity and nonlinearity at the same time. The data set we use is from Levine, Loayza and Beck [12]. It consists of observation for 66 countries for the period 1961-1995. The IV-PLR regression model employes an additive structure to investigate the marginal effect of financial development on economic growth after controlling for simultaneity. We use the marginal integration method proposed by Linton and Nielsen [13] and Fan et al. [5] to obtain consistent estimators. Our results show that the effects of finance on economic growth vary in different types of countries, depending on how we measure the level of development of the financial sector. The new methodological approach is the contribution of this study to the existing literature.

The remainder of the paper is organized as follows. Section 2 discusses the data that we use. Section 3 provides a brief discussion of the semiparametric regression methodology that yields a graphical representation of the effect of financial development on growth. Section 4 presents and discusses the results and finally we conclude in Section 5.

2 Data

The data set we use is from Levine, Loayza and Beck [12]. It consists of observations for 66 countries for the period 1961-1995. The data are averaged over five-year intervals: 1961-1965, 1966-1970, , 1991-1995, so there are seven observations per country. Table 1 presents the list of countries that are included in our sample and Table 2 provides summary statistics on the variables used in this paper and their correlations with each other.

There are different measures of financial development in the empirical literature, and different indicators will proxy different aspects of the financial system. Each has particular strengths and weaknesses. Since it is impossible to construct accurate, comparable measures of financial services for a broad cross-section of countries over the past 35 years, following Levine, Loayza and Beck [12] we use three measures of financial intermediary development: Private Credit (PC), Commercial versus Central Bank (CCB), and Liquid Liabilities (LL). Private Credit is the credit issued to the private sector as a percentage of GDP. It measures the role of financial intermediaries in channelling funds to the private sector, as opposed to governments, government agencies and public enterprises. The assumption is that financial systems that allocate more credit to private firms are more engaged in research and development by firms, providing risk management services, mobilizing savings and facilitating transactions. Commercial versus Central Bank is defined as commercial bank assets divided by commercial bank plus central bank assets. It measures the relative importance of commercial banks vis-a-vis the Central bank in allocating society's savings. It assumes implicitly that commercial banks are better at evaluating the potential returns and risks of various projects. Finally, Liquid Liabilities is defined as currency plus demand and interest-bearing liabilities of banks and non-bank financial intermediaries as percent of GDP. This variable, like Private Credit, is a measure of financial depth and thus of the overall size of the financial intermediary sector. The underlying assumption is that the quality of financial services is positively correlated with the size of the financial intermediary sector.

3 Econometric Methodology

Semiparametric methods are quite useful in econometric modeling. To study the effect of financial development on economic growth we apply a particular version of the PLR model which allows for the (unknown) nonlinear components to enter additively, namely the additive PLR model. The advantage it has over the more widely used semiparametric PLR model, see Robinson [17], is that the additive model allows for the explicit estimation of the marginal effects of these non-linear components on the dependent variable, whereas the traditional semiparametric PLR formulation treats the variables that enter the (unknown) nonlinear part of the model as nuisance variables. We can also graphically present the nonparametric component of the different measures of financial development to shed light into their nonlinear shape and offer guide to a more suitable parametric specification.

Argentina	United Kingdom	Norway
Australia	Ghana	New Zealand
Austria	Gambia, The	Pakistan
Belgium	Greece	Panama
Bolivia	Guatemala	Peru
Brazil	Guyana	Philippines
Canada	Honduras	Papua New Guinea
Switzerland	Haiti	Portugal
Chile	India	Paraguay
Cameroon	Ireland	Rwanda
Congo	Israel	Sudan
Colombia	Italy	Senegal
Costa Rica	Jamaica	El Salvador
Germany	Japan	Sweden
Denmark	Kenya	Syria
Dominican Republic	Korea, Republic of	Togo
Algeria	Sri Lanka	Thailand
Ecuador	Mexico	Trinidad and Tobago
Egypt, Arab Rep.	Mauritius	Uraguay
Spain	Malaysia	United States
Finland	Niger	Venezuela
France	Netherlands	South Africa

Table 1. Country List and Order in Data Sets: 66-Country Sample.

The semiparametric PLR model can be written as

$$y_{i,t} = \alpha y_{i,t-1} + \beta' X_{i,t} + f(F_{i,t}) + \varepsilon_{i,t} \tag{1}$$

where y is the logarithm of real per capita GDP, X represents the set of explanatory variables (other than lagged per capita GDP and indicators of development of financial intermediation) that controls for other factors associated with economic growth, ε is the error term, and the subscripts i and t represent country and time period, respectively. F refers to indicators of financial intermediary development.

As mentioned in the introduction many theoretical models show that financial development is likely endogenous (e.g. Greenwood and Jovanovic [7]), which implies that $E(\varepsilon_{i,t} \mid F_{i,t}) \neq 0$. Estimating model (1) directly will generate biased estimators. We can handle this problem by introducing a set of instruments for F.[3] Then we can express $F_{i,t}$ in terms of these instruments $G_{i,t}$ as

$$F_{i,t} = g(G_{i,t}) + u_{i,t} \tag{2}$$

---

[3]The approach below has been used in the context of a system of Engel curves by Lyssiotou, Pashardes and Stengos [14] to examine the effect of endogenous expenditures on budget shares.

Variable	GDP growth	Initial income per capita	Average Years of Sec. schooling	Private credit	Commercial Central bank	Liquid liabilities	Government size	Openness To trade	Inflation rate	Black Market Premium
Mean	1.8183	4127.4741	1.2396	38.2606	78.3954	41.8294	14.7932	57.6398	13.8396	36.1045
Maximum	9.8585	20134.8073	5.1500	205.9511	100.0000	191.4396	44.9718	314.5206	222.3284	4467.1100
Minimum	-10.0209	173.7998	0.0000	0.9059	12.2742	6.4407	4.0636	9.4113	-3.0551	-5.3540
Standard deviation	2.7691	4873.9960	0.9615	32.9257	19.5452	25.7119	5.8124	37.5822	25.0886	222.6186
Correlations										
GDP growth	1									
Initial income per capita	0.0702	1								
Avg. years of sec. schooling	0.0865	0.7183	1							
Private Credit	0.1324	0.7708	0.6258	1						
Commercial-central Bank	0.2477	0.4733	0.2723	0.5247	1					
Liquid Liabilities	0.1532	0.6189	0.5014	0.8345	0.403	1				
Government size	0.0034	0.3683	0.26	0.1906	0.1848	0.1955	1			
Openness to trade	-0.0045	-0.0725	-0.0103	-0.0382	0.1037	0.0381	0.1978	1		
Inflation rate	-0.2059	-0.1208	-0.0031	-0.1904	-0.2322	-0.2089	-0.0903	-0.1777	1	
Black market premium	-0.2345	-0.1039	-0.0663	-0.1067	-0.2205	-0.0365	-0.0592	0.0303	0.0863	1

Table 2. Descriptive statistics, 1960-1995, 66 countries.

where, for simplicity, $g(G_{i,t})$ is assumed to be parametric, say $g(G_{i,t}) = b'G_{i,t}$. We choose lagged explanatory variables as instruments. Thus, (2) can be written as

$$F_{i,t} = b'Z_{i,t-1} + u_{i,t} \qquad (3)$$

where Z represents all the explanatory variables in (1)

We assume that $E(\varepsilon_{i,t} \mid Z_{i,t-1}, u_{i,t}) = E(\varepsilon_{i,t} \mid u_{i,t})$. It then follows that $E(\varepsilon_{i,t} \mid u_{i,t}) \neq 0$, since $E(\varepsilon_{i,t} \mid F_{i,t}) \neq 0$. Hence, one can decompose $\varepsilon_{i,t}$ into $\xi_i(u_{i,t}) + \varepsilon_{i,t}$, where $\xi_i(u_{i,t}) = E(\varepsilon_{i,t} \mid u_{i,t})$ and $\varepsilon_{i,t} = \varepsilon_{i,t} - E(\varepsilon_{i,t} \mid u_{i,t})$. Equation (1) then becomes

$$y_{i,t} = \alpha y_{i,t-1} + \beta' X_{i,t} + f(F_{i,t}) + \xi_i(u_{i,t}) + \varepsilon_{i,t} \qquad (4)$$

We replace the unobservable $u_{i,t}$ by the observable $\widehat{u}_{i,t} = F_{i,t} - \widehat{b}'Z_{i,t-1}$. Then equation (4) becomes

$$y_{i,t} = \alpha y_{i,t-1} + \beta' X_{i,t} + f(F_{i,t}) + \xi_i(\widehat{u}_{i,t}) + \varepsilon_{i,t}^* \qquad (5)$$

where the error $\varepsilon_{i,t}^* = \varepsilon_{i,t} + \xi_i(u_{i,t}) - \xi_i(\widehat{u}_{i,t})$.

One can use Robinson's [17] estimator to obtain root-n-consistent estimation of parameters α and β in model (5), say $\widehat{\alpha}$ and $\widehat{\beta}$. Then substitute $\widehat{\alpha}$ and $\widehat{\beta}$ into the model (5):

$$y_{i,t} - \widehat{\alpha} y_{i,t-1} - \widehat{\beta}' X_{i,t} = f(F_{i,t}) + \xi_i(\widehat{u}_{i,t}) + \varepsilon_{i,t}^{**} \qquad (6)$$

where $\varepsilon_{i,t}^{**}$ denotes the new composite error term that accounts for the estimation of α and β. We use the marginal integration method proposed by Linton and Nielsen [13] and Fan et al. [5] to obtain consistent estimates of $f(F_{i,t})$ and $\xi_i(\widehat{u}_{i,t})$, say $\widehat{f}(F_{i,t})$ and $\widehat{\xi}_i(\widehat{u}_{i,t})$. It is of course $\widehat{f}(F_{i,t})$ the estimated function that we are interested in, since it captures the marginal effects of the financial intermediary variable on per capita growth clean of any endogeneity.

The important result from applying marginal integration to the additive PLR model (5) is that the asymptotic distribution of $(\widehat{f}(F_{i,t}) - f(F_{i,t}))$ is the same as if the other components were known. In other words, $\widehat{f}(F_{i,t})$ behaves in the same way as if it were an one dimensional local non-parametric estimator and avoids the so-called curse of dimensionality that plagues many non-parametric and semiparametric applications. This is one of the strongest supporting arguments in flavor of the above method vis-a-vis the more traditional non-parametric estimation methods.

In this paper we will use the estimates of $f(F_{i,t})$ and its graphical representation to detect the possible non-linear shape of $f(F_{i,t})$ in the context of a growth regression.

For estimation purposes we have used the Gaussian kernel. The choice of bandwidth is according to the formula $c \cdot s_{z_s} \cdot n^{-\frac{1}{6}}$, where s_{z_s} is the standard deviation of F and $\widehat{u}$, respectively, c is a constant, and n is the number of observations. We use different values of c to check for the sensitivity of our results to different bandwidth choices.

Regressors	(1)priv	(2)btot	(3)lly
Initial income per capita[a]	**-0.0000**	**-0.0000**	**-0.0000**
	(−3.0905)	(−4.6154)	(−3.2183)
Avg yrs of sec. schooling	**0.0033**	**0.0036**	*0.0027*
	(1.7030)	(1.9519)	(1.3740)
Goverment size[a]	-0.0011	0.0010	0.0009
	(−0.2578)	(0.2443)	(0.2249)
Openness to trade[a]	-0.0029	-0.0004	**-0.0044**
	(−1.1578)	(−0.1566)	(−1.7530)
Inflation[b]	*-0.0150*	**-0.0172**	-0.0070
	(−1.5640)	(−1.8248)	(−0.6930)
Black market premium[b]	**-0.0227**	**-0.0172**	**-0.0250**
	(−5.5683)	(−4.0659)	(−6.4617)
Liquid Liabilities[a]			
Comm. vs. Central Bank[a]			
Private Credit[a]			
Dummy OECD	**0.0158**	**0.0235**	**0.0132**
	(2.7556)	(4.4795)	(2.2016)

[a] In the regression, this variable is included as log(variable). [b] In the regression, this variable is included as log(1+variable). The t-statistics are given in parentheses. The number in **Bold** is significant at 5% level, and that in *Italics* is significant at 10% level.

Table 3. Semiparametric Regression for Growth Rates.

4 Empirical Results

Following Levine, Loayza, and Beck [12] we use a set of explanatory variables that make up the standard human-capital augmented endogenous growth model. These include the standard controls that have been used in the literature in addition to the financial intermediation variables described above. They are initial income, educational attainment, government size, openness to trade, inflation, the black market exchange rate premium, as well as the indicator of financial development. The dependant variable is GDP per capita growth. We take all the explanatory variables except for the financial indicators to be part of the linear part of the model, whereas the financial indicators make up the non-linear components of the model. There are three regression functions in which we use three different indicators of financial development respectively.

Table 3 presents the regression results. From the table we can see that most explanatory variables are significant at 5% significant level although their magnitude is smaller than what was obtained by Levine, Loayza, and Beck [12]. The coefficient on the logarithm of initial income is negative and significant, supporting the hypothesis of conditional $\beta-$ convergence. Government size is not significant in all three cases. Openness to trade is only significant in the third regression where Liquid Liabilities is used as an indicator of financial development. Black market premium is insignificant in the third regression.

The estimates of the nonlinear effect of the financial development indices on economic growth with their 95 percent confidence bands are presented graphically in

Figures 1-3. The horizontal axis shows the indicators of financial development (Liquid Liabilities, Private Credit and Commercial versus Central Bank, respectively), and the vertical axis their marginal effect on growth, $f(F_{it})$. For comparison in each figure we also include the benchmark line that corresponds to the linear effect under a standard parametric specification. The relationship between financial development and growth depends on how the financial development is measured. The relationship is apparently non-linear in Figure 1 where the indicator is Liquid Liabilities. The effect of financial development on growth varies according to the level of financial development of the country. The curvature of the graph implies that, on average, in the countries with low to intermediate levels of financial development, improving financial services has a large, positive effect on growth. In the high level of financial development region, additional financial improvements may have a negative effect on growth.

The negative effect of financial development on growth at high levels of financial intermediation may appear surprising and requires some discussion. One possible explanation is the improper assumption of the positive correlation of the quality of financial services and the size of the financial sector. The Liquid Liabilities indicator assumes that the quality of financial services is positively correlated with the size of the financial intermediary sector. This is true at low levels of Liquid Liabilities. However, when Liquid Liabilities have reached a certain level, financial intermediaries may find it more difficult to finance profitable projects and to maintain their growth. As a result they would have to finance some projects that are less profitable, something that implies that resources are allocated less efficiently resulting in lower economic growth.

In Figure 2 where Private Credit is used a the measure of financial intermediary development, the effect on growth is almost linear and not different statistically from zero. Financial development has little effect on growth when Private Credit is used. Figure 3 presents an ambiguous relationship between financial development and growth probably due to the poor measurement of Commercial -Central Bank index as an indicator of financial development. The banking sector is just one of sources of financial intermediation. There are other important sources of financial intermediation, such as insurance companies, private pension funds and the securities market which is not accounted for. In countries with regulatory restrictions on financial intermediaries and in countries with undeveloped legal systems that do not effectively support formal financial development, firms frequently act as financial intermediaries. Petersen and Rajan [15] show that firms frequently act as financial intermediaries in providing trade credit to related firms. Banks may simply lend to the government or public enterprises where they don't care too much about potential returns and risks. Furthermore, the definition of a bank and of a non-bank are not always consistent across countries, and it is sometime difficult to distinguish development banks from commercial banks in many countries. As in Levine, Loayza and Beck [12], we note that this measurement is not a direct measure of the quality and quantity of financial services provided by financial intermediaries.

Our results show that the effect of financial development on economic growth depends crucially on the definition and measurement of the financial development index. Economic theory suggests that financial systems influence growth by easing information and transactions costs and thereby improving the allocation of capital, corporate governance, risk management, resource mobilization, and financial exchanges. However these three common empirical measures of financial development do not directly measure these financial functions. They are all bank based measures and only rough proxies for financial development. Lack of accurate measures of financial development is one of the common problems that plague the empirical study of finance and growth nexus. The role of other important financial intermediaries should not be ignored.

5 Conclusion

In this paper we employ an additive IV-PLR model to study the potential nonlinearity of the effect of financial development on growth. We did discover that financial intermediary affects growth in a nonlinear way. However, this effect is highly dependent on how the financial intermediary development is measured. We use three common measurement of financial development and the results are different. Financial development affects economic growth nonlinearly using a Liquid Liabilities index, while the effect of Private Credit is almost linear and insignificant. The effect is ambiguous when Commercial -Central Bank is used as an index. Our result suggest that these three measurements capture different functions of the financial sector that have different effects on growth. Search for better variables measuring financial development will help to improve our understanding of the finance growth nexus.

Appendix

Fan, Härdle, and Mammen [5] applied marginal integration to the following general additive partially linear regression model:

$$Y_i = \alpha + X_i^T \beta + g_1(Z_{1i}) + g_2(Z_{2i}) + \cdots + g_p(Z_{pi}) + u_i \qquad i = 1, \cdots, n \qquad (\text{A1})$$

where X_i is a discrete variable of dimension q, β is a $q \times 1$ vector of parameters, α is a scalar parameter, Z'_{si}s are univariate continuous variables, and $g_s(\cdot)$ ($s = 1, \ldots, n$) are unknown smooth functions. The observations $\{Y_i, X_i, Z_{1i}, \ldots Z_{pi}\}_{i=1}^n$ are independently and identically distributed (i.i.d). One needs also the identification restriction that $E[g_s(Z_z)] = 0$ for $s = 1, \ldots, p$.

Fan and Li [6] allow for X_i to be continuous as well as discrete. The important result from applying marginal integration to the extended additive regression model (A1) is that the asymptotic distribution of $(\widehat{g}_s(z) - g_s(z))(s = 1, \ldots, p)$ is the same as if the other components $g_l(\cdot)$ for $l \neq s$ and β were known. In other words, $\widehat{g}_s(z)$ behaves in the same way as if it were a one-dimensional local smoother. For details about the asymptotic properties of the estimators of parameters α β and $g_s(z)(s = 1, \ldots, p)$, see Fan and Li [6] and Fan, Härdle, and Mammen [5].

The idea behind marginal integration can be illustrated in the following additive regression model with two regressors:

$$Y_i = \alpha + g_1(Z_{1i}) + g_2(Z_{2i}) + u_i \qquad i = 1, \cdots, n \qquad (A2)$$

where $\{Y_i, Z_{1i}, Z_{2i}\}_{i=1}^n$ are $i.i.d$ random variables, $E(u_i \mid Z_{1i}, Z_{2i}) = 0$, α is an unknown parameter, $g_1(\cdot)$ and $g_2(\cdot)$ are unknown univariate functions that obey the identifiability condition that $E[g_1(Z_1)] = 0$ and $E[g_2(Z_2)] = 0$.

As shown by Stone [18, 19] the additive components $g_s(z)(s = 1, 2)$ in (A2) can be consistently estimated at the same rate as a fully nonparametric regression with only one regressor. In other words the additive regression model in some sense provides a way of tackling the "curse of dimensionality" problem that is one of the most important weaknesses of nonparametric estimation methods. In recent papers Linton and Nielsen [13], Fan, Härdle, and Mammen [5] and Fan and Li [6] employ marginal integration as a way of obtaining estimates of the components of the additive regression model. Linton and Nielsen's [13] paper deals with a simple additive model with two components as in equation (A2), whereas Fan, Härdle, and Mammen [5] and Fan and Li [6] extend the regression function to allow for a more general partially linear formulation as in equation (A1).

The idea behind marginal integration in the context of equation (A3) can be described as follows. Let $E(Y \mid Z_1 = z_1, Z_2 = z_2) = \alpha(z_1, z_2)$. One can estimate $\alpha(z_1, z_2)$ by a non-parametric local smoother, say $\widehat{\alpha}(z_1, z_2)$, and then obtain an estimator of $\{\alpha + g_1(z_1)\}$ by integrating $\widehat{\alpha}(z_1, z_2)$ over z_2, i.e. $\widetilde{m}_1(z_1) = n^{-1} \sum_{j=1}^n \widehat{\alpha}(z_1, Z_{2j})$. Since $E[g_1(Z_1)] = 0$, we can obtain the estimator of $g_1(z_1)$ by subtracting the sample mean of $\widetilde{m}_1(\cdot)$ from $\widetilde{m}_1(z_1)$, i.e. $\widetilde{g}_1(z_1) = \widetilde{m}_1(z_1) - n^{-1} \sum_{j=1}^n \widetilde{m}_1(Z_{1i})$. Similarly, we can obtain an estimator for $g_2(z_2)$.

Equation (A2) can be extended to allow for an additive linear component. In that case we have

$$Y_i = \alpha + X_i^T \beta + g_1(Z_{1i}) + g_2(Z_{2i}) + u_i \qquad (A3)$$

where X_i is a variable (discrete or continuous) of dimension q, β is a $q \times 1$ vector of parameters, α is a scalar parameter as before. We can obtain a $\sqrt{n}$-consistent estimator of β using Robinson's [17] approach. Let us denote such an estimator by $\widehat{\beta}$. Equation (A3) can be then written as

$$Y_i - X_i^T \widehat{\beta} = \alpha + g_1(Z_{1i}) + g_2(Z_{2i}) + u_i + X_i^T(\beta - \widehat{\beta}) \qquad (A4)$$

where $u_i + X_i^T(\beta - \widehat{\beta})$ is the new composite error term. In a similar fashion as with equation (A2) we can apply marginal integration to equation (A4) to obtain estimates of $g_1(z_1)$ and $g_2(z_2)$.

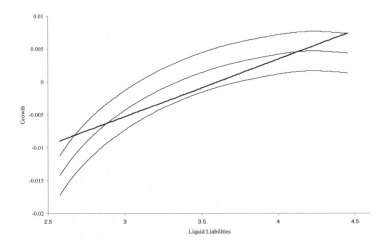

Fig. 1. Effect of liquidity-liabilities index on economics growth.

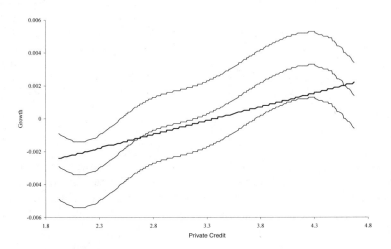

Fig. 2. Effect of private-credit index on economics growth.

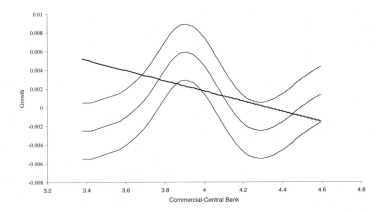

Fig. 3. Effect of commercial-central bank index on economics growth.

References

1. Beck T, Levine R, Loayza N (2000) Finance and the sources of growth. Journal of Financial Economics 58: 261-300
2. Bencivenga VR, Smith BD (1991) Financial intermediation and endogenous growth. Review of Economics Studies 58: 195-209
3. Deidda L, Fattouh B (2002) Non-linearity between finance and growth. Economics Letters 74: 339-345
4. Diamond DW (1984) Financial Intermediation and delegated monitoring. Review of Economic Studies 51: 393-414
5. Fan J, Härdle W, Mammen E (1998) Direct estimation of low dimensional components in additive models. Annals of Statistics 26: 943-971
6. Fan Y, Li Q (2004) A new kernel based method for estimating additive partially linear models. Statistica Sinica (forthcoming).
7. Greenwood J, Jovanovic B (1990) Financial development, growth, and the distribution of income. Journal of Political Economy 98: 1076-1107
8. Khan A (2001) Financial development and economic growth. Macroeconomic Dynamics 5: 413-433

9. King RG, Levine R (1993) Finance and growth: Schumpeter might be right. Quarterly Journal of Economics 108: 717-738

10. King RG, Levine R (1993) Finance, entrepreneurship, and growth: theory and evidence. Journal of Monetary Economics 32: 513-542

11. Levine R (2004) Finance and growth: Theory, evidence, and mechanisms. In Aghion P, Durlauf S (eds) Handbook of Economic Growth, Amsterdam: Nort-Holland Elsevier Publishers (fortcoming)

12. Levine R, Loayza N, Beck T (2000) Financial intermediation and growth: Causality and causes. Journal of Monetary Economics 46: 31-77

13. Linton OB, Nielsen JP (1995) A kernel method of estimating structural nonparametric regression based on marginal integration. Biometrika 82: 93-100

14. Lyssiotou P, Pashardes P, Stengos T (1999) Testing the rank of Engel curves with endogenous expenditure. Economics Letters 64: 61-65

15. Petersen MA, Rajan RG (1997) Trade credit: Some theories and evidence. Review of Financial Studies 10: 661-692

16. Rioja F, Valev N (2003) Does one size fit all?: A reexamnation of the finance growth relationship. Journal of Development Economics (forthcoming)

17. Robinson P (1988) Root-N-consistent semiparametric regression. Econometrica 56: 931-954

18. Stone CJ (1985) Additive regression and other nonparametric models. Annals of Statistics 13: 685-705

19. Stone CJ (1986) The dimensionality reduction principle for generalized additive models. The Annals of Statistics 14: 592-606

20. Xu Z (2000) Financial development, investment, and growth. Economic Inquiry 38: 331-344

Bridging the Gap: Linking Economics and Econometrics*

David F. Hendry

Economics Department, Oxford University, Manor Road Building, Manor Road, Oxford, OX1 3UQ, UK. david.hendry@nuffield.ox.ac.uk

Summary. The marked gap that exists between macroeconomic theory models and applied econometric findings arises because most observed data variability in macro-econometrics is due to factors that are absent from economic theories, but which econometric models have to tackle (particularly various non-stationarities). *Ceteris paribus* may be fine for theoretical reasoning, but is unacceptable for empirical modelling. A 'minor influence' theorem is needed instead which can only be established empirically. Thus, the chapter considers an automatic selection approach to bring objectivity and credibility to empirical econometric modelling.

1 Introduction

The marked gap that exists between macro-economic theory models and applied econometric findings arises because much observed data variability in macroeconomics is due to factors that are absent from economic theories. Various sources of non-stationarity impinge on macroeconomic data, deriving from technical progress, new legislation, institutional change, financial innovation and political factors including conflicts, inducing both evolution and structural breaks which change the distributional properties of the data. In macroeconomics, forecast failure (defined as a significant deterioration in forecast performance relative to its anticipated outcome, usually based on historical performance) is the norm, and is almost certainly due to structural breaks (see e.g., Clements and Hendry [5, 6]).

Apart from general equilibrium theory (see e.g., Kirman [48], on its evolution) – where sameness would result, not non-stationarity – few economic theories claim completeness. Thus, theory relies on many implicit *ceteris paribus* clauses. These

---

*Financial support from the ESRC under a Professorial Research Fellowship, RES051270035, is gratefully acknowledged. I am indebted to Sule Akkoyunlu, Gunnar Bårdsen, Øyvind Eitrheim, Vivien Hendry, Eilev Jansen, Katarina Juselius, Søren Johansen, Sophocles Mavroeidis, Grayham Mizon, Ragnar Nymoen, Tore Schweder, Bernt Stigum and participants at the Econometric Methodology Conference at the Norwegian Academy of Science and Letters, Oslo for helpful comments on an earlier draft.

may seem valid for theoretical reasoning, but are not an acceptable basis for empirical modelling. Even if the impounded variables are strongly exogenous, it is meaningless to appeal to *ceteris paribus* when the potential effects are non-stationary, since 'other things' cannot be 'equal' (i.e., unchanged). Instead, 'minor influence' theorems or empirical evidence (preferably both) are needed, specifying why omitted factors can be neglected, not because they will not change, but because changes in them are of a smaller order of importance than the included effects. At present such results rarely exist.

Generalizations about 'macroeconomic theory' are hazardous, as a huge range of approaches and issues are addressed in the literature. Nevertheless, some generic aspects seem open to discussion. Many economic theory models are derived from constrained optimization, dating from the classic treatment in Samuelson [64]. Other approaches regard the fundamental laws of economics as being entailed by heterogeneity of endowments, (see e.g. Hildenbrand [39, 40]), perhaps with agents having incomplete information, or holding imperfect-knowledge expectations (see e.g., Aghion et al. [1]). Yet others advocate real-business cycle theories with rational expectations (see e.g., Kydland and Prescott [16, 51]). Dynamic stochastic general equilibrium (DSGE) models abound (see e.g., Smets and Wouters [66], for a recent implementation); yet Stiglitz [69] proposes the foundations of a new macroeconomics in asymmetric information inducing Keynesian effects, and derives completely different implications for economic policy from those of 'new classical' theories. Moreover, some aspects of economic theory models are *au choix*, such as forms of utility functions: but with non-stationary data, at best one transformation will be able to characterize the evidence in a constant relationship. For example, linear relationships between variables often arise from Euler equations (as in Hall [23]), but seem unlikely to be congruent descriptions in growing economies.

The absence from economic theories of the main forces for variability is common across different research arenas, but differs in form. In micro-economics, low R^2 values, usually ascribed to individual heterogeneity and idiosyncracies, reveal that most of the variability is not accounted for by the postulated models. Heterogeneity can generate high levels of unexplained variability, but there has to remain considerable doubt that all the major factors have been included. Likewise, in panel-data studies, most of the observed data variance is attributed to persistent 'individual effects' which need to be removed by (e.g.) differencing or deviations from individual means. Such evidence that most micro variability is due to individual heterogeneity hardly sustains using 'representative' agent theories for macro behaviour. Finally, cross-country studies rarely account for key institutional differences between the constituent economies, and often use averages of data over historical epochs where considerable changes occurred between periods (see e.g., Sala-i Martin [63], and the criticisms in Hoover and Perez [42], and Hendry and Krolzig [35]).

In the absence of clear and complete theoretical guidance on all relevant and irrelevant variables, functional forms, exogeneity, dynamics, and non-stationarities, empirical determination is essential. Economists are well aware of the importance of changes in constraints and in institutions, and devote considerable effort to modelling them, as in the vast literatures on credit rationing, policy rules, and economic crises, yet in most empirical studies, *ad hoc* solutions have to be adopted. Thus, large gaps exist between theory and evidence, and this chapter describes some of their sources and possible solutions. For earlier analyses, see Spanos [67], Juselius [44], Hendry [25], and Nymoen [60].

Its structure is as follows. Section 2 discusses the roles of two important forms of non-stationarity, namely unit roots, with the associated topics of cointegration and data transforms, then structural breaks. Next, section 3 considers the substantive issue of relating theory and evidence, focusing on links between means and variances in sub-section 3.1, with the role of time in the specific guise of short-run versus long-run theory being discussed in sub-section 3.2. The implications for theories based on implicit or explicit *ceteris paribus* clauses are noted in sub-section 3.3, expectations are considered in 3.4, and the consequences for economic forecasting derived in sub-section 3.5. Section 4 then asks what determines the credibility of empirical econometric evidence, before section 5 describes an automatic modelling tool which makes model selection both objective and non-distortionary, given a congruent, if potentially over-parameterized, initial general model. The role of theory in that approach is to specify the general formulation and its parameterization, where detailed implementation depends on institutional and historical contingencies, and previous empirical evidence—hopefully encompassed by the new specification. Section 6 concludes.

2 Non-Stationarities

A time-series process is non-stationary if its moments or distributional form change over time. Two main forms of non-stationarity will be considered here. First, sub-section 2.1 discusses unit roots which induce stochastic trends, with the associated possibility of cointegrating relations that remove those unit roots, and retain linear combinations of levels of the variables. The role of data transforms will be emphasized, as unit roots and cointegration are only invariant under linear transformations. Since the topic is now the subject of a vast and well-known literature, the analysis will be illustrative, using empirical time series. Then, in sub-section 2.2, for the same data, we will consider structural breaks which induce location shifts in the processes under analysis, together with the concept of co-breaking.

2.1 Data Transforms, Unit Roots, and Cointegration

Consider a typical group of macroeconomic variables like prices, P, money, M, income, Y, and interest rates, R_L, respectively the price deflator of Y, nominal broad money (M4), real net national income, and the long-term nominal interest rate, as shown in Figure 1 (graphs are usually shown in blocks of four, denoted a, b, d, c, clockwise from top left, as labelled in Figure 1 for illustration). All four series are manifestly non-stationary, with huge ranges of variation apparent over the period 1870–2000, the maximum/minimum ratios of the series being respectively 73, 1010,

14 and a relatively small 6.5 *fold*. Linear models could never characterize such behaviour homogeneously.

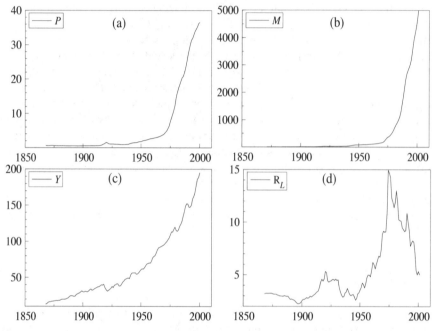

Fig. 1. P, M, Y, R_L.

However, as all four variables are inherently positive, log transformations are feasible, yielding series that are somewhat 'better behaved' (in lower case, denoted p, m, y, r_L): see Figure 2. To facilitate empirical modelling, economic theory would have to derive such log transformations of the aggregates from agents' optimizing behaviour. Such a result might hold for some specific utility or profit functions, but cannot be a generic property: and theories rarely deliver the requisite transforms. In practice, log transformations are successful in 'standardizing' behaviour of long-run time series merely because percentage changes are more stable than absolute for strongly trending series. Aggregates are linear cumulations, so the means thereof have smaller variances than levels: if $x_{i,t} \sim \text{IN}\left[\mu_t, \sigma_t^2\right]$ then $\bar{x}_t = M_t^{-1} \sum_{i=1}^{M_t} x_{i,t} \sim \text{IN}\left[\mu_t, M_t^{-1}\sigma_t^2\right]$. Log transforms of totals and means only differ by population size, which is relatively constant ($\ln \sum_{i=1}^{M_t} x_{i,t} = \ln \bar{x}_t + \ln M_t$), so standard deviations of log aggregates are proportional to scaled standard deviations of means: $\text{SD}[\ln \sum_{i=1}^{M_t} x_{i,t}] \simeq M_t^{-1}\sigma_t/\mu_t$ (see e.g., Hendry [24], Chap. 2.17). Such a transformation implements a dramatic variance reduction, independently of the underlying individual economic behaviour.

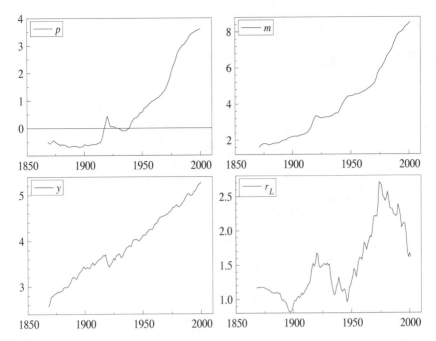

Fig. 2. p, m, y, r_L.

This is not a minor issue, as an economic theory that M is a function of P, Y, R_L could be rejected simply because incorrect data transforms were used: for example, M and m are not cointegrated. What economics does successfully deliver is that real money, M/P, and inverse velocity, M/PY, will be better behaved, especially the last of these: figure 3 confirms those implications for both M/PY and $m - p - y$, and somewhat for $m - p$, but not for M/P. Even so, the range of the inverse velocity series remains about 2.4 fold, from 65% of the mean to 160%: and this against a current UK inflation target of $2\% \pm 1\%$. Moreover, the hypothesis of a unit root in $m - p - y$ cannot be rejected despite the variance reduction of the log-velocity transform. Nevertheless, a reduction by 3 orders of magnitude from a little reasoning is impressive, even if not perfect, and indicates the potential advantages of cointegration as one bridge.

The series in Figure 1 may have stochastic trends, but differencing alone is insufficient to induce stationarity. The changes in all four level series in Figure 4 are highly non-stationary and unlikely candidates for agents to reason about, or base their decisions on—or econometricians to model. Yet many Euler-based equations are formulated in differences of levels.

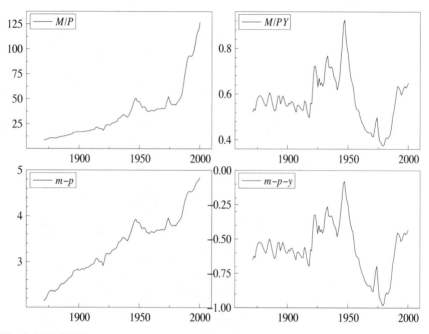

Fig. 3. M/P, M/PY, $m - p$, $m - p - y$.

However, even growth rates can be non-stationary, with means and variances evolving across epochs: see Figure 5, where panel b shows the means of Δm over successive 25-year periods (log interest rates have no obvious finance meaning, but are approximately equal to $\Delta R_L / R_L$, an appropriate heteroscedasticity-reducing transformation). More generally, Figure 6 below shows changes in the 20-year means of some UK time series.

How has economics coped? Many theories entail unit roots, including arbitrage pricing, efficient markets and Euler equations. For example, ΔR_L should be close to a martingale difference sequence to avoid creating a money machine from knowing future bond price movements, and is approximately so (although badly behaved, as Figure 4d demonstrates). Growth theory tries to explain the trending nature of output series, but even endogenous growth models (see e.g., Crafts [11]) would be pushed to explain trending growth rates. And equilibrium theories, of course, predict universal cointegration.

How has empirical econometrics coped? By independently developing statistical models of non-stationarity. These are still in their infancy, but unit roots and cointegration have proved successful tools. A key result is that *both* follow from a reduced-rank condition on the agent's decision system – specifically, that there are fewer controls than targets – and do not need to be separately postulated: see Engle

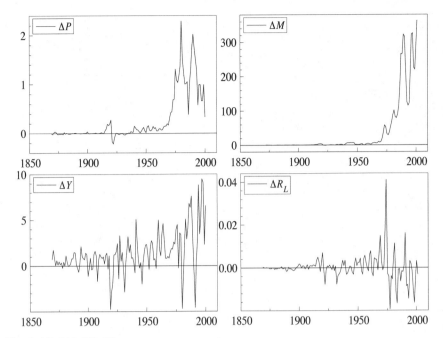

Fig. 4. ΔP, ΔM, ΔY, ΔR_L.

and Granger [3]. Other models of non-stationarity are less developed, but are a major focus of research effort, so we turn to these. An important issue for both economics and econometrics is the need to simultaneously model all the non-stationarities if the resulting theory or model is to be useful.

2.2 Location Shifts

Figures 1–3 not only manifest stochastic trends, their transforms in Figures 4 and 5 reveal clear evidence of location shifts. One can remove one unit root in an integrated process by differencing, yet the series often remains non-stationary: Figure 5b highlights the location shifts for Δm, but also consider the mean and variance of Δp pre and post 1914; or pre and post 1939.

How has empirical econometrics coped with this problem? By 'modelling' special effects. Here, institutional knowledge and economic history become essential ingredients, highlighting the contingency of economics. Consider the findings in Hendry [26], which sought to reveal why earlier attempts at modelling food demand had gone awry:

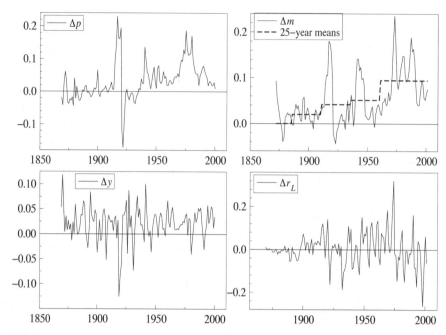

Fig. 5. Δp, Δm, Δy, Δr_L.

For the period 1912–1989, [...] there was World War I (WWI); the 1920–21 flu' epidemic that killed even more people than the war; prohibition (affecting the drinks expenditure component); the Great depression from 1929–35 (approximately, but lingering on to 1939); World War II (WWII); the Korean war (which dramatically spurred demand and inflation); the Vietnam war; and the Oil crises of the mid and late 1970s. Throughout, there was a steady decline in family size, and an increase in average age of death. Such factors need to be handled to avoid contaminating inference.

Other contributors to Magnus and Morgan [55] had eschewed modelling the 1930's data because models seemed non-constant over the combined inter-war and post-war samples. However, one dummy for a period that seems to coincide with a food program, and one for the immediate post-war de-rationing allowed a constant equation to be developed over the sample 1931–1989. Certainly an indicator variable is a crude level of measurement, but the converse strategy of not modelling major institutional changes seems even less attractive. Theory does show that food programs and switches in rationing matter; but few theory models allow for such factors in a way suitable for empirical implementation (although Tobin [72], the original analyst of this data, also published on rationing in Tobin [73]).

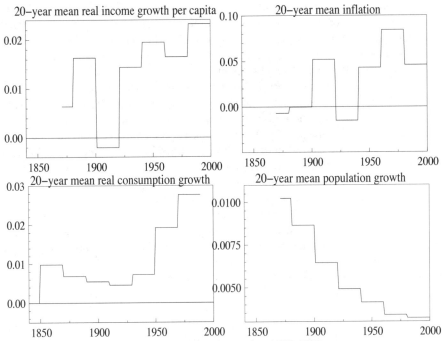

Fig. 6. 20-year mean growth rates of four UK time series, 1850–2000.

The longer the historical epoch spanned by the data sample, the greater the likely number of changes. For a second example, Hendry [30] initially needed 26 indicator variables for modelling inflation over the period 1875–1991, which witnessed not only all the factors in the above quote, but several other important conflicts, the general strike, as well as major legislative, social, and technological changes, and many policy regime shifts, including the end of the gold standard and the breakdown of Bretton Woods. Despite the large number of measures proposed for all the factors that might influence inflation, most 'extreme event' indicators proved significant (as well as some for data mis-measurement): the theory examining their combination into an 'index' is explored in Hendry and Santos [38].

Nevertheless, lest it be thought that the effort of modelling long historical periods is not worthwhile, other studies manage without many indicators despite analyzing the same long time period. For example, the equation first proposed for money demand in Hendry and Ericsson [32] for data over 1878–1975, updated in Ericsson et al. [17] to 1993, and then extended to the end of the twentieth century by Escribano [18] was found to be constant (using the data series shown in the figures above). Yet it only required one dummy for World Wars I and II combined, and one that was unity over 1971–1975 (zero otherwise) for deregulation of the banking sector following Competition and Credit Control (CCC) regulations. Other than CCC, the postulated relationship captured all other major financial innovations (from the telegraph economizing on transported cash, through the introduction of the cheque book, the massive expansion of the building-society movement, credit cards and ATMs, to interest-bearing retail sight deposits), as well as many different monetary control policies and exchange rate regimes. Consequently, while unmodelled location shifts are pernicious, they can be captured in general models, and empirical evidence is essential to establish which breaks matter.

Underlying these two very different cases is the absence or presence of co-breaking, namely the elimination of location shifts by linear combinations of variables (just as cointegration eliminates unit roots): see Clements and Hendry [6] (Chap. 9) and Massmann [57]. A causal link between variables should entail that shifts in one of the causes induces corresponding shifts in the outcomes. A major role for economic theory is to specify such causal links. Unfortunately, when location shifts are common, incomplete theories will fail empirically: co-breaking seems more likely in general than in over-simplified models.

Indeed the import of this chapter should now be clear: far from diminishing the importance of economic reasoning as a basis for empirical econometrics, modelling the profusion of 'contaminants' and non-stationarities in macroeconomic data is the only way to reveal the underlying economic behaviour. Conversely, theorists need to devote greater effort to models of the likely behavioural reactions of economic agents to major changes of the kind noted above, so that their practical treatment becomes less *ad hoc*. As macrodata are simply the aggregates of the economic microcosm, the same problems must afflict all empirical econometric studies, and are not merely an endemic problem for time-series analysts alone.

3 Linking Economics and Econometrics

Five aspects are considered. First, we discuss the relationships between means and variances in sub-section 3.1: economics is primarily about the former and econometrics about the latter, so explicit links are essential. Economic theories postulate connections between latent or unobservable variables, whereas econometric models estimate the parameters from second moments of observables: this might be a bridge too far. Secondly, the role of time, and more specifically the short run versus the long run, is noted in sub-section 3.2. Thirdly, the viability of *ceteris paribus* clauses is evaluated in sub-section 3.3. Fourthly, sub-section 3.4 considers expectations. Finally, sub-section 3.5 briefly considers the implications of the present framework for economic forecasting.

3.1 Means versus Variances

Although much of modern finance concerns variances, most economic theory is implicitly about relationships between means such as:

$$\mu_y = \beta\mu_z. \tag{1}$$

The most famous example is the permanent income hypothesis (PIH), where μ_y is permanent consumption and μ_z is permanent income, so the income elasticity of consumption is unity. However, other instances abound: most demand and supply functions relate means; expectations and Euler-equation models relate conditional first moments, as do GMM approaches; and so on. Constructs like μ_y and μ_z are inherently unobservable, so additional assumptions are needed to complete the model. For example, Friedman [22] uses:

$$y_t = \mu_y + \varepsilon_{y,t} \text{ and } z_t = \mu_z + \varepsilon_{z,t}$$

together with $\mathsf{E}\left[\varepsilon_{y,t}\varepsilon_{z,t}\right] = 0$ where $\mathsf{E}\left[\cdot\right]$ denotes an expectation. However, much more general mappings could be used without affecting the point of this section.

In contrast, econometrics is a science of second moments. Consider the simplest setting of a linear regression model of a random variable y_t where there are n regressor variables $\mathbf{z}_t' = (z_1 \ldots z_n)$ over a sample $t = 1, \ldots, T$:

$$y_t = \sum_{i=1}^{n} \gamma_i z_{i,t} + v_t \text{ where } v_t \sim \mathsf{IN}\left[0, \sigma_v^2\right] \tag{2}$$

when (2) is congruent (so matches the data evidence in all relevant respects). Also, $\mathsf{E}\left[\mathbf{z}_t v_t\right] = 0$, so:

$$\mathsf{E}\left[y_t \mid \mathbf{z}_t\right] = \gamma' \mathbf{z}_t, \tag{3}$$

which can be written in model form as in (2), or in matrix notation as:

$$y_t = \gamma' \mathbf{z}_t + v_t. \tag{4}$$

Hence from (4):

$$\mathsf{E}\left[y_t\right] = \gamma' \mathsf{E}\left[\mathbf{z}_t\right], \tag{5}$$

which is precisely of the form of (1) when β and μ_z are vectors:

$$\mathsf{E}\left[y_t\right] = \mu_y = \gamma' \mathsf{E}\left[\mathbf{z}_t\right] = \gamma' \mu_z. \tag{6}$$

At first sight, deriving the linear representation in (6) from (2) may suggest (2) is of the appropriate form for throwing light on (1). However, if $\mathbf{y}' = (y_1 \ldots y_T)$ and $\mathbf{Z}' = (\mathbf{z}_1 \ldots \mathbf{z}_T)$ then:

$$\hat{\gamma} = \left(\mathbf{Z}'\mathbf{Z}\right)^{-1} \mathbf{Z}'\mathbf{y} \tag{7}$$

which uses the second moments to estimate the parameters connecting the means. Implicitly, (2) entails:

$$\mathsf{E}\left[y_t \mathbf{z}_t'\right] = \gamma' \mathsf{E}\left[\mathbf{z}_t \mathbf{z}_t'\right],$$

which (having removed an intercept), implies a link between the variances:

$$\sigma_{yz} = \gamma' \Sigma_{zz}. \tag{8}$$

Thus, comparing (1) and (8), means and variances must be connected in exactly the same way to infer about parameters of interest in models of means using estimates based on second moments. One route is to assume some form of weak exogeneity

(Engle et al. [15]), either directly as with the parameter γ linking (6) with (8), or indirectly by postulating 'valid instrumental variables' which satisfy an equivalent weak exogeneity condition. Such a restriction would not be valid for the PIH as formulated in Friedman [22]. Much research remains to be done into when linking means and variances is feasible in non-stationary processes: the current paradigm is to transform the problem to a 'stationary' representation via cointegration, then link the means to variances in the resulting model (such as a vector autoregression, VAR, or a conditional system).

3.2 Short Run versus Long Run

A further discrepant factor which often precludes direct application of even dynamic economic theory is the lack of a clear definition of 'time'. Continuous-time formulations suggest one solution, but most agents' decisions are made discretely, and 'economic time' need not map 1–1 onto 'clock time'. This issue is paramount in understanding what aspects of econometric models are constrained by theoretical reasoning. Often, only the long-run is specified, for a hypothetical steady state, leaving open the adjustment behaviour. There are few viable theoretical models extant for adjustment costs, and the main contender—quadratic adjustment costs—often does not make sense: why would a super tanker, or a skyscraper ever be built if costs grew quadratically with the size of the investment? The large coefficients on lagged dependent variables found empirically (see e.g., Kennan [45]) are sometimes taken to entail that adjustment costs are far from trivial, but that interpretation is not unique. First, panel data studies suggest that 'individual effects' are persistent, and that differencing provides a viable solution, which would lead to coefficients on lagged dependent variables being unity. Secondly, the theory of forecasting shows that differenced-data models are more robust to location shifts (see e.g., Clements and Hendry [6]), with the same implication.

   Cointegration may be thought to have endowed equilibrium approaches with a second life by generalizing that notion to non-stationary processes. Unfortunately, the most pernicious failing in an econometric model is that occasioned by a shift in the equilibrium mean, an event that seems to happen all too often, and thereby induces significant forecast failure. Such shifts are undoubtedly due to other factors changing: money demand equations because of the introduction of new competing assets; savings behaviour because of changes in legislation about health care provision in old age; consumption decisions because of changes in credit rationing – the list could continue endlessly as non-stationarities abound. Thus, unless the theory model is complete, correct, and immutable, there are no grounds for according it a status beyond a cognitive guide. This has not stopped most referees and editors ascribing to a false approach to what they call 'science' in which empirical models must be derived from (their version of) economic theory. But if the theory model was complete, correct and immutable, economics would be at an end: there would be no 'economic theory research' – which the same editors happily continue to publish. A major difficulty to be overcome to bridge any gap is to first acknowledge that such a gap exists.

3.3 *Ceteris paribus* in a Non-Stationary World

In theoretical reasoning, a *ceteris paribus* clause could legitimately impound those potential forces that were not caused by the variables under analysis (i.e., were at least strongly exogenous): but that is not an acceptable basis for empirical modelling of non-stationary processes. To cite Cartwright [4], and in a context where she believes *ceteris paribus* has some value because of its explicit acknowledgment of important procedures that must be taken to control experiments:

> The too optimistic view supposes that theory can in principle always provide us with non-causal concepts to cash out the concept of interference. I argue that our best evidence suggests that that is wishful thinking.

Cartwright views *ceteris paribus* as roughly equivalent to 'if nothing interferes then .... some regularity is observed'. Thus, theories remain testable, albeit that a rejection outcome could be rationalized by a failure of *ceteris paribus* rather than the invalidity of the theory itself. In non-stationary processes that is precisely the problem: nothing will interfere only if other factors are irrelevant, not because they do not change. Econometric modellers are gradually uncovering various sources of non-stationarity, and while there has been a significant attempt by economists to take on board the unit root–cointegration revolution, this cannot yet be said of other sources of non-stationarity, particularly structural breaks inducing location shifts. In effect, it is meaningless to appeal to a *ceteris paribus* clause when the potential effects are non-stationary even if they are strongly exogenous (and so do not change because of changes in the variables under analysis). Instead, a 'minor influence' theorem is needed, which must specify on theoretical or evidential grounds why omitted factors can be neglected, not because they will not change, but because changes in them are of a smaller order of importance than the included effects.

Many theories in economics already postulate that the economic system is a general equilibrium in which everything depends on everything else, so *ceteris paribus* is itself theoretically suspect. Partial equilibrium analysis therefore, requires both a 'minor influence' theorem for feedback responses from affected variables, and a *ceteris paribus* condition within the partial equilibrium model for all variables not explicitly taken into account. Indeed, as sub-section 3.2 noted, when theory models are not complete, correct, and immutable, additional factors will invariably matter. That suggests embedding such theory models in more general systems that allow for all the empirically-known influences, as well as the many historical contingencies that have happened. Consequently, we should again expect to find models which involve many, rather than few, factors in macroeconomics, an implication pursued in section 5.

3.4 Models of Expectations

Another major area yet to be adequately bridged is that between theory models of expectations and the realities of economic forecasting. Economists often assume agents hold 'rational' expectations (RE), namely the correct conditional expectation $E[\cdot]$ of the variable in question (y_{t+1}) given the available information (I_t), written as:

$$y_{t+1}^{re} = E[y_{t+1} \mid I_t]. \tag{9}$$

The usual argument, often loosely worded to avoid contradiction, is that otherwise there would be arbitrage opportunities, or unnecessary losses. But expectations are formed for a purpose, not an end in themselves—so are instrumental—and agents should therefore equate the marginal benefits of improved forecasting accuracy against the additional costs of achieving it. That leads to 'economically rationally expectations' (ERE), as in Feige and Pearce [21]. In turn, ERE highlights that RE implicitly assumes free information, free computing power, and free discovery of the form of $E[y_{t+1}|I_t]$. Model consistent expectations suffer the serious additional drawback of imposing an invalid specification on the expectations formation process, unless the model is otherwise already perfect.

While ERE are more realistic than RE, they also suffer from the most serious lacuna in (9), namely the assumption that agents can do the relevant calculations. Explicitly, (9) should be written as:

$$y_{t+1}^{e} = E_{t+1}[y_{t+1} \mid I_t] = \int y_{t+1} f_{t+1}(y_{t+1} \mid I_t) \, dy_{t+1} \tag{10}$$

since only then will y_{t+1}^{e} even be an unbiased predictor of y_{t+1}. But (10) requires agents to have crystal balls that genuinely see into the future since it involves the *future* conditional density function $f_{t+1}(y_{t+1}|I_t)$. The best that any agent can do in this framework is form the 'sensible expectation', y_{t+1}^{se}, based on also forecasting $f_{t+1}(\cdot)$ by $\widehat{f}_{t+1}(\cdot)$:

$$y_{t+1}^{se} = \int y_{t+1} \widehat{f}_{t+1}(y_{t+1} \mid I_t) \, dy_{t+1}. \tag{11}$$

Even more unfortunately, when $\{y_t\}$ is non-stationary, there are no guaranteed good rules for estimating $f_{t+1}(y_{t+1}|I_t)$; in particular, when the conditional moments of $f_{t+1}(y_{t+1}|I_t)$ are changing in unanticipated ways, $\widehat{f}_{t+1}(\cdot) = f_t(\cdot)$ need not be a good choice, yet underlies most of the formal derivations of RE of which I am aware. Agents cannot actually do what (9) asserts outside of a stationary environment (see e.g., Hendry [31]).

The drawbacks of (9) and (10), and the relative success of robust forecasting rules are examples of imperfect-knowledge expectations (IKE: see Aghion et al. [1]). Agents cannot know how I_t enters $f_t(\cdot)$ (let alone $f_{t+1}(\cdot)$) when processes are evolving in a non-stationary manner. This gap is only bridgeable once extremely unrealistic assumptions are abandoned in favour of models that reflect the non-stationarity of economic data. Of course, one might attempt to collect systematic evidence on agents' expectations (see e.g., Nerlove [59]) to replace the unobservables by outcomes rather than postulates.

Another under-investigated aspect links back to sub-section 3.1. Re-consider (4), and take expectations conditional on the available information set I_{t-1}:

$$E[y_t \mid I_{t-1}] = \gamma' E[\mathbf{z}_t \mid I_{t-1}] \tag{12}$$

as $E[v_t|I_{t-1}] = 0$. Then, the conditional model, with valid weak exogeneity, implies a form of expectational representation, although the converse is false.

3.5 Implications for Economic Forecasting

Attempts by economists to forecast confirm the force of the preceding arguments: forecast failure is common. Either economists themselves uniquely fail their own assumptions about other agents, or their assumptions are incorrect more generally. The latter seems all too obvious.

In macro-economics, forecast failure is almost certainly due to location shifts in time series (see e.g., Clements and Hendry [5, 6]). Most location shifts seem to be unanticipated *ex ante*, and hence unforecastable. Once such shifts have occurred, all forms of equilibrium-correction specifications will suffer forecast failure, which class includes the vast majority of theories and models in economics. Whether failure is due to omitting relevant observable variables which shift, or internal shifts in location, the outcome is the same.

Worse still, unanticipated location shifts are common (see e.g., Stock and Watson [70]; Clements and Hendry [9]) and are pernicious for forecasting (see e.g., Clements and Hendry [10]). Surprisingly, other (i.e., zero-mean) changes are less damaging to forecasts (see e.g., Hendry [29]). Nevertheless, once it becomes likely that $f_{t+1}(\cdot) \neq f_t(\cdot)$, then forecasting devices that are robust to location shifts tend to dominate in forecasting competitions: see the theoretical analysis in Clements and Hendry [7], the interpretation of the outcomes of the M3 forecasting competitions (see e.g., Makridakis and Hibon [56]) by Clements and Hendry [8], and the empirical corroboration by Eitrheim et al. [13]. Differencing converts step shifts to impulses, as well as removing unit roots and lowering the orders of deterministic polynomials by unity, so the apparent success of differenced models is probably due to their robustness, and while consistent with theories that deduce the presence of unit roots, does not confer corroboration.

Two asides. First, on realizing the impossibility of forming RE, agents may well opt for robust predictors, which should influence the specification of expectations in theory models: see Favero and Hendry [20]. Secondly, the framework just sketched also suggests that attempts to test the rationality (or even unbiasedness) of past forecasting models may not be valid. If unanticipated location shifts occurred, any evaluation period that included such a shift would make the corresponding forecasting rule appear to be irrational, even if it was optimal before the break and the break could not be predicted.

4 Credibility

This section concerns what makes econometric evidence credible. There are two key dimensions to credibility, 'persuasiveness' and 'verisimilitude'. The former relates to whether or not scholars will deem the evidence credible relative to their belief system; the latter whether or not they should do so.

'Theory-driven' approaches, where a model is derived from *a priori* theory and calibrated from data evidence, are often deemed by economists to be credible because they are consistent with the basic axioms of economic theory. However, such models suffer from theory dependence: their credibility depends on the credibility of the theory from which they arose, and when that theory is discarded, so is the associated evidence (see e.g., Hendry [25]). Since economic theory is progressing rapidly, theory dependence is likely to induce transient and non-structural evidence. Economists do not seem to feel the need to justify the principle of deriving empirical models from theory—indeed they simply assert it is essential—but appear less persuaded by the converse of deriving theoretical models from empirical findings. Partly as a consequence, a substantial proportion of empirical econometric evidence is 'high level' in that its credibility depends directly on the prior credibility of the theoretical model from which it was derived.

The distinction in Karl Popper [62] between conjectures and refutations is helpful. Given any conjecture, we can usually test its empirical validity, thereby sustaining a destructive approach, although issues of inference from small and heterogeneous data samples complicate the analysis. What happens with rejections in the theory-based approach? If an implementation is discarded when it cannot explain the empirical evidence, the underlying theory should lose credibility; whereas if it is not discarded, the theory must be altered to avoid maintaining two contradictory propositions. In practice, the empirical model, the measurement instruments and the associated theory may all be revised till 'consistency' is achieved. Depending on how that is implemented, the result may or may not lack credibility. But postulating an endless sequence of models and theories that get rejected in turn fails to incorporate learning from the evidence. Our proposed solution is to conduct research in a progressive framework of successively encompassing, congruent models consolidated by empirically-relevant theories.

Constructing models is another matter. Empirical econometric models are designed to satisfy various criteria (including theory consistency or data coherency), so thereby acquire no excess content. Nevertheless, validity is an intrinsic property of a model independently of how it was discovered or of the initial credibility of the selection (which might depend on the discovery route). Yet how a model was selected is often claimed to affect its 'credibility': at its extreme, we find the claim in Leamer [53] that 'the mapping is the message', emphasizing the selection process over the properties of the final choice. Some economists have even come to doubt the value of empirical evidence, to the extent of referring to it as a 'scientific illusion' (Summers [71]). Many estimated models certainly lack credibility in my second sense, because they are almost untested, imposing a variety of arbitrary and unjustifiable restrictions, but I doubt that was his point. However, by performing as anticipated against new data, larger samples, new rival models or new tests, they should acquire objective credibility. Since the apparently problematic issue is data-based model selection, we consider that in more detail.

5 An Objective and Non-Distortionary Modelling Tool

Model selection is another contentious topic. To bridge the gap between fact and fiction in this arena, Hendry [28] discusses and rebuts nine claimed model selection difficulties spanning complaints from Keynes [46] and Koopmans [49], through Judge and Bock [43], Leamer [52, 53] and Lovell [54] to Pagan [61] and Faust and Whiteman [19]. As established in Hendry [27], their criticisms are neither fundamental nor inevitable, and all have counter criticisms noted in section 6. Since the best antidote is a procedure that works, section 5.4 describes the properties of our approach, which we first outline in the next three sub-sections.

5.1 The *PcGets* Algorithm

PcGets is an Ox Package (see Doornik [12]) implementing automatic general-to-specific (*Gets*) modelling based on the theory of reduction, as in Hendry [24] (Chap. 9). The present implementation is for linear regression models, but extensions to dynamic, cointegrated, simultaneous systems are clear (see e.g., Hendry and Krolzig [34]). Given the available theoretical, historical, institutional, and measurement information, as well as previous empirical evidence, a general unrestricted model (GUM) should be formulated carefully, preferably with a near-orthogonal parameterization. There are two obvious mistakes that could be made when specifying a GUM: it may have no subject-matter basis (non-encompassing of existing models), and it may fail to describe the data (non-congruent). Both need rectified by better thinking and more congruent specification before going further. The GUM is then estimated from all the available evidence, and rigorously tested for congruence. If it fails, a new formulation is required: but at least one has learned the general inadequacy of a class of models. If congruence is accepted, it is then maintained throughout the selection process by diagnostic checking (using the same statistics) at every putative simplification, thereby ensuring a congruent final model.

Statistically-insignificant variables are eliminated by selection tests, both in blocks and individually. Many reduction paths are searched, as in Hoover and Perez [41], to prevent the algorithm from becoming stuck in a sequence that inadvertently eliminates a variable that actually matters, and thereby retains other variables as proxies (as in step-wise regression). Such path searches terminate when no variable meets the pre-set elimination criteria, or any diagnostic test becomes significant. Non-rejected (terminal) models are collected, then tested against each other by encompassing: if several remain acceptable, so are congruent, undominated, mutually-encompassing representations, the reduction process recommences from their union (providing that is a reduction of the original GUM), the entire sequence repeating till a unique outcome is obtained. Otherwise, or if all selected simplifications re-appear, the search is terminated using (e.g.) the Schwarz [65] information criterion. The significance of retained variables in sub-sample is then used as a reliability check.

By making the procedure algorithmic, it can be subject to simulation studies with no human intervention. In the latest Monte Carlo experiments reported in Hendry and Krolzig [36], commencing from highly over-parameterized GUMs (between 8 and

40 irrelevant variables; zero and 8 relevant), *PcGets* recovers the DGP with an accuracy close to what one would expect if the DGP specification were known initially, but nevertheless coefficient tests were conducted. Empirically, *PcGets* selects (in seconds) models at least as good as those developed over several years by their authors (see Ericsson [16], for several examples). Although automatic model selection is in its infancy, exceptional progress has been achieved for reasons we now explain.

5.2 Costs of Search and Costs of Inference

The header alludes to a key distinction. Costs of search arise from commencing with an over-parameterized GUM, necessitating a search for a parsimonious undominated model of the DGP. Costs of inference always confront empirical investigators—even if they commence from the DGP, but do not know that their specification is correct, and so have to test for congruence and significance. Costs of inference are inevitable if tests have non-zero size and non-unit power: surprisingly in view of the multitude of criticisms noted above, costs of search are small in comparison to costs of inference—the key problem is not model selection, but the vagaries of sampling.

We assume that a congruent GUM has been achieved, so now must select a model from that GUM; and again there are two obvious mistakes. The first is including variables that do not actually matter in the DGP; the second is omitting variables that do: type I and II mistakes respectively. Since the first cannot arise if the DGP is the GUM, it is purely a cost of search. The second, however, could plague a study that commenced from the DGP, so is primarily a cost of inference, with possible additional search costs if there are lower probabilities of retaining relevant variables when commencing from the GUM.

When the nominal rejection frequency of individual selection tests is set at the conventional 5%, on average one irrelevant variable will be retained as adventitiously significant out of 20 candidates, so 19 out of the 20 will be eliminated. However, the 5% critical value of a t-test (approximately 2) entails only a 50% chance of keeping a variable with a non-centrality of 2. Thus, there is little difficulty in eliminating almost all of the irrelevant variables when starting from the GUM (a cost of search), and a small chance of retaining such relevant variables even if commencing from the DGP (a cost of inference). A more stringent critical value (say at 1%, so 2.625) worsens the latter dramatically for little gain in the former: now one irrelevant variable out of 20 will be retained on average once in 5 exercises, whereas the retention probability of the relevant variable becomes 27%, even when the correct specification is known. Costs of inference usually exceed costs of search, the exception being when all relevant variables have non-central t-statistics in excess of 5.

5.3 Choice of Strategy

The contrast in the previous section between 5% and 1% reveals the crucial nature of the testing strategy, albeit a topic little discussed in the literature. *PcGets* offers a 'Liberal' and a 'Conservative' strategy with different baselines, roughly 5% and

1% as above, but using sample-size dependent critical values. In the above illustration, 1% eliminates all 20 irrelevant variables four times out of five, and 19 on the fifth occasion: hardly a serious 'data mining' problem. Unfortunately, inference costs increase as shown: the choice of an appropriate strategy for the analysis at hand is essential. *PcGets* using the 'Liberal' strategy applied to a GUM with say 25 irrelevant variables will on average come closer to the DGP than the 'Conservative' strategy beginning from the DGP unless all t-statistics are large.

However, empirical and subject-matter knowledge can be invaluable: if there are 40 irrelevant variables and almost no relevant (as in Lovell [54], say) the 'Conservative' strategy may be best, although pre-simplifying the GUM could be better still.

5.4 Actions Speak Louder than Words

How well does the algorithm do in practice? Hendry and Krolzig [36] summarize of all the simulation findings to date for *PcGets*: see Hoover and Perez [41, 42] for additional evidence.

'Over-fitting' as measured by a downward biased estimate of the equation standard error, denoted $\hat{\sigma}$, for the true value σ, does not occur: *PcGets* selection is not based on fit, but a minimal congruent encompassing model will be best fitting for the chosen significance level. The 'Liberal' strategy has a slight downward bias from irrelevant variables retained by chance (under 5% of σ), whereas the 'Conservative' is upward biased by a similar amount as it eliminates relevant variables.

Further, the rejection frequencies for the two strategies are close to their intended significance levels of 5% and 1%. Thus, type I errors per test are well controlled. If n irrelevant variables are included at significance level α then αn variables will be retained adventitiously, and $(1 - \alpha) n$ eliminated. Some researchers think in terms of the 'size' of the selection procedure, namely $1 - (1 - \alpha)^n$, which can be large, but is uninformative about the success of simplification. Adventitiously retaining αn irrelevant variables could also be deemed over-fitting, but that seems unhelpful when the associated under-fitting of omitting relevant variables is ignored.

The average rejection frequencies of the nulls for relevant variables depend on their non-centralities. The 'Conservative' strategy never has higher power than the 'Liberal', confirming that the costs of avoiding 'spurious' variables can be high. Adding up to 8 irrelevant orthogonal variables reveals only a small impact on power, especially for the 'Liberal' strategy, confirming low search costs.

The probabilities of locating the DGP commencing from the GUM are reasonably close to the corresponding outcomes when the search commences from the DGP. Thus, often the problem attributed to a search algorithm is actually a cost of inference, since the DGP is sometimes never retained even when it is the initial specification. When population t-values are 2 or 3, the 'Liberal' strategy does best, and in practice can outperform commencing from the DGP with a 1% significance level: the two strategies cannot be ranked as their relative performance depends on the unknown state of nature.

Finally, they show that a bias correction is feasible if desired to offset the selection impact from only retaining variables whose t-test exceeds the criterion. This induces a slight increase in root mean square errors (RMSEs) when variables are relevant, but a substantial reduction in RMSEs when variables are irrelevant: see Hendry and Krolzig [36]. Thus, near unbiased estimates can be reported, despite data-based selection. Moreover, since $\hat{\sigma}$ is nearly unbiased for σ, in orthogonal problems, the reported standard errors of estimated coefficients in selected models are close to the sampling standard deviations of the corresponding coefficients in the estimated DGP.

The main application for unbiased estimates is policy analysis. If a variable is wrongly excluded, then a policy avenue may be missed, but no serious losses should result. If a variable is wrongly included, false policy may ensue, but a small coefficient will decrease the chance of an 'over-reaction' by policy makers. If a variable is correctly included, but with a biased coefficient, again incorrect policy could result, so unbiased coefficients seem valuable in this arena. As noted above, there is little RMSE cost from bias correction for relevant variables (the bias reduction being partly offset by a variance increase), and a substantive RMSE reduction for irrelevant variables.

Overall, their findings confirm that the two strategies are close to their desired operating characteristics, that 'size' is well controlled; that search costs are low; and that over-fitting does not result.

5.5 Role of Theory

Variables deemed potentially relevant to the policies under analysis can be forced to enter all specifications, including the final selected model. In Hendry and Krolzig [33], we recommend that a user run the program both with and without such 'fixed variables', and if the models differ, conduct an encompassing test between them. Naturally, the 'null' is the restricted formulation, as that is deemed theoretically preferable, so a stringent critical value is allowable, but equally, there must exist some level of significance at which the theory—and entailed policy—should be questioned. Further, note that the forcibly-retained variables need not be significant—and may even have signs that clash with the theory, although the algorithm can be designed to seek models satisfying sign constraints if such exist under the initial GUM.

We have come full circle to the role of theory, but with a more level playing field. Theory cannot be the arbiter of empirical specifications no matter how beautiful and general the framework from which it is derived. As *ceteris paribus* is not valid in a non-stationary world, a much closer interaction between theory and evidence is needed than econometrics simply being a tool for providing quantitative cloth on a fully-formed theory (Kirman [47], discusses the absence of clothes on our present emperor). This problem is compounded by the absence of a clear specification of decision time, the lack of good theories of dynamic economic behaviour, and an absence of guidance on definitive functional forms.

Most economic theories are ahistorical, and hence do not 'predict' that the behaviour of variables should depend on actual calendar time: consumption smoothing theories are typical in that regard. Of course, theorists recognize that special factors may intrude (changes in credit rationing, technological change, wars, financial innovation, deregulation, price controls etc.), but such special factors can dominate when accounting for data variability, so the empirical modelling problem cannot be surmounted simply by estimating theory-derived models: see Morgan [58], Spanos [68], and Hendry and Mizon [37] on the problems involved in testing theories using non-experimental data.

Thus, the role of theory becomes one of specifying the general formulation where detailed implementation then depends on institutional and historical contingencies, and previous empirical evidence—hopefully encompassed by the new specification. If there are competing theory models of a given variable, *PcGets* could be used to select the 'best representative' of each, conditional on the specifications of their information sets and hence GUMs. Then encompassing tests could be used to determine their relative performance. This would automate the type of approach adopted by (e.g.) Bean [3] and Ahumada [2], and ensure an objective and reproducible outcome. Still, a parsimonious encompassing test of the best against the union remains advisable.

6 Conclusion

We have argued that the marked gap between macroeconomic theory models and applied econometric findings arises because much of the observed data variability in macroeconomics is due to various non-stationarities that are absent from most economic theories, but which empirical models have to tackle. *Ceteris paribus* conditions can sometimes be justified for theoretical reasoning, but are unacceptable as a basis for empirical modelling. A 'minor influence' theorem is needed instead which can only be established empirically. This suggests formulating a general initial model consistent with all the evidence: theory, institutions, history, and data. Once a congruent encompassing general model is established, an automatic model selection approach based on general-to-simple principles is proposed to bring objectivity and credibility to empirical econometric modelling.

Such an approach is not a tract for mindless modelling of data. Our observations are far from perfect, are subject to revision, and even to conceptual changes: it is only *ex post*, for example, that M4 is the obvious choice of monetary measure. Key series are often missing, and many proxies are adopted for want of the original. There are major gaps between theory constructs (e.g., consumption, or the user cost of capital), and the measured series (consumers' expenditure or after-tax real interest rates adjusted for depreciation). Aggregation introduces a further gap.

Lest it be mis-understood, nor is this chapter an anti-economics tract: quite the opposite. Economics has delivered a vast range of invaluable insights into individual decision taking, why some markets function well and others do not, how economies as a whole behave, why trade is beneficial, and so on. It has created an impressive edifice of theory, made rapid technical and intellectual progress, and looks like doing so for some time to come. And that is one of the main points: economic theory is not complete, correct, and immutable – and never will be. But that is precisely the condition needed to justify an insistence on deriving empirical models from theory.

Rather, because theory is improving, we cannot appeal to *ceteris paribus* in a non-stationary world, and there is no generic 'minor influence' theorem, our theoretical insights should be embedded in empirically congruent representations, not forced on the data: marriage is required, not data rape.

Why have good bridges not been constructed previously? Perhaps because of a misplaced fear that data basing was mindless data mining. Unfortunately, the present theory-based paradigm encourages the latter covertly, so we do not actually know how credible much of our 'evidence' really is. Data basing was shown above not to have the pernicious properties ascribed to it by some: the general theory-model embedding GUM can have many additional potentially relevant variables without risking a 'garbage in, garbage out' approach. At 1% significance, one variable out of one hundred will be significant by chance, yet all relevant factors with t-ratios in excess of ± 2.65 will be retained.

Another factor may have been a belief that 'parsimony' is good: it is, but in the final model, not in the starting point when that is achieved by arbitrarily excluding many potentially relevant contenders. The time requirements for investigating large models may also have seemed sufficiently daunting to dissuade all but the most persistent investigators – that too is history. Indeed, so is the need for fewer candidate variables than observations: see Hendry and Krolzig [34]. There is now no case against general-to-specific modelling, and a strong case in favour. At the same time, that should not be interpreted as a case against the maximum use of our best available theory to guide our empirical endeavours.

References

1. Aghion P, Frydman R, Stiglitz J, Woodford M (2002) Knowledge, Information and Expectations in Modern Macroeconomics. Princeton, New Jersey: Princeton University Press
2. Ahumada H (1985) An encompassing test of two models of the balance of trade for Argentina. Oxford Bulletin of Economics and Statistics 47: 51-70
3. Bean CR (1981) An econometric model of investment in the United Kingdom. Economic Journal 91: 106-121
4. Cartwright N (2003) In favour of laws that are not ceteris paribus after all. Mimeo, Department of Philosophy, Logic and Scientific Method, London School of Economics
5. Clements MP, Hendry DF (1998) Forecasting economic time series. Cambridge: Cambridge University Press
6. Clements MP, Hendry DF (1999) Forecasting non-stationary economic time series. Cambridge, Mass.: MIT Press
7. Clements MP, Hendry DF (1999) On winning forecasting competitions in economics. Spanish Economic Review 1: 123-160
8. Clements MP, Hendry DF (2001) Explaining the results of the M3 forecasting competition. International Journal of Forecasting 17: 550-554
9. Clements MP, Hendry DF (2001) An historical perspective on forecast errors. National Institute Economic Review 177: 100-112
10. Clements MP, Hendry DF (2002) Explaining forecast failure in macroeconomics. In Clements MP, Hendry DF (eds) A companion to economic forecasting. Oxford: Blackwells

11. Crafts NFR (1997) Endogenous growth: Lessons for and from economic history. In Kreps DM, Wallis KF (eds) Advances in Economics and Econometrics: Theory and Applications. Seventh World Congress. Vol. 2. Cambridge: Cambridge University Press
12. Doornik JA (2001) Object-oriented matrix programming using Ox. London: Timberlake Consultants Press. 4th edition
13. Eitrheim Ø, HusebøTA, Nymoen R (1999) Equilibrium-correction versus differencing in macroeconometric forecasting. Economic Modelling 16: 515-544
14. Engle RF, Granger CWJ (1987) Cointegration and error correction: Representation, estimation and testing. Econometrica 55: 251-276
15. Engle RF, Hendry DF, Richard JF (1983) Exogeneity. Econometrica 51: 277-304. Reprinted in Hendry DF (ed) Econometrics: Alchemy or science? Oxford: Blackwell Publishers, 1993, and Oxford University Press, 2000; and in Ericsson NR, Irons JS (eds) Testing exogeneity, Oxford: Oxford University Press, 1994
16. Ericsson NR (2004) Econometric modeling. Oxford: Oxford University Press. Forthcoming
17. Ericsson NR, Hendry DF, Prestwich KM (1998) The demand for broad money in the United Kingdom, 1878–1993. Scandinavian Journal of Economics 100: 289-324
18. Escribano A (2002) Non-linear error correction models. Mimeo, Universidad Carlos III, Madrid
19. Faust J, Whiteman CH (1997) General-to-specific procedures for fitting a data-admissible, theory-inspired, congruent, parsimonious, encompassing, weakly-exogenous, identified, structural model of the DGP: A translation and critique. Carnegie-Rochester Conference Series on Public Policy 47: 121-161
20. Favero C, Hendry DF (1992) Testing the Lucas critique: A review. Econometric Reviews 11: 265-306
21. Feige EL, Pearce DK (1976) Economically rational expectations. Journal of Political Economy 84: 499-522
22. Friedman M (1957) A Theory of the Consumption Function. Princeton: Princeton University Press
23. Hall RE (1978) Stochastic implications of the life cycle-permanent income hypothesis: Evidence. Journal of Political Economy 86: 971-987
24. Hendry DF (1995) Dynamic econometrics. Oxford: Oxford University Press
25. Hendry DF (1995) Econometrics and business cycle empirics. Economic Journal 105: 1622-1636
26. Hendry DF (1999) An econometric analysis of US food expenditure, 1931-1989. In Magnus JR, Morgan MS (eds) Methodology and tacit knowledge: Two Experiments in econometrics, Chichester: John Wiley and Sons.
27. Hendry DF (2000) Econometrics: Alchemy or Science? Oxford: Oxford University Press. New Edition
28. Hendry DF (2000) Epilogue: The success of general-to-specific model selection. In Hendry DF (ed) Econometrics: Alchemy or Science? Oxford University Press
29. Hendry DF (2000) On detectable and non-detectable structural change. Structural Change and Economic Dynamics 11: 45-65. Reprinted in Hagemann H, Landesman M, Scazzieri (eds.) The Economics of Structural Change, Edward Elgar, Cheltenham, 2002
30. Hendry DF (2001) Modelling UK inflation, 1875-1991. Journal of Applied Econometrics 16: 255-275
31. Hendry DF (2002) Forecast failure, expectations formation, and the Lucas critique. Annales d'Économie et de Statistique 67-68: 21-40

32. Hendry DF, Ericsson NR (1991) An econometric analysis of UK money demand in Monetary Trends in the United States and the United Kingdom' by Milton Friedman and Anna J Schwartz. American Economic Review 81: 8-38

33. Hendry DF, Krolzig H-M (2001) Automatic econometric model selection. London: Timberlake Consultants Press

34. Hendry DF, Krolzig H-M (2004) Resolving three 'intractable' problems using a Gets approach. Oxford Bulletin of Economics and Statistics 66: 799-810

35. Hendry DF, Krolzig H-M (2004) We ran one regression. Unpublished paper, Economics Department, University of Oxford

36. Hendry DF, Krolzig H-M (2005) The properties of automatic Gets modelling. Economic Journal, forthcoming

37. Hendry DF, Mizon GE (2000) Reformulating empirical macro-econometric modelling. Oxford Review of Economic Policy 16: 138-159

38. Hendry DF, Santos C (2005) Regression models with data-based indicator variables. Oxford Bulletin of Economics and Statistics, forthcoming

39. Hildenbrand W (1994) Market demand: Theory and empirical evidence. Princeton: Princeton University Press

40. Hildenbrand W (1998) How relevant are the specifications of behavioural relations on the micro-level for modelling the time path of population aggregates? European Economic Review 42: 437-458

41. Hoover KD, Perez SJ (1999) Data mining reconsidered: Encompassing and the general-to-specific approach to specification search. Econometrics Journal 2: 167-191

42. Hoover KD, Perez SJ (2004) Truth and robustness in cross-country growth regressions. Oxford Bulletin of Economics and Statistics 66: forthcoming

43. Judge GG, Bock ME (1978) The Statistical implications of pre-test and Stein-Rule estimators in econometrics. Amsterdam: North Holland Publishing Company

44. Juselius K (1993) VAR modelling and Haavelmo's probability approach to econometrics. Empirical Economics 18: 595-622

45. Kennan J (1979) The estimation of partial adjustment models with rational expectations. Econometrica 47: 1441-1455

46. Keynes JM (1939) Professor Tinbergen's method. Economic Journal 44: 558-568. Reprinted in Hendry DF, Morgan MS (eds) The foundations of econometric analysis, Cambridge: Cambridge University Press, 1995

47. Kirman A (1989) The intrinsic limits of economic theory: The emperor has no clothes. Economic Journal 99: 126-139

48. Kirman A (1995) The evolution of economic theory. In d'Autume A, Cartelier J (eds) L'Economie devient-elle une science dure?, Paris: Economica. Reprinted in English as: Is economics becoming a hard science? Edward Elgar, 1997.

49. Koopmans TC (1947) Measurement without theory. Review of Economics and Statistics 29: 161-179

50. Kydland FE, Prescott EC (1990) Business cycles: Real facts and a monetary myth. Federal Reserve Bank of Minneapolis, Quarterly Review 14: 3-18

51. Kydland FE, Prescott EC (1991) The econometrics of the general equilibrium approach to business cycles. Scandinavian Journal of Economics 93: 161-178

52. Leamer EE (1978) Specification searches. Ad-Hoc inference with non-experimental data. New York: John Wiley

53. Leamer EE (1983) Let's take the con out of econometrics. American Economic Review 73: 31-43. Reprinted in Granger CWJ (ed) Modelling economic series, Oxford: Clarendon Press, 1990

54. Lovell MC (1983) Data mining. Review of Economics and Statistics 65 1-12
55. Magnus JR, Morgan MS (1999) Methodology and tacit knowledge: Two Experiments in econometrics. Chichester: John Wiley and Sons.
56. Makridakis S, Hibon M (2000) The M3-competition: Results, conclusions and implications. International Journal of Forecasting 16: 451-476
57. Massmann M (2001) Co-breaking in macroeconomic time series. Unpublished paper, Economics Department, Oxford University
58. Morgan MS (1990) The history of econometric ideas. Cambridge: Cambridge University Press
59. Nerlove M (1983) Expectations, plans, and realizations in theory and practice. Econometrica 51: 1251-1279
60. Nymoen R (2002) Faulty watch towers: Structural models in Norwegian monetary policy analysis. Unpublished paper, University of Oslo
61. Pagan AR (1987) Three econometric methodologies: A critical appraisal. Journal of Economic Surveys 1: 3-24. Reprinted in Granger CWJ (ed) Modelling economic series, Oxford: Clarendon Press, 1990.
62. Popper KR (1963) Conjectures and refutations. New York: Basic Books
63. Sala-i Martin XX (1997) I have just run two million regressions. American Economic Review 87: 178-183
64. Samuelson PA (1947) Foundations of economic analysis. Harvard: Harvard University Press
65. Schwarz G (1978) Estimating the dimension of a model. Annals of Statistics 6: 461-464
66. Smets F, Wouters R (2002) An estimated stochastic dynamic general equilibrium model of the Euro area. ECB Working Paper No 171, European Central Bank, Frankfurt
67. Spanos A (1989) On re-reading Haavelmo: A retrospective view of econometric modeling. Econometric Theory 5: 405-429
68. Spanos A (1995) On theory testing in econometric modelling with non-experimental data. Journal of Econometrics 67: 189-226
69. Stiglitz J (2003) Is Keynes dead? Reviving a sensible macroeconomics. Clarendon lectures, Department of Economics, University of Oxford
70. Stock JH, Watson MW (1996) Evidence on structural instability in macroeconomic time series relations. Journal of Business and Economic Statistics 14: 11-30
71. Summers LH (1991) The scientific illusion in empirical macroeconomics. Scandinavian Journal of Economics 93: 129-148
72. Tobin J (1950) A statistical demand function for food in the U.S.A. Journal of the Royal Statistical Society, Series A 113: 113-141
73. Tobin J (1952) A survey of the theory of rationing. Econometrica 26: 24-36

Revenue Smoothing in an ARIMA Framework: Evidence from the United States[*]

Periklis Gogas[1] and Apostolos Serletis[2]

[1] Department of Economics, University of Abertay-Dundee, North College Campus and A. Michailides S.A., Agricultural Industries, Thessaloniki, 56430, Greece.
perrygogas@usa.net
[2] University of Calgary, Department of Economics, Calgary, Alberta, T2N 1N4, Canada.
serletis@ucalgary.ca

Summary. This paper tests Mankiw's [9] revenue-smoothing hypothesis, that the inflation rate moves one-for-one with the marginal tax rate in the long run, using the new average marginal tax rate series constructed by Stephenson [16] and the long-horizon regression approach developed by Fisher and Seater [5]. It reports considerable evidence against revenue-smoothing.

Key words: : Optimal seigniorage, Integration, Long-run derivative

JEL classification: C22, F31

1 Introduction

A crucial implication of Mankiw's [9] revenue-smoothing (or optimal seigniorage) hypothesis is that higher tax rates are associated with higher inflation rates (and nominal interest rates). There have been many attempts to test this hypothesis. For example, Mankiw [9] and Poterba and Rotemberg [14] using the OLS method find support of the hypothesis. However, more general tests (based on the cointegration and/or VAR methodology) by Trehan and Walsh [17], Ghosh [6], Evans and Amey [4], and Serletis and Schorn [15] generally reject revenue smoothing.

The present paper extends the literature by testing whether the inflation rate moves one-for-one with the marginal tax rate in the long run, using the new average marginal tax rate series constructed by Stephenson [16] and the long-horizon regression approach developed by Fisher and Seater [5]. Long-horizon regressions have received a lot of attention in the recent economics and finance literature, because studies based on long-horizon variables seem to find significant results where short-horizon regressions commonly used in economics and finance have failed.

[*]Serletis gratefully acknowledges support from the Social Sciences and Humanities Research Council of Canada.

In what follows, we provide a brief summary of Mankiw's [9] theory of optimal seigniorage (Section 2) and of the econometric approach developed by Fisher and Seater [5] (Section 3). In Section 4, we discuss the data, investigate the integration properties of the variables, and present the results. The paper closes with a brief summary and conclusion (Section 5).

2 The Theory of Optimal Seigniorage

Following Mankiw [9], let Y be the exogenous level of real output and τ the tax rate on output. The revenue raised by this tax is τY. It is assumed that the government finances expenditure in excess of taxes from seigniorage. Assuming that the demand for money is described by the quantity equation, $M/P = kY$, the real revenue from seigniorage is

$$\frac{\dot{M}}{P} = \frac{\dot{M}}{M}\frac{M}{P} = (\pi + g)kY$$

where π is the inflation rate and g is the growth rate of real output. The total real tax revenue, T, is therefore the sum of the receipts from direct taxation, τY, and seigniorage, $(\pi + g)kY$. That is, $T = \tau Y + (\pi + g)kY$.

The social costs of taxation and inflation are assumed homogenous in output and denoted by $f(\tau)Y$ and $h(\pi)Y$, respectively, where $f' > 0$, $h' > 0$ and $f'' > 0$, $h'' > 0$. The government's goal is to minimize, with respect to τ and π, the expected present value of the social losses

$$E_t \sum_{j=0}^{\infty} \beta^j \left[f(\tau_{t+j}) + h(\pi_{t+j}) \right] Y$$

subject to the present value budget constraint

$$\sum_{j=0}^{\infty} \beta^j G_{t+j} + B_t = \sum_{j=0}^{\infty} \beta^j T_{t+j}$$

where G_t is real government expenditure at time t (taken to be exogenous), B_t is real government debt at time t, and β is the real discount factor, assumed constant over time.

The first-order conditions necessary for optimal intertemporal monetary and fiscal policy are (see Mankiw [9])

$$E_t \left[f'(\tau_{t+j}) \right] = f'(\tau_t), \tag{1}$$

$$E_t \left[h'(\pi_{t+j}) \right] = h'(\pi_t), \tag{2}$$

$$h'(\pi_t) = k f'(\tau_t). \tag{3}$$

The intertemporal first-order conditions (1) and (2) equate the marginal social cost of taxation and inflation, respectively, today and in the future. The static first-order condition (3), which relates the tax rate to the rate of inflation, equates the marginal social cost of raising revenue through taxation and the marginal social cost of raising revenue through seigniorage. This last condition expresses a crucial implication of the theory of optimal seigniorage. Increases in the government revenue requirement increase both taxation and inflation. Hence, over time higher tax rates are associated with higher inflation rates and higher nominal interest rates.

3 Econometric Methodology

As already noted, we test the theory of optimal seignioarge using the long-horizon regression approach developed by Fisher and Seater [5]. One important advantage to working with the long-horizon regression approach is that cointegration is neither necessary nor sufficient for tests on the long-run derivative. We start with the following bivariate autoregressive representation

$$\alpha_{\pi\pi}(L)\Delta^{\langle\pi\rangle}\pi_t = \alpha_{\pi\tau}(L)\Delta^{\langle\tau\rangle}\tau_t + \varepsilon_t^{\pi}$$
$$\alpha_{\tau\tau}(L)\Delta^{\langle\tau\rangle}\tau_t = \alpha_{\tau\pi}(L)\Delta^{\langle\pi\rangle}\pi_t + \varepsilon_t^{\tau}$$

where $\alpha_{\pi\pi}^0 = \alpha_{\tau\tau}^0 = 1$, $\Delta = 1 - L$, where L is the lag operator, π is the inflation rate, τ is the marginal tax rate, and $\langle z \rangle$ represents the order of integration of z, so that if z is integrated of order γ, then $\langle z \rangle = \gamma$ and $\langle \Delta z \rangle = \langle z \rangle - 1$. The vector $(\varepsilon_t^{\pi}, \varepsilon_t^{\tau})'$ is assumed to be independently and identically distributed normally with zero mean and covariance $\sum_{\varepsilon}$, the elements of which are $\text{var}(\varepsilon_t^{\pi})$, $\text{var}(\varepsilon_t^{\tau})$, $\text{cov}(\varepsilon_t^{\pi}, \varepsilon_t^{\tau})$.

According to this approach, revenue smoothing can be tested in terms of the long-run derivative of π with respect to a permanent change in τ, which is defined as follows. If $\lim_{k\to\infty} \partial\tau_{t+k}/\partial\varepsilon_t^{\tau} \neq 0$, then

$$LRD_{\pi,\tau} = \lim_{k\to\infty} \frac{\partial\pi_{t+k}/\partial\varepsilon_t^{\tau}}{\partial\tau_{t+k}/\partial\varepsilon_t^{\tau}}$$

Thus, in the present context $LRD_{\pi,\tau}$ expresses the ultimate effect of an exogenous marginal tax rate disturbance on π, relative to that disturbance's ultimate effect on the marginal tax rate τ. When $\lim_{k\to\infty} \partial\tau_{t+k}/\partial\varepsilon_t^{\tau} = 0$, there are no permanent changes in τ and thus $LRD_{\pi,\tau}$ is undefined. In terms of this framework, revenue smoothing requires that $LRD_{\pi,\tau} = 1$.

The above bivariate autoregressive system can be inverted to yield the following vector moving average representation

$$\Delta^{\langle\pi\rangle}\pi_t = \theta_{\pi\tau}(L)\varepsilon_t^{\tau} + \theta_{\pi\pi}(L)\varepsilon_t^{\pi}$$
$$\Delta^{\langle\tau\rangle}\tau_t = \theta_{\tau\tau}(L)\varepsilon_t^{\tau} + \theta_{\tau\pi}(L)\varepsilon_t^{\pi}$$

In terms of this moving average representation, Fisher and Seater [5] show that $LRD_{\pi,\tau}$ depends on $\langle\tau\rangle - \langle\pi\rangle$, as follows

$$LRD_{\pi,\tau} = \frac{(1-L)^{\langle\tau\rangle-\langle\pi\rangle}\,\theta_{\pi\tau}(L)|_{L=1}}{\theta_{\tau\tau}(1)}$$

Hence, meaningful long-horizon regression tests of the revenue smoothing hypothesis can be conducted if both π_t and τ_t satisfy certain nonstationarity conditions. In particular, long-horizon regression tests require that both π_t and τ_t are at least $I(1)$ and of the same order of integration. In fact, when $\langle\pi\rangle = \langle\tau\rangle = 1$, the long-run derivative becomes

$$LRD_{\pi,\tau} = \frac{\theta_{\pi\tau}(1)}{\theta_{\tau\tau}(1)}$$

where $\theta_{\pi\tau}(1) = \sum_{j=1}^{\infty}\theta_{\pi\tau}^j$ and $\theta_{\tau\tau}(1) = \sum_{j=1}^{\infty}\theta_{\tau\tau}^j$. Above, the coefficient $\theta_{\pi\tau}(1)/\theta_{\tau\tau}(1)$ is the long-run value of the impulse-response of π with respect to τ, suggesting that $LRD_{\pi,\tau}$ can be interpreted as the long-run elasticity of π with respect to τ.

Under the assumptions that $\mathrm{cov}(\varepsilon_t^\pi, \varepsilon_t^\tau) = 0$ and that the marginal tax rate is exogenous in the long-run, the coefficient $\theta_{\pi\tau}(1)/\theta_{\tau\tau}(1)$ equals the zero-frequency regression coefficient in the regression of $\Delta^{\langle\pi\rangle}\pi$ on $\Delta^{\langle\tau\rangle}\tau$ — see Fisher and Seater (1993, note 11). This estimator is given by $\lim_{k\to\infty} b_k$, where b_k is the coefficient from the regression

$$\left[\sum_{j=0}^{k}\Delta^{\langle\pi\rangle}\pi_{t-j}\right] = a_k + b_k\left[\sum_{j=0}^{k}\Delta^{\langle\tau\rangle}\tau_{t-j}\right] + e_{kt}$$

In fact, when $\langle\pi\rangle = \langle\tau\rangle = 1$, consistent estimates of b_k can be derived by applying ordinary least squares to the regression

$$\pi_t - \pi_{t-k-1} = a_k + b_k\left[\tau_t - \tau_{t-k-1}\right] + e_{kt}, \qquad k = 1, \ldots, K. \tag{4}$$

The null of revenue smoothing is $b_k = 1$. If the null is not rejected across a range of k-forecast horizons, the data supports the theory of optimal seigniorage.

4 Empirical Results

4.1 The Data

We examine two variables in this paper — the inflation rate, π_t, and the average marginal tax rate, τ_t. As a measure of the average marginal tax rate we use Stephenson's [16] average marginal effective tax rate on personal income ($AMETR$). The data is annual from 1934 to 1994 (a total of 61 observations).

It is to be noted that Mankiw [9] mostly uses federal government receipts as a percent of GNP (TAX), as a measure of the average tax rate, and his analysis is over the 1951 to 1985 period (that is, over 35 observations). He also uses the average marginal tax rate (MAR) on labor income (including social security) as estimated by Barro and Sahasakul [1], and finds a positive relation to both the inflation rate and nominal interest rate. However, only the relation to the nominal interest rate is statistically significant, with the coefficient on MAR (in a regression of ΔINT on a constant and ΔMAR) being 0.50.

Of course, as Mankiw ([9], p. 339) puts it "[i]t is not clear *a priori* which of the two tax measures, TAX or MAR, is preferable. One might argue that the average marginal tax rate is the best measure of the marginal social cost of raising revenue. Yet consider what makes these two variables different. Changes in the mix of taxes, such as a shift between personal and corporate taxes, would change MAR without changing TAX. It is not obvious whether such a change in the tax mix should be associated with a change in the reliance on seigniorage as a source of revenue. Resolving this issue requires a model more extensive than that presented here." With this in mind, in what follows we use Stephenson's [16] average marginal effective tax rate on personal income ($AMETR$) as a measure of the average tax rate.

4.2 Integration Tests

As it was argued in the introduction, meaningful long-run revenue-smoothing tests can only be conducted if both the π_t and τ_t variables satisfy certain nonstationarity conditions. In particular, revenue-smoothing tests require that both π_t and τ_t are at least integrated of order one and of the same order of integration. Hence, the first step in conducting revenue-smoothing tests is to test for stochastic trends (unit roots) in the autoregressive representation of each individual time series. In doing so, in what follows we use four alternative testing procedures, to deal with anomalies that arise when the data are not very informative about whether or not there is a unit root.

In Table 1 we report p-values (based on the response surface estimates given by MacKinnon [8]) for the augmented Weighted Symmetric (WS) unit root test (see Pantula et al. [11]), the augmented Dickey-Fuller (ADF) test (see Dickey and Fuller [44]), and the nonparametric, $Z(t_{\widehat{\alpha}})$, test of Phillips [124] and Phillips and Perron [125]. We also report the KPSS (see Kwiatkowski et al. [71]) $\widehat{\eta}_\mu$ and $\widehat{\eta}_\tau$ t-statistics.[3] For the WS and ADF tests, the optimal lag length is taken to be the order selected by the Akaike Information Criterion (AIC) plus 2 - see Pantula et al. [11] for details regarding the advantages of this rule for choosing the number of augmenting lags. The $Z(t_{\widehat{\alpha}})$ test is done with the same Dickey-Fuller regression variables, using no augmenting lags.

Based on the p-values for the WS, ADF, and $Z(t_{\widehat{\alpha}})$ unit root tests reported in Table 1, the null hypothesis of a unit root in levels cannot be rejected. Also, the t-statistic $\widehat{\eta}_\mu$ that tests the null hypothesis of level stationarity is large relative to the 5% critical value of .463 given in Kwiatkowski et al. [71], for the τ_t series. However, the t-statistic $\widehat{\eta}_\tau$ that tests the null hypothesis of trend stationarity does not exceed the 5%

---

[3]Kwiatkowski et al. [71] argue that unit root tests have low power against relevant alternatives and they propose tests (known as the KPSS tests) of the hypothesis of stationarity against the alternative of a unit root. They argue that such tests should complement unit root tests and that by testing both the unit root hypothesis and the stationarity hypothesis, one can distinguish series that appear to be stationary, series that appear to be integrated, and series that are not very informative about whether or not they are stationary or have a unit root.

	p-values			KPSS	
Variable	WS	ADF	$Z(t_{\widehat{\alpha}})$	$\widehat{\eta}_\mu$	$\widehat{\eta}_\tau$
π_t	.666	.741	.072	.154	.081
τ_t	.946	.128	.501	.671	.146

Notes: Numbers in the WS, ADF, and $Z(t_{\widehat{\alpha}})$ columns are tail areas of tests.

Table 1. Unit Root Tests in the Levels.

critical value of .146 (also given in Kwiatkowski et al. [71]), for both series. Although the series do not appear to be very informative as to their integration properties, combining the results of our tests of the stationarity hypothesis with the results of our tests of the unit root hypothesis, we conclude that both series have at least one unit root.

To test the null hypothesis of a second unit root, in Table 2 we test the null hypothesis of a unit root [using the WS, ADF, and $Z(t_{\widehat{\alpha}})$ tests] as well as the null hypotheses of level and trend stationarity in the first differences of the series. Clearly, the differenced series appear to be stationary, since the unit root null is rejected and the level and trend stationarity null hypotheses cannot be rejected.

	p-values			KPSS	
Variable	WS	ADF	$Z(t_{\widehat{\alpha}})$	$\widehat{\eta}_\mu$	$\widehat{\eta}_\tau$
π_t	.000	.000	.000	.136	.086
τ_t	.003	.000	.074	.296	.081

Notes: Numbers in the WS, ADF, and $Z(t_{\widehat{\alpha}})$ columns are tail areas of tests.

Table 2. Unit Root Tests in the First Differences of Levels.

4.3 Cointegration Tests

Although cointegration is neither necessary nor sufficient for tests on the long-run derivative, for information purposes we also test the null hypothesis of no cointegration (against the alternative of cointegration) between π_t and τ_t using the Engle and Granger [3] two-step procedure. In particular, we regress one variable against the other (including a constant and a trend variable in the regression) to obtain the OLS regression residuals $\widehat{\zeta}_t$. A test of the null hypothesis of no cointegration is then based on testing for a unit root in $\widehat{\zeta}_t$, using the ADF test (with the number of augmenting lags being chosen based on the AIC+2 rule mentioned earlier) and asymptotic *p*-values using the coefficients in MacKinnon [8].

The cointegration tests are first done with π_t as the dependent variable in the cointegrating regression and then repeated with τ_t as the dependent variable.[4]. When π_t is the dependent variable the p-value of the null hypothesis of no cointegration is .511 and when τ_t is the dependent variable the p-value is .143. Clearly, the null hypothesis of no cointegration between π_t and τ_t cannot be rejected (at the 5% level).

4.4 Long-Horizon Regression Tests

We start by estimating equation (4) for values of k ranging from 1 to 30, as in Fisher and Seater [5], and present the estimates of b_k along with the 95% confidence bands (using the Newey and West [100] procedure) in Figure 1. The evidence shows that the null hypothesis that $b_k = 1$ can be rejected for any $k \in [1, 30]$. Thus, we find strong evidence that revenue-smoothing does not hold.

To investigate the robustness of this result, we also examine the relationship between the three-month Treasury bill rate, R_t, and τ_t. In particular, we investigate the univariate time series properties of R_t and ΔR_t, we test for cointegration between R_t and τ_t, and estimate equation (4) with $R_t - R_{t-k-1}$ as the dependent variable. The integration tests in Table 3 indicate that the time series properties of R_t are very similar to those of τ_t, investigated in Tables 1 and 2. Also, when we test the null hypothesis of no cointegration between R_t and τ_t, we cannot reject the null (irrespective of which variable is treated as the dependent variable).

Finally, we present the estimates of b_k along with the 95% confidence bands in Figure 2. The evidence shows that again the null hypothesis that $b_k = 1$ can be rejected for most values of $k \in [1, 30]$.

Variable	p-values			KPSS	
	WS	ADF	$Z(t_{\widehat{\alpha}})$	$\widehat{\eta}_\mu$	$\widehat{\eta}_\tau$
R_t	.575	.730	.396	.690	.101
ΔR_t	.000	.000	.001	.159	.115

Notes: Numbers in the WS, ADF, and $Z(t_{\widehat{\alpha}})$ columns are tail areas of tests.

Table 3. Unit Root Tests in R_t and ΔR_t.

---

[4]We should wary of a result indicating cointegration using one series as the dependent variable, but no cointegration when the other series is used as the dependent variable.

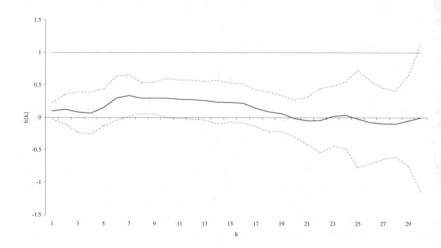

Fig. 1. The LRD for the Inflation Rate.

5 Conclusion

We have tested the revenue-smoothing hypothesis using annual data for the United States over the period from 1934 to 1994. In doing so, we have used the Fisher and Seater [5] methodology, paying particular attention to the integration properties of the data, since meaningful long-horizon refression tests critically depend on these properties. Overall, although Mankiw [9] and Poterba and Rotemberg [14] found evidence supporting revenue-smoothing in the United States using contemporaneous ordinary least squares regressions, the evidence presented here, as well as in Trehan and Walsh [17], Ghosh [6], Evans and Amey [4], and Serletis and Schorn [15], does not support the theory of optimal seigniorage.

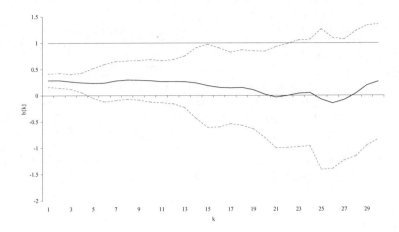

Fig. 2. The LRD for the Interest Rates.

References

1. Barro RJ, Sahasakul C (1983) Measuring the average marginal tax rate from the individual income tax. Journal of Business 56: 419-452
2. Dickey DA, Fuller WA (1981) Likelihood ratio statistics for autoregressive time series with a unit root. Econometrica 49: 1057-72
3. Engle RF, Granger CW (1987) Cointegration and error correction: Representation, estimation and testing. Econometrica 55: 251-276
4. Evans JL, Amey MC (1996) Seigniorage and tax smoothing: Testing the extended tax-smoothing model. Journal of Macroeconomics 18: 111-125
5. Fisher M, Seater J (1993) Long-run neutrality and superneutrality in an ARIMA framework. American Economic Review 83: 402-415
6. Ghosh AR (1995) Intertemporal tax-smoothing and the government budget surplus: Canada and the United States. Journal of Money, Credit, and Banking 27: 1033-1045
7. Kwiatkowski D, Phillips PCB, Schmidt P, Shin Y (1992) Testing the null hypothesis of stationarity against the alternative of a unit root. Journal of Econometrics 54: 159-178
8. MacKinnon JG (1994) Approximate asymptotic distribution functions for unit-root and cointegration tests. Journal of Business and Economic Statistics 12: 167-176

9. Mankiw NG (1987) The optimal collection of seigniorage: Theory and evidence. Journal of Monetary Economics 20: 327-341
10. Newey W, West K (1987) A simple positive semi-definite, heteroskedasticity and auto-correlation consistent covariance matrix. Econometrica 55: 703-708
11. Pantula SG, Gonzalez-Farias G, Fuller WA (1994) A comparison of unit-root test criteria. Journal of Business and Economic Statistics 12: 449-459
12. Phillips PCB (1987) Time series regression with a unit root. Econometrica 277-301
13. Phillips PCB, Perron P (1988) Testing for a unit root in time series regression. Biometrica 75: 335-346
14. Poterba JM, Rotemberg JJ (1990) Inflation and taxation with optimizing governments. Journal of Money, Credit, and Banking 22: 1-18
15. Serletis A, Schorn R (1999) International evidence on the tax- and revenue-smoothing hypotheses. Oxford Economic Papers 51: 387-396
16. Stephenson EF (1998) Average marginal tax rates revisited. Journal of Monetary Economics 41: 389-409
17. Trehan B, Walsh CE (1990) Seigniorage and tax smoothing in the United States: 1914-1986. Journal of Monetary Economics 25: 97-112

What VAR Tell us about DSGE Models?[*]

Fabio Canova[1] and Joaquim Pires Pina[2]

[1] IGIER Bocconi, Universitat Pompeu Fabra, and CEPR, IGIER-Universit Bocconi, via Salasco 5, 20136 Milano, Italia. fabio.canova@uni-bocconi.it

[2] University Nova of Lisbon, Faculty of Economics, Campus de Campolide, 1099-032 Lisboa, Portugal. jagl@fct.unl.pt

Summary. We examine the consequences of extracting structural shocks in VAR models using standard standard inertial restrictions, when the data has been generated by two stochastic dynamic general equilibrium (DSGE) models featuring different types of microfundations and different sources of sluggishness. We find that, in general, misspecification is substantial: short run coefficients often have wrong signs; impulse responses and variance decompositions give misleading representations of the dynamics; inexistent puzzles are created. We show that an omitted variables bias accounts for the results and propose an alternative identification technique which can cope with the inherent underidentification displayed by the DSGE models currently used in macroeconomics.

Key words: General equilibrium, Monetary Policy, Identification, Structural VARs

JEL Classification: C32, C68, E32, E52

> Per questo non abbiamo niente da insegnare: su cio' che piu' somiglia alla nostra esperienza non possiamo influire, in cio' che porta la nostra impronta non sappiamo riconoscerci.
> *Mr. Palomar, Italo Calvino*

---

[*]We would like to thank Harald Uhlig, Lucrezia Reichlin, Jerome D'Adda, Morten Ravn, Vincenzo Quadrini, John Faust, David Bowman and the participants of seminars at a number of universities, conferences and summer schools for comments and suggestions. Canova acknowledges the financial support of DGYCIT grants; Pina acknowledges financial support from *Sub-Programa Ciência e Tecnologia do 2° Quadro Comunitário de Apoio*. An earlier version of this paper has circulated with the title "Monetary policy misspecification in VAR models".

1 Introduction

The high correlation between monetary and real aggregates over the business cycle has attracted the attention of macroeconomists for at least forty years. Friedman and Schwartz [17] were among the firsts to provide a causal interpretation of this relationship: they showed that the comovements of money with output were not due to the passive response of money to the developments in the real and financial sides of the economy and argued that changes in money were good approximations to policy disturbances. Since their seminal work, several generations of macroeconomists have tried either to empirically refute Friedman and Schwartz's causal interpretation or to provide theoretical models which can account for such a relationship (see for examples, Lucas [20]; Cooley and Quadrini [11]; Chari, Kehoe and McGrattan [5]).

The empirical side of the literature has documented that unforecastable movements in money produce responses in macroeconomic variables, in particular interest rates, that are difficult to interpret - they generate the so-called liquidity puzzle (see Leeper and Gordon [19]). To remedy these problems Sims [25], Bernanke and Blinder [1] suggested to use short term interest rate innovations as indicators of monetary policy disturbances. However, also in this case, the responses of certain variables to policy disturbances are difficult to justify (in particular, the responses of the price level (Sims [26]). As a consequence of these difficulties, the last ten years have witnessed a considerable effort in trying to identify monetary policy disturbances using parsimoniously restricted multivariate time series models (see Gordon and Leeper [18]; Christiano, Eichenbaum and Evans [8]; Bernanke and Mihov [2]; Uhlig [31]).

This literature has stressed the pitfalls of an incorrect choice of variables and identification schemes and carefully documented the type of central bank reaction function in place in various historical episodes. However, by concentrating on the identification of monetary policy disturbances, this literature has disregarded possible feedbacks due to the general equilibrium nature of shocks. In particular, conventional "inertial" constraints are routinely imposed on equations other than the one under consideration in order to obtain the minimum number of restrictions needed to identify the full system of equations.

This paper examines the consequences of imposing (false) inertial restrictions on the inference a VAR econometrician draws when two classes general equilibrium models are used to generate the data. In particular, we are interested in knowing whether it is possible to recover the underlying policy rule and whether statistics characterizing the transmission properties of monetary policy shocks and the importance of policy disturbances in generating real fluctuations are reliable or not.

The mechanics underlying the transmission properties of monetary disturbances are as elusive as ever and current theoretical models, although a bit more microfunded and articulated than those used in the past, still fall short in accounting for many aspects of the monetary phenomena. For example, existing paradigms have difficulties in accounting for the unconditional correlation of output, interest rates, real balances and inflation observed in the last 40 years both in the US and Europe and for the persistence of inflation. Rather than taking a position in the dispute of what model better represents the data, we prefer to be agnostic: we take two prototype models with different microfundations off-the-shelf (a version of the limited participation model of Christiano, Eichenbaum and Evans [7] and a version of the sticky price, sticky wage model of Erceg, Henderson and Levin [12]), simulate them under two different monetary policy rules and examine what structural VAR analysis can tell us about their properties.

These two classes of models use different frictions to produce real effects of monetary policy. Because of their internal structure, they generate different inter-relationships between the real and the monetary side of the economy and different intensity and timing in the transmission of shocks. Despite these differences they are, approximately, equivalent in their poor fit to the data. On the other hand, both models display desirable features which makes them good candidates for the experiments we are interested in. First, they have built-in a liquidity effect, i.e. a surprise increases in nominal interest rates produces negative responses of real balances. Second, depending on the parametrization used, the response of prices to shocks may be made instantaneous or sluggish. Third, most of the variations in the policy instrument are accounted for by responses to the state of the economy and not by random disturbances to policy. Finally, at least in the first model, the contribution of monetary policy shocks to the variability of real variables can be made either modest or sizable, depending on the policy rule used.

Using data simulated from these two models, we estimate a 4-variable VAR model with output, inflation, interest rates and real balances and identify structural disturbances by imposing exclusion restrictions on the contemporaneous impact of innovations according to two schemes, a recursive and a non-recursive one. The first scheme imposes that the estimated monetary policy rule is of a feedback (Taylor) type while the second allows interest rates to partially accommodate movements in real balances. Both schemes impose stringent "inertial" restrictions on the data: policy disturbances are assumed not to affect output and inflation contemporaneously and the static aggregate demand curve is assumed to cross a vertical aggregate supply curve.

We compare theoretical and the estimated structural models using impact coefficients, impulse responses and the variance decomposition. We find that identified VARs provide a poor characterization of the data generating process (DGP) and that our conclusions are, to a large extent, robust to the choice of the DGP and of the policy rule. Misspecifications occur at all levels. Estimated short run coefficients often have the wrong sign and, in same cases, are estimated to be the same regardless of the monetary rule generating the data. The sign and the significance of impulse responses differ across DGP, policy rules and identification schemes but there is a widespread tendency to misrepresent the true dynamics. The variance decomposition underestimates the importance of monetary policy shocks as sources of real variability in one case and, in at least another, attributes most of the fluctuations to the wrong source of disturbance.

We argue that the parametrization of the theoretical economy, the small size of the sample and the failure to include state variables in the VAR can not account for the poor behavior of the estimated structural models. To understand the reasons for the poor performance of structural VARs note that, although based on different principles, the two economies (and many other variants of these) share one important feature: the matrix of impact coefficients has several blocks of non-zero elements and these elements are forced to be zero with both identification approaches. That is to say, there equations which are not identifiable using contemporaneous zero restrictions. Structural VAR analyses which employ inertial restrictions in an underidentified system omit important variables from certain equations when estimating structural shocks and this omission biases inference in the entire system. As a result, impact coefficients are mismeasured; the sign and the shape of impulse responses misspecified; the contribution of monetary shocks to the variability of real variables distorted. These outcomes obtain even when the estimated policy rule correctly recognizes the inputs of the theoretical policy rule and problems are more severe whenever contemporaneous feedbacks are stronger.

Economies where dynamic general equilibrium effects occur within one period are therefore not suited to be analyzed with standard identification procedures because there is no natural "inertial" restriction one can appeal to recover the disturbances. Frictions due to price and wage stickiness or adjustment costs may reduce the extent of the underidentification present in the system but, as our simulations show, they do not solve the problem. Stronger type of restrictions, for example, one period in advance labor decisions, may induce sluggishness in the data but, by restricting the response of one variable to *all* shocks, they leave unresolved the inherent underidentification of the data. Furthermore, while certain frictions currently used may have some intuitive appeal (e.g. habit persistence), other do not. In general, DSGE models seldomly provide the full array of inertial restrictions typically used to identify VARs and when they do, as in Sims and Zha [29] or Rotemberg and Woodford [22]), it is because of rather ad-hoc formulations.

Given the large body of empirical VAR literature which claimed success in recovering structural disturbances, one may be tempted to conclude that our results obtain because the class of models we consider provides a poor characterization of the data, in terms of sources of shocks, contemporaneous impacts and richness of the dynamics - after all, the world is different from our toy laboratories. While both models have problems, we are not aware of any alternative and fully articulated DSGE paradigm which would give a significantly better match with the data. Furthermore, we have not rigged the data so that VAR econometricians would stumble at the first hurdle: the models are both standard and simple; they have been widely used in the theoretical literature; and last but not least, they generate a considerable variety of contemporaneous and dynamic effects.

The conclusion we would like to stress is different. If one takes the point of view that general equilibrium feedbacks are important, inertial identification constraints should be treated with care since misspecification is widespread and generic and that answers to interesting economic questions can misleading. Clearly, this does not mean that VAR analyses should be abandoned; it simply means that a different style of identification should be used. Both models, in fact, contain a wealth of restrictions which, although rarely used, can be employed for identification purposes. In the latter part of the paper, we show that approaches along the lines of Canova and De Nicoló [4], Faust [14] and Uhlig [32], where identification is obtained by means of sign restrictions on the cross correlation function of certain variables in response to shocks, do not suffer misspecification problems: estimated policy shocks produce dynamics which reproduce the theoretical ones and correctly characterize their importance for movements in real variables, regardless of the DGP and the policy rule we employ. That is, VAR econometricians which use model based restrictions can learn about the underlying features of the data, no matter how strong the contemporaneous interrelationships across the reduced form innovations are. Hence, our criticism is not directed to the VAR methodology per-se but to a particular type of identification restrictions routinely used in applied work.

Several papers have examined misspecification problems in VARs (see e.g. Sargent [24]; Cooley and LeRoy [9]; Hansen and Sargent [16]; Rudebusch [23]). Our work looks at this issue from a different perspective: we show that inertial assumptions are inconsistent with the restrictions implied by a large class of general equilibrium models and that the outcomes of the exercises conducted with conventional identification scheme can be highly distorted. As far as we know, this last point has not been sufficiently appreciated in the literature and only Cooley and Dwyer [10] have produced an example where conventional long run restrictions may badly distort inference when applied to data generated from a simple DSGE model.

The rest of the paper is organized as follows. Section 2 briefly describes the two models, the calibration and discusses the properties of the theoretical economies. Section 3 describes the results obtained using identified VARs on data simulated from the artificial economies. Section 4 provides explanations for the results. Section 5 present results obtained with an identification approach based on sign restrictions. Section 6 concludes.

2 Models

Since the models we employ in our exercises are standard, we only describe their main features and quickly proceed to the calibration and to the examination of their properties. We use a richer probabilistic structure than it is typically assumed to have a data generating process with more realistic features and an economy which has the same number of shocks as the variables we will consider later on in the VAR.

2.1 A Limited Participation (LP) Model

The economy we use is a version of the model used by Christiano, Eichenbaum and Evans[7]. There are five types of agents (households, firms, a bank, a government and the monetary authority) and all markets are competitive. Since the behavior of the fiscal and monetary authorities is similar in the two models we postpone the description of their action to a later subsection.

The representative household maximizes the expected discounted sum of instantaneous utilities (with discount factor $\beta \in (0,1)$) derived from consuming an homogenous good, C_t and from enjoying leisure. The timing of the decision is the following: agents choose deposits, I_t, at the beginning of the period out of money held, M_{t-1} before observing the shocks ; then all the shocks are realized, and the monetary injection, X_t^A, is fed into the bank. At this point households choose the number of hours to work, and how much capital to rent to firms. The time endowment is normalized to one; capital is in fixed supply and normalized to one. At the end of production time, households collect the wage payment, $W_t N_t$, and uses it with the money left, $M_{t-1} - I_t$, to buy goods. After goods are purchased agents receive income from holding one-period government bonds, $R_t^b B_{t-1}$, from renting capital to the firm, $r_t K_{t-1}$, from owning shares in the firms and in the bank, and from deposits, $R_t^M I_t$ and pay taxes, where R_t^M is gross return on money deposits (and credit) and R_t^b is gross nominal return on bonds. Out of disposable income the household decides the composition of its portfolio (money, capital and bonds) to be carried over next period. The program solved is

$$Max_{\{C_t, I_t, N_t, K_t, M_t, B_t\}} E_0 \sum_{t=0}^{\infty} \beta^t [\xi_t (\ln(C_t)) + \gamma \ln(1 - N_t)] \tag{1}$$

subject to

$$P_t C_t \leq M_{t-1} - I_t + W_t N_t \tag{2}$$

$$M_t + P_t K_t + B_t \leq W_t N_t + P_t r_t K_{t-1} + R_t^M (I_t + X_t) + R_t^b B_{t-1}$$
$$+ M_{t-1} - I_t - P_t (C_t + T_t) \tag{3}$$

where ξ_t is a preference shock, M_{-1}, B_{-1}, K_{-1} are given and E_0 is the expectation conditional on information at time 0. Equation (2) is the cash-in-advance constraint and equation (3) is the budget constraint. Given local nonsatiation, both constraints are assumed to hold with equality.

There exists a continuum of identical firms, facing a constant returns to scale technology perturbed by an exogenous technology shock v_t. Each firm maximizes profits subject to the given technology and to a cash-in-advance constraint, since wages are paid before the firm collects revenues from the sales of the product. Profits are measured by the difference between the receipts from selling the good, Y_t, at price P_t, and the costs associated with renting capital, $P_t r_t K_t$, and paying wages, $(1 + R_t^M) W_t N_t$. Given the technology shock v_t , the problem solved by the firm is

$$Max_{\{N_t, K_t\}} \text{Profits}_t = P_t Y_t - (1 + R_t^M) W_t N_t - P_t r_t K_t \tag{4}$$

subject to

$$W_t N_t \leq I_t + X_t \tag{5}$$

$$Y_t \leq v_t N_t^\alpha K_t^{1-\alpha} \tag{6}$$

Also here we assume that the constraints (5)-(6) hold with equality.

Banks collect deposits from the households, I_t^A, pay R_t^M of gross interest and receive X_t^A from the monetary authority, issued at zero cost and supplied at zero price. They then rents these funds to firms at the price R_t^M. Profits from financial intermediation, $R_t^M X_t^A$, are paid-out to the household in the form of dividends. (The superscript A indicates aggregate variables).

2.2 A Sticky Price, Sticky Wage (SPSW) Model

The economy is a version of the one studied by Erceg, Hendeson and Levine [12]. There are five agents also in this economy (households, intermediate and final good producing firms, a government and a monetary authority). Household are monopolistic competitive in selling labor and intermediate firms are monopolistic competitive in selling their product. Consumer maximize a separable utility function defined over consumption (C_t), leisure $(1 - N_t)$ and real balances $(\frac{M_t}{p_t})$ given by $\ln(c_t) + \xi_t ln(1 - N_t) + \frac{\mu}{1-\mu}(\frac{M_t}{p_t})^{1-\mu}$ where ξ_t is a preference shock. The household constraint is

$$P_t c_t(h) + M_t(h) + P_t K_t(h) + B_t(h) \leq W_t(h)N_t(h) + P_t r_t K_{t-1}(h)$$
$$+ R_t^b B_{t-1}(h) + M_{t-1}(h) + \Gamma_t(h) + T_t(h)$$

where $\Gamma_t(h)$ is the household h share of firms profits, $T_t(h)$ is a lump sum tax and all the other variables have been already defined. Also in this case we assume that capital is in fixed supply and normalized to 1. The labor demand aggregator N_t is given by $[\int_0^1 N_t(h)^{1/(1+\theta_w)}dh]^{1+\theta_w}$ where $\theta_w > 0$. Since the cost of a unit of labor index to the production sector is $W_t = [\int_0^1 w_t(h)^{-1/\theta_w}dh]^{-\theta_w}$, the demand for labor of household h is $N_t(h) = [\frac{W_t(h)}{W_t}]^{-\frac{1+\theta_w}{\theta_w}}N_t$. We assume that a fraction $1 - \zeta_w$ of the households renegotiate their wage contract in each period and they choose W_t to maximize utility. Optimization implies:

$$E_t \sum_j \beta^j \zeta_w^j (\frac{1}{1+\theta_w}\frac{\pi^j w_t(h)}{p_{t+j}}c_{t+j}^{-1} - \xi_{t+j}(1 - N_{t+j}(h)^{-1})N_{t+j}(h) = 0 \qquad (7)$$

When a consumer is not allowed to change the wage $W_{t+j}(h) = \pi^j W_t(h)$ where π is the steady state gross inflation rate.

The output index is assembled using a constant returns to scale technology $Y_t = [\int_0^1 Y_t(f)^{1/(1+\theta_p)}df]^{1+\theta_p}$. Units of output are sold at the price $P_t = [\int_0^1 P_t(f)^{-1/\theta_p}df]^{-\theta_p}$ and the demand function for each good f is $Y_t(f) = [\int_0^1 \frac{P_t(f)}{P_t}]^{-(1+\theta_p)/\theta_p}Y_t$. The production function of each intermediate good is $Y_t(f) = v_t N_t^\alpha K_t^{1-\alpha}$ where v_t is a technology shock. A fraction $1 - \zeta_p$ of the firms can reset their price at each t to maximize their profits. Optimization implies

$$E_t \sum_j \psi_{t,t+j}\zeta_p^j(\frac{1}{1+\theta_p}\pi^j p_t(f) - MC_{t+j})Y_{t+j}(f) = 0 \qquad (8)$$

where MC_{t+j} is the marginal costs at $t + j$ and $\psi_{t,t+h}$ is the Arrow-Debreu price at t of a unit of profit at $t + j$. If a firm is not allowed to change its price $p_{t+j}(f) = \pi^j p_t(f)$.

2.3 Fiscal and Monetary Policy and Shocks

Fiscal and Monetary policy actions are similar in the two models. Stochastic government consumption G_t^A, is financed by issuing one-period bonds, B_t^A, after repaying outstanding debt, $R_t^b B_{t-1}^A$, and lump sum taxes. That is, $P_t(G_t^A - T_t) = B_t^A - R_t^b B_{t-1}^A$.

The monetary authority issues cash at no costs every period and transfers to the bank in the limited participation model or to the consumers in the sticky price, sticky wage model in the form of an "helicopter drop" of money. The policy rule can take two forms: a partial accommodation rule or a feedback rule. At this stage, we specify it in an implicit form as $f(R_t, M_t, P_t, Y_t, \varepsilon_t) = 0$ where ε_t governs the non-systematic part and monetary injections are defined as $X_t^A = M_t^A - M_{t-1}^A$

In both specifications fluctuations are driven by four types of shocks: technology, monetary policy, government expenditure and preference shocks. Structural shocks are assumed to be uncorrelated at all leads and lags and represented with the following AR processes

$$\ln(\xi_t) = (1 - \psi)\ln(\xi) + \psi \ln(\xi_{t-1}) + u_t, \text{ with } u_t \sim iid(0, \sigma_u^2), |\psi| < 1$$

$$\ln(v_t) = (1 - \rho)\ln(v) + \rho \ln(v_{t-1}) + \vartheta_t, \text{ with } \vartheta_t \sim iid(0, \sigma_\vartheta^2), |\rho| < 1$$

$$\ln(\varepsilon_t) = (1 - \phi)\ln(\varepsilon) + \phi \ln(\varepsilon_{t-1}) + \omega_t, \text{ with } \omega_t \sim iid(0, \sigma_\omega^2), |\phi| < 1$$

$$\ln(G_t) = (1 - \theta)\ln(G) + \theta \ln(G_{t-1}) + \varphi_t, \text{ with } \varphi_t \sim iid(0, \sigma_\varphi^2), |\theta| < 1$$

2.4 Calibration and Computation of Equilibrium

To generate time series out of the model, we choose standard parametrizations. The time unit of the model is a quarter. The parameters common to the two specifications are:

$\bar{N}$	α	$\bar{\Pi}$	β	$\bar{c}/\bar{y}$
0.33	0.65	1.005	0.99	0.80

where $\bar{c}/\bar{y}$ is the share of consumption in output, $\bar{N}$ is hours worked and $\bar{\Pi}$ is gross inflation in the steady states, α is exponent of labor in the production function, β is the discount factor. These parameters imply, for example, that in steady-state the gross real interest rate is 1.01, output is 0.46, real balances 0.37 and the real (fully flexible) wage 0.88. Moreover, for the limited participation model these parameters imply that the share of leisure in utility is 0.65, and $\gamma = 1.86$, which are in line with those used in the literature.

For the sticky price, sticky wage model we select the degree of price and wage rigidity to be the same and set $\zeta_p = \zeta_w = 0.75$, a standard value in the literature (it implies that on average firms (consumers) change their price (wage) every three quarters). Lower values for these parameters imply that the economy is approaching the flexible price situation. Also, we choose the elasticity of money demand μ to be 7. The value of this parameter is uninfluential on our conclusions: any choice between 2 and 100 would produce the same results.

We parametrize the stochastic processes for the four shocks to all have the same persistence and the same standard deviation. The conclusions we draw are robust to the exact choice of the persistence parameters within the range [0.8, 0.98]. In the benchmark case we set:

v	ε	ξ	ρ	ϕ	ψ	θ	σ_ϑ	σ_ω	σ_u
1.0	1.0	1.0	0.95	0.95	0.95	0.95	0.71	0.71	0.71

where v, ε, ξ are the steady state value of the shocks, ρ, ϕ, ψ, θ are the AR parameters and σ_ϑ, σ_ω, σ_u are the standard deviations for the shocks. We choose the standard deviation of G shocks so that the coefficient of variation is the same as for other processes, i.e., $\sigma_\varphi = G^A * 0.71$ where G^A is the steady state value of G. Note that this parsimonious selection ties our hands since it reduces the number of degrees of freedom we have to fine tune the data to the idiosyncracies of the identification schemes.

To solve the model we transform the variables in real terms. This ensures, along with the assumed parametrization, stationarity of simulated data. The policy rule is of the form

$$m_t^{\delta_0} = \kappa \Pi_t^{\delta_1} R_t^{\delta_2} y_t^{\delta_3} \varepsilon_t \tag{9}$$

where κ is a constant. In percentage deviation from steady state, a partial accommodation (PA) rule is obtained setting $\delta_2 = -1, \delta_0 = 0.3, \delta_1 = \delta_3 = 0$; and a feedback (FB) Taylor-type rule is obtained setting $\delta_2 = -1.0; \delta_1 = 0.5; \delta_3 = 0.1, \delta_0 = 0$. Note that in both cases the supply of real balances is upward sloping in the (m, R) space [3]. A solution to the model is obtained log-linearizing the equilibrium conditions around the steady state and using Uhlig's [31] approach.

2.5 Policy Rules and the Dynamics of the Model

Inspection of the equilibrium policy functions and of the dynamics generated by the model provides useful information on the characteristics of our economies. We present the equilibrium policy functions as follows:

Limited Participation - Partial Accommodative Policy

$$
\begin{bmatrix} \widehat{m}_t \\ \widehat{i}_t \\ \widehat{y}_t \\ \widehat{R}_t \\ \widehat{\Pi}_t \end{bmatrix} =
\begin{bmatrix} 0.0000 & -0.0000 \\ 0.0000 & 0.0000 \\ 0.0000 & 0.0000 \\ 0.0000 & 0.0000 \\ 5.1118 & -4.1118 \end{bmatrix}
\begin{bmatrix} \widehat{m}_{t-1} \\ \widehat{i}_{t-1} \end{bmatrix} +
\begin{bmatrix} 0.9732 & 0.4428 & -0.4428 & -0.1061 \\ 0.4399 & 0.2123 & -1.3934 & 0.1420 \\ 0.7786 & 0.3543 & -0.3543 & 0.1151 \\ 0.2920 & 0.1328 & 0.8672 & -0.0318 \\ -2.9741 & -1.3532 & -2.7586 & 1.1465 \end{bmatrix}
\begin{bmatrix} \widehat{v}_t \\ \widehat{\omega}_t \\ \widehat{\varepsilon}_t \\ \widehat{g}_t \end{bmatrix}
$$

Limited Participation - Feedback Policy

$$
\begin{bmatrix} \widehat{m}_t \\ \widehat{i}_t \\ \widehat{y}_t \\ \widehat{R}_t \\ \widehat{\Pi}_t \end{bmatrix} =
\begin{bmatrix} -0.4960 & 0.3990 \\ -1.0039 & 0.8075 \\ -0.3968 & 0.3192 \\ 0.9713 & -0.7813 \\ 2.0219 & -1.6264 \end{bmatrix}
\begin{bmatrix} \widehat{m}_{t-1} \\ \widehat{i}_{t-1} \end{bmatrix} +
\begin{bmatrix} 1.3034 & 0.5930 & -0.1941 & -0.2257 \\ 1.1459 & 0.5621 & -1.4786 & -0.1260 \\ 1.0427 & 0.4744 & -0.1552 & 0.0194 \\ -0.3545 & -0.1613 & 0.3800 & 0.2025 \\ -0.9175 & -0.4175 & -1.2089 & 0.4011 \end{bmatrix}
\begin{bmatrix} \widehat{v}_t \\ \widehat{\omega}_t \\ \widehat{\varepsilon}_t \\ \widehat{g}_t \end{bmatrix}
$$

[3] The reason to choose low feedback from inflation in the FB rule is that in the LP economy, explosive roots are generated whenever δ_1 approximate one from below. Since any value of δ_1 is consistent with determinate equilibrium in the SPSW economy, we use the same specification in both cases to keep the message clear and simple.

Sticky Price, Sticky Wage - Partial Accommodative Policy

$$
\begin{bmatrix} \widehat{w}_t \\ \widehat{y}_t \\ \widehat{R}_t \\ \widehat{m}_t \\ \widehat{\Pi}_t \end{bmatrix} = \begin{bmatrix} 0.0012 \\ 0.5571 \\ 0.1082 \\ 0.1293 \\ 0.1050 \end{bmatrix} \begin{bmatrix} \widehat{w}_{t-1} \end{bmatrix} + \begin{bmatrix} 0.5823 & 0.3857 & -0.0970 & -0.0005 \\ 0.2756 & -0.4910 & 0.1235 & 0.0009 \\ -0.3633 & 0.0832 & -0.0197 & 1.0001 \\ 0.0957 & -0.1275 & -0.0040 & -0.1410 \\ -0.7817 & 0.2646 & -0.0641 & 0.0027 \end{bmatrix} \begin{bmatrix} \widehat{v}_t \\ \widehat{\xi}_t \\ \widehat{\varepsilon}_t \\ \widehat{g}_t \end{bmatrix}
$$

Sticky Price, Sticky Wage - Feedback Policy

$$
\begin{bmatrix} \widehat{w}_t \\ \widehat{y}_t \\ \widehat{R}_t \\ \widehat{m}_t \\ \widehat{\Pi}_t \end{bmatrix} = \begin{bmatrix} 0.0012 \\ 0.5571 \\ 0.0416 \\ 0.1386 \\ 0.1050 \end{bmatrix} \begin{bmatrix} \widehat{w}_{t-1} \end{bmatrix} + \begin{bmatrix} 0.5823 & 0.3857 & -0.0970 & -0.0005 \\ 0.2756 & -0.4911 & 0.1236 & 0.0008 \\ 0.0128 & -0.0333 & -0.0020 & 0.9595 \\ 0.0427 & -0.1111 & -0.0065 & -0.1351 \\ -0.7812 & 0.2644 & -0.0641 & 0.0025 \end{bmatrix} \begin{bmatrix} \widehat{v}_t \\ \widehat{\xi}_t \\ \widehat{\varepsilon}_t \\ \widehat{g}_t \end{bmatrix}
$$

The responses of the endogenous variables for the two different policy rules following monetary policy and technology shocks in Figure 1 for the LP economy and Figure 2 for the SPSW economy. Table 1 reports the variance decomposition for output, inflation, nominal interest rate and real balances at the 16-periods horizon for each model and each rule.

Few features of the policy rules should be highlighted. First, the dynamics generated with a feedback (FB) rule are richer than those obtained with a partial accommodative (PA) rule in the LP economy but not in the SPSW economy. Second, the sign of certain impact coefficients changes with the nature of the policy rule. For example, in the LP economy, switching from a PA rule to a FB rule changes the signs of the impact coefficients of three shocks on the interest rate. In the SPSW economy, switching rules changes the sign of the instantaneous responses of the nominal interest rate and of real balances to technology and preference shocks. Third, in the LP economy, the instantaneous response of the nominal rate to a monetary policy shock is smaller in magnitude when a FB rule is employed. That is, nominal interest rates are worse indicators of the stance of monetary policy with a FB rule than with a PA rule (see also Bernanke and Blinder [1]). Fourth, in both economies inflation instantaneously reacts to technology and preference shocks. Also, while it reacts instantaneously and with a large coefficient to monetary and government expenditure shocks in the LP economy, this is not the case in the SPSW economy. In this latter model, sluggishness induced by price and wage rigidities implies little contemporaneous effect of demand shocks on inflation. Note also that monetary policy shocks have a sizable instantaneous impact on output in the LP economy while this is not the case in the SPSW economy, regardless of the policy rule. Hence, instantaneously monetary policy shocks in the SPSW economy have measurable effects only on real balances, while in the LP economy they also have effects on inflation and real variables. These different features should be kept in mind when interpreting structural VAR results.

	Y	Π	R	m
Limited Participation - Partial Accommodative Policy				
Technology shocks	69.7	37.1	10.0	70.2
Preference shocks	14.4	7.3	2.1	14.5
Monetary shocks	14.4	50.6	87.8	14.5
Government shocks	1.5	5.0	0.1	0.8
Limited Participation - Feedback Policy				
Technology shocks	52.4	5.0	1.7	52.2
Preference shocks	11.8	0.7	0.2	11.7
Monetary shocks	35.2	93.6	97.9	35.1
Government shocks	0.6	0.7	0.2	1.0
Sticky Price Sticky Wage Economy - Partial Accommodative Policy				
Technology shocks	81.7	83.6	0.2	43.2
Preference shocks	17.1	16.3	0.1	10.5
Monetary shocks	0.0	0.0	99.6	45.5
Government shocks	1.2	0.1	0.1	0.8
Sticky Price Sticky Wage Economy - Feedback Policy				
Technology shocks	81.1	82.0	23.7	56.7
Preference shocks	17.6	16.9	3.3	13.6
Monetary shocks	0.0	0.0	72.9	29.7
Government shocks	1.3	1.1	0.1	0.1

Table 1. Variance Decomposition at the 16-Period Horizon.

Figures 1 and 2 indicate that, regardless of the specification, surprise increases in interest rates generate a liquidity effect. In the LP economy this obtains because increases in nominal interest rates contracts employment, output and consumption and decreases real and nominal wages and prices. In the SPSW economy, increases in the nominal interest rates reduce the amount of real balances needed to support a given volume of transactions, because they change the opportunity cost to hold money - negligible aggregate demand effects are generated in this model. In fact as Figure 2 shows, monetary disturbances have no real demand side effects either in the short or in the medium run.

A technology shock has the standard effects on output, inflation and real balances in both economies while, because of the lack of intertemporal smoothing opportunities, hours fall as their dynamics are dominated by a wealth effect. There are some differences in the responses of the nominal interest rate depending on the policy rule used, but this difference is common to the two setups: it increases when a partial accommodative rule is used and decreases when a feedback type rule is employed. This is not surprising: with the latter rule nominal interest rates fall as inflation fall, while with a partial accommodation rule interest rate rise with real balances.

Perhaps unsurprisingly given the dynamics we have just described, the contribution of shocks to the variability of output, inflation, real balances and nominal rate dramatically differs in the two economies. In the LP economy most of the dynamics at the 16-periods horizon in all variables are due to technology and monetary shocks, regardless of the policy rule. Interestingly, monetary shocks explain a larger portion of the variability of output in the FB economy then in the PA economy and their size (35% vs. 14%) roughly corresponds to the range of estimates obtained in the literature (see e.g. Uhlig [31]).

In the SPSW economy, technology shocks drive the majority of the fluctuations in all variables but the nominal interest rate. Preference shocks also play some role for all variables but the nominal interest rate. On the other hand, monetary shocks have negligible explanatory power for output and inflation fluctuations, regardless of the policy rule employed. This result is robust: increasing in the degree of nominal rigidity does not quantitatively change this conclusion. The problem, as pointed out by Farmer [13] or Neiss and Pappa [21], is that in this model real rigidities are too small to make monetary policy shock matter. Note that because monetary policy shocks have no effects on output and inflation either in the short or in the long run, this economy displays a block recursive structure with output and inflation preceeding interest rates and real balances. As we will see, the presence of feedbacks in the first two equations still creates problems, even in this special setup.

To summarize, both models have desirable and undesirable features. Among the latters one should include, for example, that in the LP economy the instantaneous response of inflation to monetary shock is probably too large, while, monetary shocks in the SPSW economy play no role in generating real fluctuations. There are several other features of the data that these models have hard time to reproduce. Table 3, which reports the contemporaneous correlation of output, nominal interest rates, real balances and inflation in the actual data and in the models, provides a glimpse of some of these problems. For example, the correlation between output and inflation is 0.35 in the US data, it is negative and large in both version of the SPSW model and negative and large in one version of the LP model. Similarly, the correlation between output and nominal interest rates is roughly zero in the data while, depending on the rule employed, it is either significantly positive or significantly negative in the two models. Rather than using these numbers to discriminate between models, we take the dynamics they produce as representative of the range of outcomes macroeconomists feel comfortable with and analyze what kind of information a structural VAR econometrician, endowed with a standard set of tools, would extract from data simulated from these models.

It is worth mentioning that while we employ very simple data generating processes, we have also experimented with economies where capital accumulation is allowed, where there are adjustment costs to capital (or investment) and where the preference specification allows for richer interactions between the arguments of util-

	(Y,R)	(Y,m)	(Y,Π)
Actual Data	0.08	0.54	0.35
Limited Participation - PA	-0.74	0.99	-0.72
Limited Participation - FB	0.49	0.99	0.05
Sticky Price Sticky Wage - PA	-0.27	0.78	-0.86
Sticky Price Sticky Wage - FB	0.24	0.68	-0.89

Note: Actual data reports correlations obtained using US data from 1960:1 to 1997:2 (150 data points) when Output, Real Balances and Inflation are detrended with Hodrick and Prescott filter. Simulated statistics are computed using 150 data points and no filtering.

Table 2. Contemporaneous Correlations.

ity. While all these additions make the dynamics of the model richer and real effects of monetary shocks more persistent, they change very little the quantitative characterization we have provided so far because the relative importance of various shocks is unaltered. In other words, the main features we have highlighted in this section would remain even when bells and whistles are added to the models to make them more realistic.

3 VAR Models

3.1 Specification

We represent the simulated economies with a set of linear dynamic equations of the form

$$A_0 z_t = A(L) z_{t-1} + e_t \tag{10}$$

where L is the lag operator, $A(L)$ is a matrix polynomial in L, $e_t = [v_t, \xi_t, \varepsilon_t, G_t]$ has a mean of zero and a diagonal covariance matrix Σ_e. We assume that A_0 is invertible so that the VAR representation of the system is

$$z_t = B(L) z_{t-1} + \zeta_t \tag{11}$$

where $\zeta_t = A_0^{-1} e_t$ has covariance matrix Σ_ζ.

Our task will be to estimate a model like (11) using data simulated from the two economies under the two monetary policy rules. Using the fact that $A_0^{-1} \Sigma_e A_0^{-1'} = \Sigma_\zeta$ and exclusion restrictions on A_0 we will extract structural disturbances. Then we examine (i) whether the sign and the magnitude of the coefficients of the estimated monetary policy rule replicate those of the generating economy, (ii) whether the estimated dynamics in response to a monetary policy shock mimic those of the generating economy, (iii) whether the variance decomposition matches the one of the theoretical economy.

Since our model has four structural shocks, we use a four variable VAR model with output, inflation, real balances and nominal interest rates as our basic structure.

Because the policy functions we presented in Section 2.5 produce restricted VAR models in 5 variables and because state variables are omitted from the estimated VAR, the DGP for the 4 variables we estimate is an ARMA of infinite length. Rather than arbitrarily choose long lags to account for such a structure, we employ AIC and SIC criteria to pick the optimal lag length, given the dynamics of simulated data. For the LP economy the two approaches selected one lag for the PA rule and two lags for the FB one. For the SPSW economy a lag length of two was chosen in both cases.

We assume that a VAR econometrician a-priori represents the monetary policy rule as

$$R_t = f(\Theta_t) + q_t \qquad (12)$$

where f is a linear function of Θ_t, the available information set, and q_t is the monetary policy innovation. We consider two specifications for Θ_t. The first, in the spirit of Christiano, Eichenbaum and Evans [8] [CEE] assumes that Θ_t includes current and lagged values of output and inflation, in addition to lagged values of real balances and interest rates. In other words, we assume a contemporaneous relationship between monetary policy shock and shocks to inflation and production of the same type as the one described by the FB rule. To complete the identification of the other disturbances (named for simplicity, aggregate supply, aggregate demand and money demand) we assume that output contemporaneously reacts only to its own innovations, that inflation responds contemporaneously to output and inflation innovations and that real balances are contemporaneously affected by innovations in all the variables. These restrictions imply a lower triangular A_0 matrix with the variables in the VAR ordered as output, inflation, interest rates and real balances. The second identification scheme is in the spirit of Sims and Zha [29] [SZ] and Leeper, Sims and Zha [?]. It assumes that Θ includes current and lagged values of real balances, in addition to lagged values of the interest rate, inflation and output. Hence the policy equation we recover is characterized by the same type of contemporaneous feedbacks we obtain with a PA rule. To complete the identification we assume that output and inflation are not contemporaneously affected by monetary policy shocks, that inflation reacts to output and inflation innovations contemporaneously and that real balances respond contemporaneously to innovations in the other three variables. It is important to stress both schemes impose stringent "inertial" restrictions: policy disturbances are assumed not to affect output and inflation contemporaneously and the static aggregate demand curve is assumed to cross a vertical aggregate supply curve.

3.2 The Results

We generate 600 data points for the endogenous variables for each specification we consider and use the last 160 as our data set. Given the quarterly frequency of the model, this corresponds to 40 years of data. VAR models are estimated by OLS, equation by equation, and for each data set we apply the two identification schemes, for a total of 8 combinations. We present estimates of the policy rules. In parenthesis are asymptotically standard errors of the estimates.

Limited Participation - Partial Accommodative Policy

$$\text{CEE} : R_t = -0.55\,\Pi_t - 0.24\,Y_t$$
$$\phantom{\text{CEE} : R_t = }(0.004)\qquad(0.001)$$
$$\text{SZ} : R_t = 0.12\,m_t$$
$$\phantom{\text{SZ} : R_t = }(0.07)$$

Limited Participation - Feedback Policy

$$\text{CEE} : R_t = -0.55\,\Pi_t - 0.24\,Y_t$$
$$\phantom{\text{CEE} : R_t = }(0.003)\qquad(0.002)$$
$$\text{SZ} : R_t = -0.30\,m_t$$
$$\phantom{\text{SZ} : R_t = }(0.01)$$

Sticky Price Sticky Wage - Partial Accommodative Policy

$$\text{CEE} : R_t = 0.96\,\Pi_t - 0.77\,y_t$$
$$\phantom{\text{CEE} : R_t = }(0.03)\qquad(0.13)$$
$$\text{SZ} : R_t = -0.15\,m_t$$
$$\phantom{\text{SZ} : R_t = }(0.66)$$

Sticky Price Sticky Wage - Feedback Policy

$$\text{CEE} : R_t = 0.87\,\pi_t + 0.17\,y_t$$
$$\phantom{\text{CEE} : R_t = }(0.05)\qquad(0.14)$$
$$\text{SZ} : R_t = 2.17\,m_t$$
$$\phantom{\text{SZ} : R_t = }(0.49)$$

Recall that in the PA economy, the interest rate responds to real balances and the contemporaneous coefficient is 0.3. With LP generated data, the SZ scheme correctly captures the sign of this coefficient but the point estimate is insignificantly different from zero. With the CEE scheme estimates of the coefficients on output and inflation, which should be theoretically equal to zero, are instead negative and significant. Hence, it appears that monetary policy is leaning against output and inflation innovations while this is not the case in the theoretical economy. In the FB economy, the coefficients on output and inflation innovations in the policy equation are equal to 0.1 and 0.5, respectively. Estimates obtained with the CEE scheme suggest that these coefficients are negative and significant. Interestingly, short run estimates of the policy parameters are very similar across data sets with the CEE scheme. With the SZ identification scheme the sign of the coefficient on interest rate innovations is negative and significant so that, in this case, this scheme fails to recover a (positively sloped) supply function for real balances.

With SPSW generated data the results are similar. With the SZ scheme, the coefficient on real balances in the PA economy is negative but insignificant while in the economy with a FB rule the coefficient, which should be zero in theory, is estimated to be positive and large. With the CEE scheme the coefficients on inflation and output have the right sign but are slightly upward biased in the FB economy. However, in an economy endowed with a PA rule, a CEE scheme gives significantly positive weight on inflation innovations and significantly negative weight on output innovations.

To summarize, regardless of the DGP used, the identification schemes we have used fail to capture the features of the true monetary policy rule in the majority of the experiments. With LP generated data, a triangular scheme is worse while with SPSW generated data, misspecification of the policy rule is larger with the SZ scheme.

Figure 3 presents the estimated dynamic response to policy (interest rate) shocks with LP data and Figure 4 the dynamic responses obtained with SPSW data. Each figure presents 68% confidence bands obtained by Monte Carlo methods together with the theoretical responses, scaled so that policy shocks in the theoretical economy and in the VAR have the same variance. Each figure has four columns corresponding to the two identification scheme for the two policy rules [4].

Consider first the CEE scheme with LP generated data. When a PA rule is used, both the sign and the magnitude of the responses to monetary policy (interest rate) shocks are wrong. For example, estimated output and real balances responses are positive while they are negative in theory and the response of inflation is insignificant throughout the range while in theory it has a jagged pattern. When a FB rule is employed, the sign of the responses are correct except for inflation, but in two of the four cases, the 68% bands do not contain the true responses at several horizons.

With a recursive identification scheme, it is possible that disturbances to real balances also capture important aspects of monetary policy shocks. Interestingly, there is very little difference in how the system reacts to interest rates and real balances disturbances. In the PA economy, they are exactly identical apart from a sign change in all the responses. In the FB economy output and real balances median responses are significantly positive while inflation and interest rates median responses are insignificant.

The median responses obtained with SZ scheme are qualitative similar to those obtained with the CEE scheme. The bands, however, are large and asymmetric reflecting the non-normality of estimated parameters in small samples. In general, when a PA rule is used, the 68% bands for output and real balances responses never

---

[4] For the just-identified CEE system, Monte Carlo bands are constructed using the standard WinRATS procedure. For over-identified SZ system we follow Sims and Zha [29], draw 1000 replications from the joint posterior distribution of the autoregressive parameters, the variance-covariance matrix of the residuals and the matrix of the structural parameters; use importance sampling to weight draws with different information and antithetic methods to speed up the calculations. We report small sample confidence bands, as opposed to their asymptotic counterparts, to allow for asymmetries in the distribution of impulse responses, if they exist.

contains the true ones, while the ones of inflation and nominal interest rates are wrong for a few quarters. Furthermore, the median responses of these variables are persistently negative after few quarters while in the model economy this is never the case. In the FB economy note that the scheme produces initially positive responses of inflation - a reminiscent of the "price puzzle" (see Sims [26]) . Furthermore, the responses of output and real balances tend to stay persistently below zero while this is not the case in the theoretical economy. Quantitatively speaking, in only less than 10% of the steps true responses are inside the (large) estimated bands for these two variables.

The estimated responses obtained with the two schemes using SPSW data are less dramatic but equally misleading. For example, when regardless of the rule employed, misspecification of the impact coefficient with the CEE scheme implies that the true responses of inflation and output fall outside the estimated 68% bands at all horizons and dynamics which are the opposite of the true ones. Furthermore, misspecification of the coefficients of the policy rule with the SZ scheme results in output and inflation responses which are outside the 68% band at several or all horizons and, in the case of inflation, have wrong signs with both data sets.

The variance decomposition (Tables 3 and 4) confirms the presence of misspecification. Recall that in the LP economy monetary shocks explain, depending on the policy rule, between 14 and 35% of the variance of output and real balances, between 50 and 93% of the variance of inflation and between 87 and 97% of the variance of interest rates.

With the triangular scheme, the contribution of monetary policy shocks to the variance of real and monetary variables at the 16 periods horizon for both data sets is negligible. Also, contrary to the theoretical decomposition, inflation innovations are the only significant source of variations in interest rates at the 16 periods horizon with both data sets. Hence, this identification scheme produces the erroneous impression that liquidity effects are short lived and that expected inflation effects dominate the variability of interest rates in the long run. Furthermore, contrary to what theory predicts, aggregate supply (output) innovations fail to explain a significant portion of inflation variability in the FB economy and aggregate demand (inflation) innovations fail to generate significant long run variations in output and real balances in the PA economy.

With the SZ scheme monetary policy innovations explain large and significant portions of the variability of real variables in both economies. With this identification scheme long run variations in interest rates appear to be driven, at least partially, by monetary policy innovations suggesting that the liquidity effect of a policy shock is much more long lived than with the CEE scheme. As with CEE scheme, however, aggregate demand (inflation) innovations explain small but significant portions of the variability of all variables while money demand (real balances) innovations play a negligible role with all data sets. Contrary to what was obtained in the theoretical economy, aggregate supply (output) innovations account for an insignificant portion of the variability of real variables which are now driven by aggregate demand and policy shocks. Finally, and quantitatively speaking, the 68% bands obtained with the two schemes do not typically include the true values.

	$Var(Y_t)$	$Var(\Pi_t)$	$Var(R_t)$	$Var(m_t)$

1) CEE Identification Scheme
A) Partial Accommodative Policy

	$Var(Y_t)$	$Var(\Pi_t)$	$Var(R_t)$	$Var(m_t)$
Innovations in y_t	$[69.5, 93.7]$	$[8.7, 17.1]$	$[1.5, 17.1]$	$[70.4, 94.1]$
Innovations in Π_t	$[0.9, 15.0]$	$[81.8, 90.3]$	$[74.7, 95.8]$	$[0.9, 14.6]$
Innovations in R_t	$[0.6, 9.5]$	$[0.1, 0.9]$	$[0.3, 5.2]$	$[0.6, 9.2]$
Innovations in m_t	$[0.7, 10.0]$	$[0.1, 1.1]$	$[0.2, 6.5]$	$[0.7, 9.5]$

B) Feedback Policy

Innovations in Y_t	$[32.4, 59.7]$	$[2.9, 7.5]$	$[1.6, 7.5]$	$[31.8, 59.2]$
Innovations in Π_t	$[15.7, 38.0]$	$[73.9, 91.3]$	$[68.3, 91.2]$	$[15.7, 37.8]$
Innovations in R_t	$[0.7, 12.2]$	$[1.5, 13.3]$	$[1.6, 17.9]$	$[0.7, 12.6]$
Innovations in m_t	$[7.2, 35.5]$	$[0.5, 9.2]$	$[0.5, 11.3]$	$[0.8, 36.2]$

2) SZ Identification Scheme
A) Partial Accommodative Policy

Innovations in AS	$[3.4, 54.1]$	$[3.4, 12.9]$	$[1.7, 12.9]$	$[3.4, 50.2]$
Innovations in AD	$[24.1, 50.1]$	$[42.9, 79.8]$	$[39.0, 67.6]$	$[24.9, 50.0]$
Innovations in MP	$[17.0, 51.8]$	$[9.2, 51.0]$	$[24.9, 53.9]$	$[18.7, 51.8]$
Innovations in MD	$[0.1, 0.2]$	$[0.1, 0.1]$	$[0.1, 0.2]$	$[0.1, 0.2]$

B) Feedback Policy

Innovations in AS	$[1.0, 36.0]$	$[0.4, 4.2]$	$[0.3, 4.4]$	$[1.0, 35.7]$
Innovations in AD	$[12.7, 50.5]$	$[45.6, 73.3]$	$[46.4, 77.2]$	$[12.3, 50.5]$
Innovations in MP	$[22.0, 55.0]$	$[21.1, 51.3]$	$[15.9, 50.9]$	$[22.2, 55.1]$
Innovations in MD	$[0.4, 22.1]$	$[0.2, 3.3]$	$[0.2, 4.3]$	$[0.4, 22.4]$

Note: AS stands for aggregate supply, AD for aggregate demand, MP for monetary policy and MD for money demand.
The numbers refer to the percentages explained at the 16 period horizon.

Table 3. Estimated Variance Decomposition - Limited Participation.

In sum, the liquidity effects of a monetary policy shock are estimated to be short lived with the CEE scheme and this type of disturbances has negligible importance in explaining real fluctuations. With the SZ scheme the opposite occurs: the liquidity effects of monetary shocks have longer lasting repercussions and this type of disturbances explain between 20 and 50% of the variability of output.

The variance decomposition obtained with CEE scheme in SPSW data provides a correct ordering of the relative importance of different sources of fluctuations with both policy rules, even though there is a tendency to underestimates the contribution to monetary shocks in the PA economy. The SZ approach also recognizes the relative importance of each shock but overestimates the contribution of monetary shocks with

	$Var(Y_t)$	$Var(\Pi_t)$	$Var(R_t)$	$Var(m_t)$

1) CEE Identification Scheme
A) Partial Accommodative Policy

	$Var(Y_t)$	$Var(\Pi_t)$	$Var(R_t)$	$Var(m_t)$
Innovations in y_t	$[71.5, 87.1]$	$[7.2, 20.2]$	$[0.2, 13.6]$	$[0.0, 0.0]$
Innovations in Π_t	$[70.2, 80.1]$	$[8.4, 19.3]$	$[0.3, 14.4]$	$[0.0, 0.0]$
Innovations in R_t	$[4.9, 28.2]$	$[0.3, 6.6]$	$[66.6, 94.8]$	$[0.0, 0.0]$
Innovations in m_t	$[23.3, 49.7]$	$[4.4, 15.2]$	$[39.7, 66.7]$	$[0.0, 0.0]$

B) Feedback Policy

Innovations in Y_t	$[72.2, 85.5]$	$[12.1, 23.1]$	$[0.5, 5.5]$	$[0.0, 0.0]$
Innovations in Π_t	$[72.2, 84.0]$	$[14.6, 24.8]$	$[0.4, 2.8]$	$[0.0, 0.0]$
Innovations in R_t	$[9.2, 26.3]$	$[5.2, 18.9]$	$[58.2, 81.7]$	$[0.0, 0.0]$
Innovations in m_t	$[29.1, 54.0]$	$[10.0, 23.2]$	$[29.4, 55.2]$	$[0.0, 0.0]$

2) SZ Identification Scheme
A) Partial Accommodative Policy

Innovations in AS	$[73.3, 89.7]$	$[5.2, 15.7]$	$[0.2, 15.5]$	$[0.0, 0.0]$
Innovations in AD	$[73.1, 87.4]$	$[8.8, 16.7]$	$[0.3, 14.3]$	$[0.0, 0.0]$
Innovations in MP	$[0.6, 11.2]$	$[0.7, 2.4]$	$[86.2, 98.8]$	$[0.0, 0.0]$
Innovations in MD	$[33.6, 59.0]$	$[4.2, 11.8]$	$[31.9, 58.5]$	$[0.0, 0.0]$

B) Feedback Policy

Innovations in AS	$[69.5, 84.7]$	$[13.2, 24.3]$	$[0.4, 8.6]$	$[1.0, 35.7]$
Innovations in AD	$[71.3, 82.1]$	$[14.9, 24.8]$	$[0.2, 6.9]$	$[12.3, 50.5]$
Innovations in MP	$[1.5, 10.4]$	$[1.3, 11.6]$	$[78.4, 95.6]$	$[22.2, 55.1]$
Innovations in MD	$[9.4, 24.9]$	$[2.2, 4.6]$	$[70.6, 86.4]$	$[0.4, 22.4]$

Note: AS stands for aggregate supply, AD for aggregate demand, MP for monetary policy and MD for money demand.
The numbers refer to the percentages explained at the 16 period horizon.

Table 4. Estimated Variance Decomposition - Sticky Price Sticky Wage.

the FB rule and underestimates that of preference shocks in the PA economy. Overall, the magnitude of the distortions in the variance decomposition obtained in the SPSW economy is smaller than the one obtained in the LP economy.

While this paper focuses on monetary policy shocks, we would like to stress that responses to the other shocks are also misspecified. For example, the aggregate demand shock partially captures both the dynamics generated by the technology and the preference shock in the SPSW economy and, as a result, tends to produce insignificant inflation responses in both economies. This means that the problems we noted here are generic; regardless of the DGP or the rule employed, one or more equations of the system may be misspecified.

We have conducted several experiments to examine the sensitivity of the results to parameter choices in the theoretical economy. In particular, we have changed the variances and the persistence of the structural shocks: we cut by half the variance of monetary innovations, we have calibrated their persistence to US data or made them iid. We have also varied the coefficient in partial accommodation rule from 0.05 (which corresponds approximately to a interest rate rule) to 0.8 and changed the parameter on inflation in the feedback rule from 0.5 to 0.8 (see Sims and Zha [29] and Taylor [30] for an empirical justification of these ranges). We found that the extent of the misspecification is robust to variations of the parameters within these ranges.

4 Explanations

The results we have obtained are somewhat surprising and contradict the conventional wisdom that (semi-)structural VARs can recover, when appropriately performed, the true dynamics of the data. It is therefore worth investigating why our results go against this commonly held perception.

One reason for why both identification schemes could fail to capture the features of monetary policy disturbances is the small sample of the data. That is, structural VAR estimates are far away from the truth - even when the estimated policy function uses the correct inputs - because the sample is too short for any asymptotic approximation to hold. While this certainly possible, small samples typically imply insignificant estimated contemporaneous parameters and error bands that include zero, which is not necessarily the case in our experiments.

To detect how important the small sample problem is, we conducted two experiments. In the first one, we use 500 observations for estimation. The qualitative features of the results are unchanged. With LP data, the coefficients of the policy function estimated with the CEE scheme are still wrong and their magnitude is independent of the data generating process. With the SZ scheme the coefficient on real balances obtained with data from the PA economy is positive and now significantly different from zero while the sign of the coefficient on real balances in the policy function is still wrong with data from the FB economy. With SPSW data, the only significant change concerns the estimate of the coefficient of real balances with the SZ scheme when a PA rule is used: it now becomes positive and significant even though it is still different from the 0.3 value we have inputted. The remaining features of the impact coefficients and of the variance decomposition are unaltered.

In the second experiment, we artificially give to the VAR econometrician the exact specification of the variance covariance matrix of reduced form VAR residuals, computed analytically from the decision rules of the equilibrium policy functions in Section 2.5 (omitting lagged deposits or lagged wage inflation from the specifications), and ask him/her to estimate the free parameters with the two identification schemes. When we input the true covariance matrix in the routine to estimate impact coefficients, we find no changes with the CEE scheme with both data sets while with the SZ scheme the coefficient on real balances in the PA economy is positive and significant with both data sets. Also, in this case the qualitative features of the variance decomposition are unchanged. Hence, the presence of estimation and/or small sample problems is unlikely to explain the pattern of results: even when the sample is large, both schemes fail to capture the structure of contemporaneous interdependencies and the pattern of lagged dynamics exactly in those cases when problems have previously emerged.

We have conducted a number of other robustness checks to examine whether results are due to improper statistical assumptions we have made at the estimation stage. In particular, for the LP economy, we have reestimated the VAR using money and prices in place of real balances and inflation and we have taken into account that, based on the policy rules presented in Table 1, the estimated VAR is misspecified - there is a state variable which is omitted - allowing 18 lags for each variable. In both cases, there are no significant changes in the qualitative features of the results. Hence, what is the reason for the poor performance of identified VARs?

To understand the nature of the problem is worth turning back to the equilibrium policy functions. Consider first the LP economy, the one for which misspecification is larger, and focus attention on the subset of the impact coefficients which correspond to the four variables used in the VAR. It is easy to check that with both rules the system is econometrically underidentified. That is, the model produces impact responses which are inconsistent with the inertial constraints imposed by the two identification schemes. In particular, the entries of the rows corresponding to $\hat{y}$ and $\hat{\pi}$ in the impact matrices are large while both identification scheme force many of them to be zero. Imposing false zero restrictions produces an omitted variable bias and the non-zero coefficients in other equations will capture the effect of omitted innovations. For example, the negative coefficients on inflation and output in the policy rule obtained with the CEE scheme results from the omission of policy shocks from the aggregate supply and the aggregate demand equations.

Sign and magnitude biases in the impact coefficients translate in distorted estimates of the dynamics, since the matrix of contemporaneous coefficients enters the matrices of estimated structural lagged coefficients. This may explain why both the variance decomposition and the impulse responses are far from the true ones and why, for example, the estimated contribution of monetary policy shocks to the variance of output is so different from the theoretical one.

One way to evaluate the soundness of this argument is to examine a recursive identification scheme in the spirit of Sims [26], where VAR variables are ordered as interest rate, real balances, inflation and output. Here the estimated policy rule is misspecified (a interest rate rule is assumed) but the aggregate demand and supply equations are more correctly characterized (inflation is allowed to respond to innovations in the nominal rate and in real balances and output responds to innovations in all variables). We report the impulses responses following an orthogonal interest rate shock in Figure 5 and estimates of the variance decomposition in Table 5. Clearly, the extent of the misspecification is reduced. For example, except for the sign of inflation responses in the FB economy, all other responses have now the correct sign. However, it is still true that the relative contribution of shocks to the variability of the four VAR variables is incorrect (see, for example, the contribution of supply and money demand shocks to the variability of output).

	$Var(\widehat{y}_t)$	$Var(\widehat{\Pi}_t)$	$Var(\widehat{R}_t)$	$Var(\widehat{m}_t)$
A) Limited Participation - Partial Accommodative Policy				
Innovations in $\widehat{y}_t$	[1.5, 14.7]	[0.2, 1.4]	[0.4, 8.5]	[1.3, 14.3]
Innovations in $\widehat{\Pi}_t$	[0.6, 6.2]	[0.2, 0.7]	[0.1, 3.5]	[0.5, 6.0]
Innovations in $\widehat{R}_t$	[3.2, 25.6]	[73.5, 80.2]	[79.7, 97.3]	[3.1, 25.2]
Innovations in $\widehat{m}_t$	[60.4, 88.3]	[18.6, 24.9]	[0.4, 10.3]	[61.4, 88.8]
B) Limited Participation - Feedback Policy				
Innovations in $\widehat{y}_t$	[8.6, 36.3]	[0.4, 7.4]	[0.5, 8.9]	[9.0, 37.0]
Innovations in $\widehat{\Pi}_t$	[0.4, 7.3]	[2.6, 20.6]	[3.7, 26.5]	[0.4, 7.4]
Innovations in $\widehat{R}_t$	[50.7, 79.0]	[21.8, 41.7]	[24.2, 47.1]	[49.9, 78.6]
Innovations in $\widehat{m}_t$	[5.0, 12.6]	[40.6, 64.6]	[31.4, 57.4]	[5.0, 12.6]

Table 5. Estimated Variance Decomposition at the 16-periods horizon - Sims (1992) Scheme.

Why is it that this scheme better? Inspection of the equilibrium policy functions in Section 2.5 indicates that the entries of the $\widehat{R}$ row in the impact matrix are much smaller than those, for example, of the $\widehat{\pi}$ row. Hence the imposition of (false) inertial constraints in the policy rule produces smaller distortions. Clearly, this outcome depends on the parametrization: if the coefficients on real balances in the PA rule is increased to 0.8 (from 0.3) also the entry of the $\widehat{R}$ row becomes large and imposing false restrictions in the $\widehat{R}$ equation is not better than imposing them in the $\widehat{\pi}$ equation.

Can the inherent underidentification of our LP system be solved by introducing additional frictions in the model? The answer is negative. First, extreme restrictions (such as one period in advance decisions) may produce zeros in the matrix of impact coefficients, but the zeros are not necessarily "in the right position". For example, with complete one-period-in advance price decisions, inflation will not move in response to **all** shocks and this produces a row of zeros in the matrix of contemporaneous impacts. Second, with the more conventional parametrizations adopted, for example, in the SPSW economy, the matrix of impact multipliers is still misspecified, exactly because of the existence of omitted variables. In that economy, the output and inflation blocks are exogenous with respect to the rest of the model but the presence of significant interrelationships between these two variables produce responses to policy and non-policy shocks which have, at times, the wrong sign.

As we have already suggested the SPSW economy is somewhat extreme, in the sense that two shocks have, by construction, no impact on two variables, while the LP economy is probably extreme in the opposite direction, since all shocks have strong contemporaneous impact on all variables. Given that some form of misspecification occurs in all setups, the issues we highlight here are general and should be taken seriously by VAR researchers who use DSGE theory to organize their thoughts. Standard DSGE models seldomly produce the full array of inertial restrictions used by applied researchers to identify structural shocks. To generate them models need to be rigged and some of the constraints that one must introduce may be difficult to justify theoretically (see e.g. the frictions imposed by Sims and Zha [29] or Rotemberg and Woodford [22]). Hence, the class of general equilibrium models which produce an underidentified matrix of impact coefficients is dense and the underidentification problems discussed here widespread and pervasive.

5 An Alternative Identification Scheme

One way to respond to our arguments is to trash both models as empirically irrelevant and suggest, as some commentators have done, the use of models which fit well known empirical regularities (such as those documented in Christiano, Eichenbaum and Evans [8]). We do not find this approach palatable for two reasons: first, empirical regularities do depend on the identification scheme used and the available evidence is obtained primarily using sluggish restrictions which have little theoretical underpinning in general equilibrium frameworks. Second, the two classes of models span the range of DSGE structures macroeconomists feel comfortable with and there are few operational alternatives to them.

A more productive approach is to take existing theoretical structures (of whatever microfundation one feels comfortable with) as given and ask if there are alternative identification schemes, which avoid the use of inertial constraints, and which could be used to recover the true structural shocks. Since the work Blanchard and Quah [3] several researchers have employed long run constraints to identify structural shocks. From our point of view these restrictions are more appealing than those based on contemporaneous constraints since they capture features present in many theoretical models. Some of these restrictions naturally emerge from models like those considered here, e.g. money neutrality, and others can be obtained by adding assumptions on the data generating process of the disturbances, e.g. permanent technology shocks. However, long run restrictions are seldomly used to identify monetary VARs; furthermore, because these restrictions are scarce, it is hard to fully identify all the equations of a medium sized VAR only with such restrictions, and in general, they may be only weakly identifying the quantities of interest, in the sense of Faust and Leeper [15]. Finally, as Cooley and Dwyer [10] have shown, also these schemes are not immune from misspecification problems.

While information on the timing of the reaction of variables to shocks - which are the basis for the inertial contemporaneous restrictions - and on the cumulative effect of disturbances - which are exploited with long run identification schemes - are typically scarce in general equilibrium models, monetary DSGE models have abundant sign restrictions on the dynamic response to shocks which can serve for identification. For example, regardless of the exact specification of the policy rule, our theoretical economies implies that a contractionary monetary policy shock produces an increase in interest rates and a decrease in real balances. Hence, an orthogonal shock can be termed "a monetary policy disturbance" if it generates a cross correlation function for interest rates and real balances which is negative for all leads and lags.

Canova and De Nicoló [4], Uhlig [31] and Faust [14] have used restrictions of this type to identify monetary shocks in the actual data. Such an approach works well with data generated by DSGE economies like the ones considered here. To illustrate the point we employ a variant of the two-step procedure suggested by Canova and De Nicoló. The procedure first requires to find an orthogonal decomposition of the covariance matrix of the reduced VAR shocks of the type $\Sigma_\zeta = PDP'$ where P is a matrix of eigenvectors and D a diagonal matrix of eigenvalues. Since the matrix P does not have any zeros and is not subject to the misspecifications we have mentioned in the previous section. In a second step, the theoretical information about the joint behavior of the variables of the system in response to a policy disturbance is used to examine whether any of the four orthogonal shocks produces the required cross-correlation pattern. If with the proposed decomposition there is no shock which fits the theoretical pattern, an alternative orthogonal decomposition can be constructed and the exercise repeated until one candidate is found [5].

In Figure 5 we present impulse responses to the orthogonalized monetary policy disturbance in the LP economies for each policy rule. The sample size used to estimates the parameters is 150 and the VAR is estimated as in Section 3. In all cases such a shock represents a contractionary monetary policy shock: it increases interest rates, it decreases real balances and output and makes inflation first decline and then increase. Since the response of output and inflation was not employed to identify the policy shock they can be used to independently check the outcomes of the identification approach. It is therefore remarkable that the method produces output responses with the right sign and in the case of the FB economy with roughly the right persistence.

Table 6 presents the percentage of the variance of output, inflation are explained by identified policy disturbances. For reference, we also repeat those of the theoretical economy. Although in some cases the importance of policy disturbances for output fluctuations is slightly overstated and for inflation fluctuations slightly understated, 68% bands are not that far from the correct values. For example, in the LP-PA economy, orthogonalized shocks to inflation explain in the median 24% of the variance of output, 63% of the variance of inflation, while in the theoretical economy these percentages were 14%, 50% respectively. In the SPSW economy, estimated bands are close to zero as are the true values in the economy.

---

[5] Since there is an infinite number of (non-recursive) orthogonal decompositions which can be obtained from a symmetric matrix Σ_ζ, all differing by an (orthonormal) matrix Q, it may be the case that many orthogonalizations may produce the required pattern. When this is the case, we select the decomposition which (a) produces the maximum number of identified shocks, (b) come closest to reproduce the sign restrictions on the whole vector of theoretical pairwise cross correlation functions considered. The reader interested in the technical details concerning the selection criteria may consult Canova and De Nicoló [4].

	$Var(\widehat{y}_t)$	$Var(\widehat{\Pi}_t)$	$Var(\widehat{R}_t)$	$Var(\widehat{m}_t)$
	A) Limited Participation Economy			
	Partial Accommodative Feedback			
Theoretical MP shocks	14.4	50.6	35.2	93.6
Identified MP shocks	[16.1,32.0]	[61.5,64.2]	[34.0, 53.1]	[74.1,86.2]
	B) Sticky Price, Sticky Wage Economy			
	Partial Accommodative Feedback			
Theoretical MP shocks	0.0	0.0	0.0	0.0
Identified MP shocks	[0.00,0.01]	[0.01,0.01]	[0.00,0.00]	[0.00,0.01]

Table 6. Variance Decomposition - Alternative Identification.

In conclusion, VAR identified with sign restrictions correctly identify monetary disturbances in both economies. Contrary to procedures that impose zero restrictions on the contemporaneous impact of shocks, such an approach is able to properly identify the monetary policy disturbance, mimic their dynamic effects on real variables and correctly measure their importance as source of fluctuations in the economy, regardless of how strong are the true contemporaneous feedbacks. It is important to stress that these results are obtained using the same sample size, the same variables, the same VAR specification and applying the same estimation approach employed in section 3. Hence, we confirm that small samples, the omission of a state variable, the nature of the variables used in the VAR are not crucial ingredients to explain why standard approaches fail.

6 Conclusions and Practical Suggestions

This paper examined whether structural VARs capture crucial features of theoretical monetary policy disturbances when two types of widely used DSGE models are employed as DGP and identification is achieved via conventional inertial constraints. The two types of models use different frictions to generate real effects of monetary policy. As a consequence, the timing and the intensity of the dynamics and the interrelationships between the real and the monetary side of the economy they produce are different. However, roughly speaking, they (mis)match existing data with the same degree of (in)accuracy.

The two economies (and many other variants of these) have one important feature in common: the matrix of impact coefficients has blocks of elements which are non-negligible but forced to be zero when conventional identification approaches are used. The imposition of zero restrictions in an underidentified equation causes an omitted variable problem which biases inference not only in the underidentified equation, but in the entire system. As a result, impact coefficients are mismeasured; the sign and the shape of impulse responses misspecified; and the contribution of monetary shocks to the variability of real variables distorted. It is important to stress that these outcomes obtain even when the estimated policy rule correctly recognizes the inputs of the theoretical policy rule. Clearly, problems are more acute in economies where the degree of misspecification of contemporaneous relationships is stronger.

If one takes the view that contemporaneous general equilibrium feedbacks are important, VAR analyses conducted with a different style of identification maybe preferable. For example, when identification is obtained by means of sign restrictions on the cross correlation function of certain variables in response to shocks, estimated policy shocks produce dynamics which mimic the theoretical ones and correctly characterize their importance for movements in real variables, regardless of the DGP and the policy rule employed.

Because standard statistics measuring the contribution of shocks to the dynamics of the endogenous variables may give an erroneous representation of the DGP, crucial economic questions may receive the incorrect answers. For example, we have seen that with at least one DGP the importance of monetary policy shocks for the variability of real variables is underestimated, and this could explain why many authors have questioned the importance of monetary policy disturbances as sources of output fluctuations. When sign restrictions are used, the contribution of various shocks to the variability of the four variables is correctly ranked, the dynamics in response to structural shocks have the right qualitative features and, to a large extent, the correct magnitude.

Most of the conclusions we have reached should not surprise sophisticated users of structural VARs. The idea that the omission of variables correlated with those included in a regression causes biases and distortions is as old as econometrics, as is the statement that theoretical systems which are underidentified can not be estimated using exclusion restrictions. What we have shown here is that these problems may be quantitatively important for several questions of interest to macroeconomists, and they can be solved using more theory based identification approaches.

One may be tempted to argue that the specifications we are using are unrealistic, that they are very far away from the real economy to allow VAR econometricians to learn from the data or that when stronger frictions in the form of adjustment costs, implementation lags or habit persistence are present, our arguments will loose steam. While we agree that such specifications may produce strong sluggishness in responses of certain variables to shocks, it is also the case that this type of sluggishness may not be helpful for identification. On the other hand, the claim that VAR econometricans are not allowed to learn from the data is untenable: those which are endowed with conventional constraints don't, but those who use theory to derive identifying restrictions do learn! We have shown that a method which uses a minimal amount of theory to guide empirical research, works reasonably well both when there are strong feedbacks across all reduced form equations. The reason why traditional VAR econometricians do not learn about the features of the underlying economy is not because the DGPs are strange or unrealistic but because the tools they use to analyze the data are inappropriate.

Whenever there are doubts about the features of the DGP and the extent of sluggishness of variables in reaction to disturbances, a case which we consider the norm in practice, one should be very careful in using inertial constraints and should instead prefer identification schemes which exploit robust and generic theory-based restrictions. The suggestion of moving away from VAR identified using contemporaneous inertial restrictions is present in a latent form in e.g. Sims [27] and recent contributions of Canova and De Nicoló [4], Faust [14] and Uhlig [31] makes the task feasible.

Limited Participation Economy

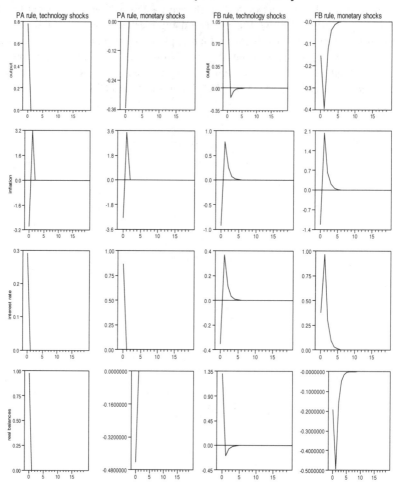

Fig. 1. Theoretical Responses.

Sticky Price Sticky Wage economy

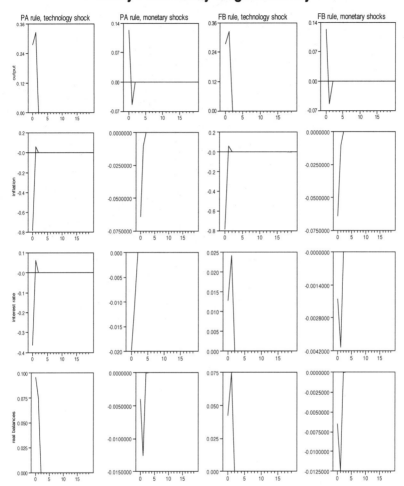

Fig. 2. Theoretical Responses.

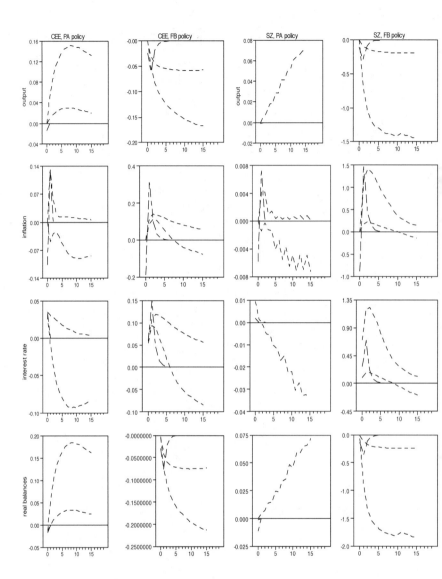

Fig. 3. Estimated and Theoretical Responses.

Sticky Price, Sticky Wage

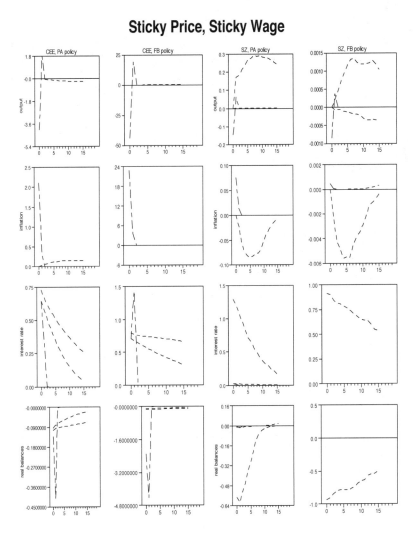

Fig. 4. Estimated and Theoretical Responses.

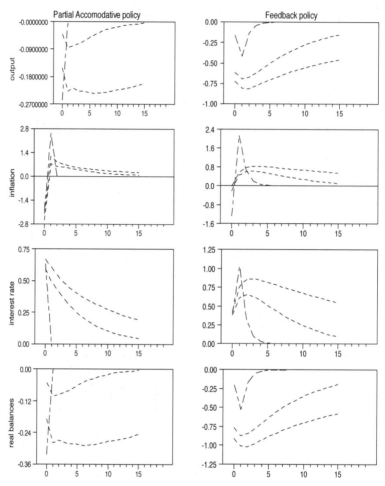

Fig. 5. Estimated and Theoretical Responses. Sims' (1992) Identification Scheme.

Limited Participation

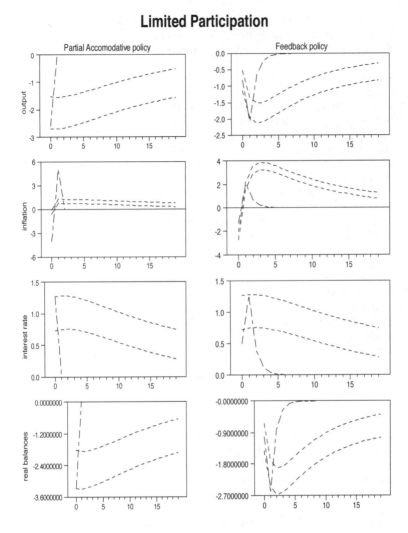

Fig. 6. Estimated and Theoretical Responses. Sign Restrictions.

References

1. Bernanke B, Blinder A (1992) The federal funds rate and the channels of monetary transmission. American Economic Review 82: 901-921
2. Bernanke B, Mihov I (1998) Measuring monetary policy. Quarterly Journal of Economics 113: 869-902
3. Blanchard O, Quah D (1989) The dynamic effects of aggregate demand and supply disturbances. American Economic Review 79: 655-673
4. Canova F, De Nicoló G (2002) Monetary disturbances matter for output for business fluctuations in the G-7. Journal Of Monetary Economics 49: 1131-1159
5. Chari VV, Kehoe P, McGrattan E (2000) Sticky price models of the business cycle: Can the contract multiplier solve the persistence problem? Econometrica 68: 1151-1179
6. Christiano L (1991) Modelling the liquidity effect of a monetary shock. Federal Reserve Bank of Minneapolis, Quarterly Review Winter: 1-24
7. Christiano L, Eichenbaum M, Evans C (1997) Sticky price and limited participation models of money: A comparison. European Economic Review 41: 1201-1249
8. Christiano L, Eichenbaum M, Evans C (1999) Monetary policy shocks: What have we learned and to what end. In Taylor J, Woodford M (eds) Handbook of macroeconomics. Elsevier Science
9. Cooley T, Leroy S (1985) Atheoretical macroeconomics: A critique. Journal of Monetary Economics 16: 283-308
10. Cooley T, Dwyer M (1995) Business cycle analysis without much theory: A look at structural VARs. Journal of Econometrics 83: 57-88
11. Cooley T, Quadrini V (1997) Monetary policy and financial decision of the firms. UPF Manuscript
12. Erceg C, Henderson D, Levin A (2000) Optimal monetary policy with staggered wage and price contracts. Journal of Monetary Economics 46: 281-212
13. Farmer R (2000) Two theories of sticky prices. Journal of Macroeconomic Dynamics 4: 1-34
14. Faust J (1998) The robustness of identified VAR conclusions about money. Carnegie Rochester Conference Series 49: 207-244
15. Faust J, Leeper E (1997) When do long run identifying restrictions give reliable results? Journal of Business and Economic Statistics 15: 345-353
16. Hansen L, Sargent T (1991) Two difficulties in interpreting vector autoregressions. In Hansen L, Sargent T (eds) Rational expectations econometrics. Boulder Press
17. Friedman M, Schwartz A (1960) A monetary history of United States. Princeton University Press
18. Gordon R, Leeper E (1994) The dynamic impact of monetary policy: An exercise in tentative identification. Journal of Political Economy 102: 1228-1247
19. Leeper E, Gordon (1992) In search for a liquidity effect. Journal of Monetary Economics : 341-370.
20. Lucas R (1990) Liquidity and interest rates. Journal of Economic Theory 50: 237-264
21. Neiss K, Pappa E (2003) Output persistence without too much stickiness. Review of Economic Dynamics forthcoming
22. Rotemberg J, Woodford M (1997) An optimization-based econometric framework for the evaluation of monetary policy. NBER Macroeconomics Annual 12: 298-361
23. Rudebusch G (1998) Do measures of monetary policy in a VAR make sense? International Economic Review 39: 907-948 (with discussion and reply)
24. Sargent T (1984) Autoregression, expectations, advice. American Economic Review 74: 408-415

25. Sims C (1980) A comparison of interwar and postwar business cycles: Monetarism reconsidered. American Economic Review 70: 250-257
26. Sims C (1992) Interpreting the macroeconomic time series facts: The effects of monetary policy. European Economic Review 36: 975-1000
27. Sims C (1998) Comment on G. Rudebusch's Do measures of monetary policy in a VAR make sense? International Economic Review 39: 933-941
28. Sims C and Zha T (1996) Does monetary policy generate recessions? Manuscript, Yale University
29. Sims C and Zha T (1999) Error bands for impulse responses. Econometrica 67: 1113-1165
30. Taylor J (1993) Discretion versus policy rules in practice. Carnegie Rochester Conference Series on Public Policy 39: 195-214
31. Uhlig H (1999) A toolkit for analyzing nonlinear dynamic stochastic models easily. In Marimon R, Scott A (eds) Computational methods for the study of dynamic economies. Oxford University Press, Oxford
32. Uhlig H (1999) What are the effects of monetary policy on output? Results from an agnostic identification procedure. Center working paper 9928, Tilburg University

Ex ante Real Returns in Forward Market Speculation in the Inter-War Period: Evidence and Prediction*

Ivan Paya[1] and David A. Peel[2]

[1] University of Alicante, Departamento Fundamentos Analisis Economico, E-03080 Alicante, Spain. ivanpaya@merlin.fae.ua.es
[2] Lancaster University Management School, Lancaster LA1 4YX, UK. d.peel@lancaster.ac.uk

Summary. The Keynes-Einzig conjecture states that discrepancies between interest parities and forward rates in the interwar period did not cause deliberate transfers through interest arbitrage on a large scale unless and until the profit on the operation was at least $1/2$ percent per anum. We further examine this conjecture by employing monthly data for six currencies against the US Dollar for the period 1921-1936. In particular, we analyse the *ex ante* real returns to uncovered forward speculation in the interwar period. We find that excess returns were predictable and that deviations from covered interest parity (CIP) were large and systematic. Evidence of nonlinear adjustment of CIP is also provided.

1 Introduction

A number of authors have investigated the properties of spot and forward exchange rates in the inter-war floating period (e.g. Hansen and Hodrick [14]; Taylor and McMahon [28]; Fraser and Taylor [13]; Baillie et al. [1]; and Byers and Peel [2]).This empirical work suggests that, as is consistent with analysis of post-war data (e.g. Fama [10]), the forward exchange rate is a biased and inefficient predictor of future exchange rates. As a consequence there are to be, at least ex-post, predictable non-zero returns to speculation. However as is now well recognised if agents are risk-averse rather than risk neutral, then speculative returns should be non-zero reflecting the required risk premium (see e.g. Hodrick and Srivastava [15]). Whilst predictable non-zero returns to speculation may be a consequence of risk premia it is also of course possible that they reflect inefficiency of expectations formation. This type of explanation is given weight by those who regard the results of the analysis of directly observed survey data on expectation formation as relevant. This work uniformly points to bias and inefficiency in expectation formation (see e.g. Frankel and Froot [11]; MacDonald and Torrance [21]; MacDonald [20]; Cavaglia et al. [3]).

*Financial support from ESRC grant under grant L/138/25/1004 is gratefully acknowledged.

Another possible explanation of nonzero speculative returns in the inter war period is the failure of covered interest arbitrage to hold. In the *Tract on Monetary Reform*, Keynes conjectured that deviations from covered interest rate parity would not be arbitraged unless a profit of at least a half of one percent on an annualised basis was available, and that larger deviations would still be moderately persistent because of the less than perfect elasticity of supply of arbitrage funds. This two-part conjecture was given further emphasis by other writers on this period, notably Einzig [6]. The following three quotations illustrate their thoughts on this issue:

1. "It may be said, therefore, that discrepancies between Interest Parities and forward rates do not cause deliberate transfers through interest arbitrage on a large scale unless and until the profit on the operation is at least 1/2 per cent per annum. This has been recognised by Mr. Keynes and by other writers, but is often overlooked by those who are not in contact with the market." Einzig [6], pp. 172-173.
2. "It must be remembered that the floating capital normally available, and ready to move from centre to centre for the purpose of taking advantage of moderate arbitrage profits between spot and forward exchange, is by no means unlimited in amount, and is not always adequate to the market's requirements..... [An] abnormal discount can only disappear when the high profit of arbitrage between spot and forward has drawn fresh capital into the arbitrage business." Keynes [17], pp. 107-8.
3. "So few persons understand even the elements of the theory of the forward exchanges that there was an occasion in 1920, even between London and New York, when a seller of spot dollars could earn at the rate of 6 per cent per annum above the London rate for short money." Keynes [17], p. 108.

The first two statements about the functioning of the exchange market during the inter-war period are known as the "Keynes-Einzig" conjecture. In a recent paper, Peel and Taylor [25] apply non-linear econometric techniques to a previously unexplored weekly data base for the period 1921-1923 for the London and New York markets. They find strong support for the conjecture of Keynes and Einzig that there were systematic deviations from covered interest arbitrage.

The purpose in this paper is to examine further the conjecture of Keynes and Einzig employing monthly data for six countries over the period 1921-1936. The monthly interest rate data for this period we have access to is taken from Einzig [6] and consists of weekly averages. Consequently the returns from covered interest arbitrage *per se* cannot be computed since, as it is now well known, it is important to measure deviations employing data recorded at the same instant in time at which a dealer could have dealt (see e.g. Sarno and Taylor [27]). Nevertheless analysis of the time series properties of this data (see Appendix 1) are consistent with the Keynes-Einzig conjecture. Naturally if there were systematic deviations from covered interest arbitrage during the inter war period the same will be true of uncovered arbitrage, *a fortiori*. Consequently, we analyse the *ex ante* real returns to uncovered forward speculation in the inter-war period where data issues are less of an issue. We examine whether agents could have made profits from forward speculation. The general framework will be to consider the case of an American investor operating in the forward market with six different currencies –British sterling, French franc, Italian lira, Swiss franc, Belgian franc and Dutch guilder– in the period 1921-1936.

The remainder of the paper is organised as follows. Section 2 sets out the determinants of real excess returns employing the inter temporal asset pricing model as developed in Frenkel and Razin [12], Engel [8], Cumby [4], and Kaminsky and Peruga [16]. The empirical tests of this hypothesis are described and the results set out in Section 3. Section 4 describes and analyses the forecast of real return from forward speculation. Section 5 concludes.

2 Excess Foreign Exchange Returns

An American investor taking a long forward position in foreign currency j at time t agrees to buy the foreign currency forward for $F_{t,k}^j$ dollars at $t+k$ for each unit of currency j purchased.[3] At maturity, $t+k$, the investor will receive S_{t+k}^j dollars for the sale of the foreign currency. The return of this forward position will be:

$$r_{t,k}^j = (S_{t+k}^j - F_{t,k}^j)/S_t^j \tag{1}$$

If financial markets are efficient, investors are risk-neutral then uncovered interest parity hypothesis states that expected profits to forward speculation are zero. That is, $E_t(r_{t,k}^j) = 0$, where E_t is the rational expectation conditional on all information available at time t. Using this framework, we can define the (nominal normalised) risk premium as the expected return to forward speculation[4], $\rho_{t,k}^j = E_t(r_{t,k}^j)$.

In this paper we extend this line of research taking into account the fact that the relationship expressed in (1) does not hold in general if investors have utility over consumption goods. As Frenkel and Razin [12] and Engel [8] point out, under equation 1, even if investors are risk-neutral (marginal utility of consumption constant), expected nominal profits to forward speculation could be nonzero but expected real profits should be zero for the optimal condition to hold as we describe below.[5] Rejection of uncovered interest parity does not provide evidence of a risk premium in the forward foreign exchange market, within this framework. Nevertheless, evidence of *ex ante* real profits would be consistent with the existence of a risk premium.

The theoretical framework we consider is based on the intertemporal asset-pricing model developed by Lucas (1982). In the international context, the first-order condition for expected utility-maximising representative investors is:

---

[3] The subscript k in our case denotes months.

[4] For a comprehensively theoretical and empirical survey of risk premium, see Lewis [18] and Engel [9].

[5] It could be the case that during the period of speculation, the domestic currency looses purchasing power, so even if the investor can make a nominal profit in the domestic currency through forward speculation, there would be no expected real profits.

$$E_t \left[\left(U'(C_{t+k})/U'(C_t) \right) \left(P_t/P_{t+k} \right) \left(S_{t+k}^j - F_{t,k}^j \right) /S_t^j \right] = 0 \qquad (2)$$

where $U'(C_t)$ is the marginal utility of real consumption, and P_t is the consumer price index in the domestic economy. Assuming that agents are risk neutral, the condition of the absence of real profit opportunities from forward market speculation can be written as:

$$E_t \left[\left((S_{t+k}^j - F_{t,k}^j)/S_t^j \right) \left(P_t/P_{t+k} \right) \right] = 0 \qquad (3)$$

defining the real return for market speculation $-e_{t,k}^j$ - in currency j as $((S_{t+k}^j - F_{t,k}^j)/S_t^j)(P_t/P_{t+k})$, we can then test for the hypothesis that expected real returns are zero. Figures 1 to 6 show $e_{t,3}^j$ –in percentage- for the six exchange rates under consideration for the 1921-1936.[6] We observe from the graphs that ex-post real profits were large and persistent in the floating periods. In Table 1 we report some summary statistics on the quarterly absolute deviations from our measure of covered interest arbitrage in the floating periods and fixed periods as well as the absolute interest rate differentials for the fixed periods. As noted above the interest rates are computed as averages of weekly data. The summary data is suggestive that there were large deviations from CIP in the floating period. The measured deviations in the fixed period were, reassuringly, of much smaller magnitude and much closer on average to the hypothesised transactions bands. The relatively high average absolute interest deviation for the Lira (0.79%) but smaller average absolute deviation of CIP, of 0.48%, is consistent with a persistent market perception of devaluation of the Lira during the fixed period. Overall the summary statistics and figures are suggestive that profitable ex-ante speculation may have been feasible in the floating periods.

3 Empirical Tests

The real return for forward market speculation, $e_{t,k}^j$, is constructed using exchange rates and forward rates expressed in dollars per unit of foreign currency and a price index in dollar terms –in particular, the retail price index RPI. We consider three month returns for six different series of exchange rates –Dollar/Sterling, Dollar/French Franc, Dollar/Lira, Dollar/Swiss Franc, Dollar/Belgian Franc, and Dollar/Dutch Guilder. The data at monthly frequency spans from 1921 to 1936. The data series are taken from Einzig [6] and described in detail in Appendix 1. During this time period the different currencies experienced several exchange rate regimes.

---

[6]In the case of the Belgian franc, observations 1926:08, 1926:09 and 1926:10 have been excluded due to their abnormal value-around 400% - which would have distorted the scale of the graph, smoothing out the shape of the rest of the graph. The shaded areas correspond to the periods considered as fixed for every currency in the sample period.

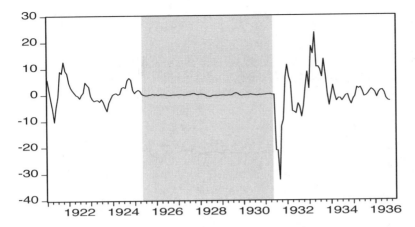

Fig. 1. Ex post real speculative returns three month rate: British Pound.

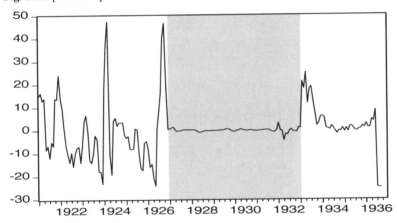

Fig. 2. Ex post real speculative returns three month rate: French Franc.

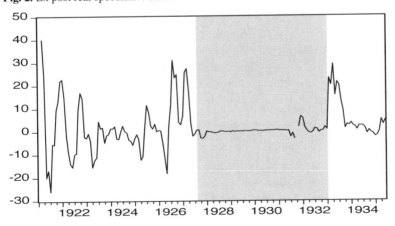

Fig. 3. Ex post real speculative returns three month rate: Italian Lira.

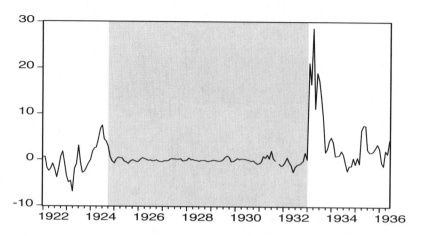

Fig. 4. Ex post real speculative returns three month rate: Swiss Franc.

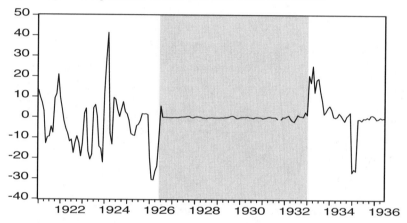

Fig. 5. Ex post real speculative returns three month rate: Belgian Franc.

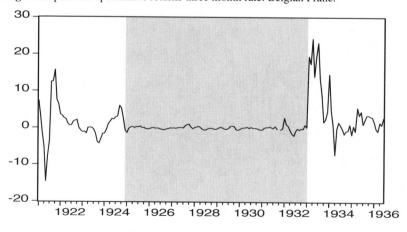

Fig. 6. Ex post real speculative returns three month rate: Dutch Guilder.

	Period	British Pound	French Franc	Italian Lira	Swiss Franc	Belgian Franc	Dutch Guilder
Average CIP dev.	Floating	0.18%	0.85%	1.06%	0.77%	0.62%	0.50%
Median CIP dev.	Floating	0.15%	0.39%	0.88%	0.35%	0.49%	0.24%
Max CIP dev.	Floating	1.58%	7.70%	5.13%	6.45%	1.97%	3.65%
Average CIP dev.	Fixed	0.12%	0.29%	0.48%	0.23%	0.19%	0.13%
Median CIP dev.	Fixed	0.12%	0.23%	0.44%	0.18%	0.13%	0.09%
Max CIP dev.	Fixed	0.41%	1.37%	1.87%	1.39%	1.65%	2.08%
Average Interest rate differential	Fixed	0.17%	0.21%	0.79%	0.20%	0.23%	0.11%
Median int. rate diff.	Fixed	0.15%	0.17%	0.89%	0.20%	0.15%	0.09%
Max int. rate diff.	Fixed	0.44%	0.52%	1.25%	0.54%	0.64%	0.41%
Without outliers in fixed regime							
Average CIP dev.	Fixed	0.12%	0.19%	0.37%	0.14%	0.12%	0.08%
Average Int. rate differential	Fixed	0.17%	0.18%	0.70%	0.17%	0.17%	0.10%

Table 1. Absolute Quarterly Deviations from CIP and Interest Rate Differentials.

In Appendix 1 we also define the periods in which each currency was under a 'floating' or a "fixed" regime.[7]

---

[7]That period was characterised by a generalised intervention by monetary authorities of the different countries in order to control the value of their currencies.
"Even during the period of inter-war stability there was, generally speaking, much more official activity in Foreign Exchanges than before 1914. Apart from other reason, this was due to the operation of the gold exchange standard in a large number of countries. Central Banks which pursued a policy of active intervention developed advanced techniques of squeezing speculators". Einzig [7], p.286.
In spite of this, we consider "fixed" regime to be the one in which the monetary authorities managed to keep the value of the currency within a very narrow band.

If equation 3 holds, $e^j_{t,k}$ should be uncorrelated with any variables in the time t information set. It must be realised that in this case we are testing the joint null hypothesis that markets are perfect; investors are risk neutral; and that they have rational expectations. Two different set of tests are considered for the estimation of the null hypothesis that $e^j_{t,k}$ cannot be explained by any information that investors have at time t.[8] The first test regresses $e^j_{t,k}$ on its own lagged values; currency j lagged forward premium, nominal interest rate changes in the US and in country j; and two "macro" variables, namely the US inflation rate and the rate of change of US industrial production; this group of variables will be named as set 1. The set of variables used in the second test, set 2, includes one lag of $e^j_{t,k}$ for every currency; lagged value of forward premia of each currency plus the 'macro' variables considered in the first set. These data are chosen since forward premia have proven useful in predicting nominal returns (e.g. Cumby [4]), whilst inflation, the rate of change of industrial production and changes in nominal interest rates are "fundamental" determinants of exchange rates and saving and investment decisions. Augmented Dickey-Fuller –ADF– and Phillips-Perron –PP– tests were performed in order to check the stationarity properties of the time series. For all the variables employed in the orthogonality regressions we were able to reject the null hypothesis of unit root[9].

Table 2 reports the results of the orthogonality tests for the three-month *ex ante* real profits from forward speculation. The estimation is carried out using Newey-West [100] covariance matrix estimator that is consistent in the presence of both heteroskedasticity and autocorrelation. This is important since monthly observations on quarterly returns ($k = 3$) used in the empirical work lead to serial correlation in the residuals and because the homoskedasticity in this case has been previously rejected in the literature (Cumby and Obstfeld [5]; Hodrick and Srivastava [15]). The F-statistic reported tests the joint hypothesis that all slope coefficient (excluding the constant) are zero.

The results of the tests for expected real profits using three-month forward rates show that the null hypothesis of the absence of un-exploited profit opportunities can be clearly rejected in every case using the second set of explanatory variables. This same result is found when we run the regression with the first set of explanatory variables, although in this case the null is not rejected for the Belgian Franc in the floating period.

This evidence suggests that from the view of an American investor, there were clear opportunities of profits in the foreign exchange market in the inter-war period that it may have been possible to exploit using the appropriate information set available at the time the investment decision had to be made. Notwithstanding, we have to bear in mind that the financial market conditions at that time were different that the ones investors face today. As was pointed out in the introduction, Keynes suggested that

---

[8] As pointed out by Engel [8], to test relationship 3 directly we would need to know the price deflator of the risk-neutral investor. The availability of data forces us to use RPI as the price index.

[9] Although the table with the result of the unit root test is not shown in this paper, they are available on request from the authors.

Currency	Set 1 Floating Period	Set 2 Floating Period
British Pound	0.048	0.000
French Franc	0.005	0.000
Italian Lira	0.001	0.000
Swiss Franc	0.005	0.018
Belgian Franc	0.128	0.008
Dutch Guilder	0.003	0.011

This table reports the p-value of the F-statistic with $q-1$ (q is the number of parameters in the regression excluding the constant) numerator degrees of freedom and $T-q$ (T number of observations) denominator degrees of freedom. The null hypothesis is that all coefficients are zero. The regression with set 1 regresses $e_{t,1}^{j}$ on a constant, four of its own lagged values-in particular $e_{t-3,k}^{j}, e_{t-4,k}^{j}, e_{t-5,k}^{j}, e_{t-6,k}^{j}$-, four lags of the currency j forward premia -$fp_{t,k}^{j} = \log(F_{t,k}^{j}/S_{t}^{j})$-, four lags of the inflation rate, four lags of industrial production growth and two lags of the interest growth of both US and country j. The regression with set 2 regresses $e_{t,1}^{j}$ on a constant and one of its own lags, and one lag of the excess return of each of the other currencies, lagged value of forward premia of each currency, four lags of inflation rate and four lags of industrial production.

Table 2. Test for the Absence of Expected Real Profits in Forward Speculation: 3-Month.

only when deviations from CIP were above $\pm 1/2$ percent on an annualised basis would arbitrage be profitable. Assuming the same band for uncovered deviations in Table 3 we report the percentage of real excess return observations, $-e_{t,k}^{j}$ that are outside that neutral band for every currency. The results overall indicate that most of the time profit opportunities were substantial for an American investor trading with these six different currencies in the FOREX market. It also appears to be the case that the British Pound, Dutch Guilder and the Belgian Franc were the most arbitraged currencies.

Currency	Floating Period
British Pound	94.38%
French Franc	100%
Italian Lira	97.40%
Swiss Franc	98.46%
Belgian Franc	89.66%
Dutch Guilder	92.86%

This table reports the percentage of observations of $e_{t,k}^{j}$ that fall outside the neutral band for every currency within the different regimes. The upper and lower limits of the band are 0.5% per annum. Therefore, in the case of the one-month rates, compounding up 0.5% per annum yields limits of 0.042%. In the case of three-month rates, the limits are 0.1247%.

Table 3. Percentage of $e_{t,k}^{j}$ Observations Outside the Neutral Band in the Case of Three Months Forward Rates.

4 Prediction

The previous section showed evidence that two different sets of economic variables were significant in explaining excess return from forward speculation during the inter-war period. The next step is to investigate whether these information sets would have been useful to forecast correctly the sign and size of those excess returns. We aim to predict whether the excess return is going to be positive and outside the neutral band - $1/2\%$ per annum-; negative and below that band; or inside the transaction cost band. According to that prediction, the speculation strategy would be to buy forward the foreign currency; to sell it forward; or do nothing, respectively.

In order to generate predictions we run sets of rolling regressions for the excess return from forward speculation for each exchange rate considered above using as regressors the economic variables used before, namely, set 1 and set 2. The sample under consideration is the respective floating periods between 1921 and 1936, and the maturity for the assets is three months[10]. The rolling forecasts -$\hat{e}_{t,k}^{j}$- begin two years after the first observations are available, so that, earlier forecasts are consistent with a certain amount of historical information. We repeat this experiment using the two different sets of explanatory variables in order to forecast the excess return.

Table 4 reports the percentage of times that the forecasts have been accurate in predicting whether the excess return was within the band, above the band and positive or below the band and negative. It is interesting to note that the forecast ability is at least fifty percent in all cases, and much higher in the case of the Swiss Franc and the Dutch Guilder when set 2 is used. Although we have evidence of predictability this does not give a measure of the profitability of the speculation, it simply implies that in all cases the excess return would have been correctly forecast more times than it would have been wrongly forecast.

Currency	Set 1	Set 2
British Pound	58%	56%
French Franc	56%	56%
Italian Lira	54%	50%
Swiss Franc	63%	69%
Belgian Franc	50%	52%
Dutch Guilder	57%	73%

Table 4. Percentage of $\hat{e}_{t+k}^{j}$ that Correctly Predicted e_{t+k}^{j} During the Floating Period in the Case of Three Months Horizon.

Consequently, we investigate the possibility of making systematic profits in the financial markets at that period of time. For that purpose, let us assume that an investor

---

[10]Due to the availability of the data, for the case of the Italian lira the sample period spans until December 1935.

had invested \$100 every period, we then add the excess returns that were correctly predicted and subtract the ones that were inaccurate, leaving out the ones when the forecast $-\hat{e}_{t,k}^{j}$- was within the band because there would not have been an investment in that case. We then divide the total return by the number of quarters in which we have speculated in the forward market of each currency, giving as a result the average quarterly real return from speculation. In the first and second rows of Table 5, we report the results when we employed set of variables 1 and 2 as regressors in the forecast equations. Except for the Belgian Franc, all currencies exhibit positive returns from forward speculation. Especially remarkable is the return in the French Franc and the Lira. Although Table 4 shows that the percentage of cases correctly predicted was not particularly high for these currencies, we could predict correctly most of the major movements of these currencies during that period, giving as a result high speculative profits. As a final check, we employ as the predicted value of $e_{t,k}^{j}$ the previous available value, $e_{t-3,k}^{j}$, since one could argue that at that time computers were not available and investors did not have the possibility of using the technique applied in the earlier tests. The results are qualitatively unchanged using this procedure as can be seen in the third row of Table 5. The final row of Table 5 reports the average of the US quarterly real return of the risk free rate computed in the periods when forward speculation was undertaken. Apart from the Belgian Franc the average real returns from speculation were consistently positive and large in relation to the average real rate of interest in the US.

	British Pound	French Franc	Italian Lira	Swiss Franc	Belgian Franc	Dutch Guilder
Speculation using set 1	0.44%	1.88%	0.84%	1.19%	-1.99%	0.61%
Speculation using set 2	0.60%	2.01%	1.68%	1.64%	-0.10%	1.02%
Speculation using $e_{t-3,k}^{j}$	0.73%	1.41%	1.45%	1.29%	-0.76%	0.77%
US risk free real rate	-0.78%	-0.57%	0.06%	-1.19%	-0.24%	-0.64%

The US real risk free rate has been calculated for the periods where forward speculation was in operation in each currency during "floating" periods.

Table 5. Average quarterly profits from forward speculation in floating periods from 1921 to 1936.

5 Conclusion

Keynes stated in the early 1920s that the functioning of the financial markets, and specifically the Forward Exchange, allowed for the possibility of excess nominal profits through absence of covered interest parity arbitrage. Absence of matched data for interest and exchange rates precludes us from examining that hypothesis directly for the six currencies. However the data based on interest rate averages is suggestive that there were significant departures from CIP which would be consistent with the evidence of Peel and Taylor [25] who employed weekly matched data for the Pound/Dollar over the period 1921-1923. In this paper we investigated the real excess returns from uncovered forward speculation in the inter-war period. We examined this hypothesis conditional on the assumption of a wide variety of information sets and found that real excess returns had a predictable structure. The large predictable rates of return in the uncovered position that we obtained would appear to be too great to explain in terms of time varying risk premia. These results seem more consistent with systematic departures from the covered condition for which we provided some empirical evidence detailed in Appendix 2.

Appendix 1. The Data

The data consists of monthly observations over the period December 1921 to June 1936, taken from Einzig [6]. The period commences in December 1921 because this is when the forward rate quotations were changed to one or three calendar months as opposed to the previous practice of quoting to the end of the current month. The forward rates are three-months (13 weeks) ahead rates and are beginning of month quotations. The corresponding future spot rates are sampled three months (13 weeks) later. These data are extracted from the weekly circular published by the Anglo-Portuguese Colonial and Overseas Bank Ltd.

The interest rate figures are based on the monthly average of market rates of discount for three months' prime bills in the various centres -New York, London, Paris, Italy, Holland, Switzerland an Belgium-[11]. The average have been compiled from the following sources: *Statistical Year Book of the League of Nations*; London and Cambridge Economic Service; Harvard Economic Service; *Statisches Jahrbuch des Deutsches Reiches*; *Bulletin Mensuel*, Banque National Suisse; *Bulletin d'information et de documentation*, Banque Nationale de Belgique; *Revue d'Economie Politique*; and Annual Report of the Netherlandsche Bank.

The sample periods considered as "fixed regime" for each currency are shown in the following table. We also report the observations that have been excluded in every case as a result of special events that would have distorted the estimation of

---

[11]"Markets rates of discount are much more suitable than Bank rates as a basis for calculating Interest Parities". Einzig [6], p. 159.

the whole model, although in any case they would affect the main conclusions we have pointed out in this paper[12]:

Currency	Fixed Regime	Excluded observations
British Pound	1925:05 1931:09	1931:07-1933:12
French Franc	1926:12 1933:01	1933:01-1933:12
Italian Lira	1927:08 1933:01	1933:01-1933:12
Swiss Franc	1924:10 1933:01	1933:01-1933:12
Belgian Franc	1926:06 1933:01	1926:08-1926:10
	1935:01 1936:12	1933:01-1933:12
Dutch Guilder	1924:12 1933:01	1933:01-1933:12

Appendix 2. Time Series Representation of Deviations from Covered Interest Parity

The Covered Interest Parity (CIP) condition can be written as:

$$f_{t,k}^{j} = i_t - i*_t^{j} \qquad (4)$$

where j = British Pound, French Franc, Italian Lira, Swiss Franc, Belgian Franc and Dutch Guilder; i_t, and $i*_t^{j}$ represent the domestic (US) and foreign –country j– interest rates on assets with maturity k, and $f_{t,k}^{j}$ is the forward premium of currency j with the same term to maturity as the assets, in our case, three months, $k = 3$[13]. If CIP holds, in the absence of transaction costs, estimation of the equation

---

[12]"When following on the crisis in Central Europe a sweeping attack on sterling developed during August 1931 the authorities hoped to cope with the situation by the time-honoured method of raising the Bank rate". Einzig [7], pp. 287-88.

"The failure of the first attempt at stabilisation (of the Belgian franc) early in 1926 was accompanied by a widening of the discount to abnormal proportions. Indeed, during the critical days of July the discount on the forward Belgian franc was even wider than the discount on the forward French franc". Einzig [6], p. 304.

Year 1932 for the British pound and year 1933 for all currencies have been excluded from the sample due to the abnormal behavior that the dollar suffered during that period as a consequence of the banking crisis: "As a result of the American banking crisis and of heavy withdrawals of foreign funds from the United States, the dollar was allowed to depreciate in 1933. Indeed the Government declared itself in favour of a deliberate depreciation of the dollar although, inconsistently enough, exchange restrictions were adopted to prevent export of capital and speculation. This marked the beginning of an international exchange depreciation race which threatened to create chaotic conditions". Einzig [6], p. 289.

[13]Even though interest rate figures are based on a monthly average and subsequently covered interest parity, CIP, cannot be computed *per se* , we believe that the analysis below will fairly reflect the adjustment process of CIP at that point in time.

$$f_{t,k}^{j} = \beta_0 + \beta_1(i_t - i*_t^{j}) + \varepsilon_t \tag{5}$$

should give estimates of β_1 that do not differ significantly from unity[14]. Table 6 displays the unit root tests for the variables involved in equation 5. The majority of interest rates and forward premia are very persistent and in fact appear to be nonstationary. Table 7 presents the results of the estimation of coefficient β_1; the Wald test of the null $\beta_1=1$; and the ADF test of the residuals, ε_t. If there is a cointegrating relationship between the forward premium and the interest rate differential, we should reject the null hypothesis of unit root in the residuals.

Interest Rate	i_{US}	i_{UK}	i_{FR}	i_{IT}	i_{SW}	i_{BE}	i_{HO}
	-4.01	-2.24	-1.21	-1.94	-1.70	-1.11	-3.03
Forward Premium		f_{UK}	f_{FR}	f_{IT}	f_{SW}	f_{BE}	f_{HO}
		-6.99	-1.60	-2.02	-3.47	-2.47	-3.20
Interest Rate Differential		i_{US}-i_{UK}	i_{US}-i_{FR}	i_{US}-i_{IT}	i_{US}-i_{SW}	i_{US}-i_{BE}	i_{US}-i_{HO}
		-1.08	-1.51	-1.50	-0.68	-1.85	-2.36

The critical value of the t-statistic at the 5% significance level reported by Perron [111] is -3.87. The corresponding DF statistic is -3.41.

Table 6. Unit Root Test of the Components of CIP for Floating Period.

Currency	β_1(t-stat)	Wald test $\beta_1 = 1$ (P-value)	ADF resids	ADF resids ($\beta_1 = 1$)
British Pound	0.88 (10.43)	0.15	-2.11**	-2.11**
French Franc	1.38 (4.81)	0.18	-2.85**	-2.64**
Italian Lira	2.90 (8.60)	0.00	-3.17**	-2.54**
Swiss Franc	1.61 (7.48)	0.00	-2.39**	-2.23**
Belgian Franc	2.21 (7.95)	0.00	-2.65**	-1.99**
Dutch Guilder	2.28 (17.42)	0.00	-3.36**	-2.24**

*(**) denotes rejection of the null hypothesis of unit root at 5%(1%) significance level according to MacKinnon [24] critical values.

Table 7. Estimation of CIP for Floating Period.

This appears to be the case for all the different exchange rates under consideration. Similar results are found when we constrain the coefficient of β_1 to be equal to 1. Given this result we can then write deviations from CIP at time t as

---

[14]This is a necessary condition for covered interest arbitrage to hold.

$$y_t^j = i_t^j - i*_t - f_{t,k}^j \tag{6}$$

Once deviations from CIP are computed, we determine the properties of y_t^j and whether it exhibits nonlinear adjustment during the period of time between 1921 and 1936 when the currencies were not at a fixed rate. The presence of transaction costs implies a non-linear process in the y_t term of identity 6. When deviations from CIP are bigger than transactions costs capital should move in order to eliminate such deviations. However, as pointed out by Keynes, the capital needed to take advantage of the arbitrage opportunity was not adequate and would depend on the size of deviations. In that case, the nonlinear adjustment process can be characterised in terms of an exponential smooth transition autoregressive (ESTAR) model[15]. Accordingly, the following step is to test for linearity of y_t^j.

Linearity Test

If the delay parameter, d, in the ESTAR model is fixed, the linearity test consists of estimating by OLS the regression,

$$y_t = \beta_{00} + \Sigma(\beta_{0j}y_{t-j} + \beta_{1j}y_{t-j}y_{t-d} + \beta_{2j}y_{t-j}y_{t-d}^2) + u_t \tag{7}$$

and testing the null hypothesis

$$H_{0L} : \beta_{1j} = \beta_{2j} = 0 \qquad j = 1, \ldots, p \tag{8}$$

We determine the delay parameter, d, as one; and p equals one as well. In order to assist in the specification of the ESTAR model, we carry out another F-test based on (7) by testing

$$H_{0k} : \beta_{1j} = 0 \qquad j = 1, \ldots, p \tag{9}$$

Also provided that (9) is valid, a more powerful test of linearity is obtained by testing the null hypothesis

$$H*_{0L} : \beta_{2j} = 0/\beta_{1j} = 0 \qquad j = 1, \ldots, p \tag{10}$$

The test statistics associated with 8-10 are denoted by F_L, F_k, $F*_L$, respectively. These tests are used for the model selection procedure. The test statistics are computed for the floating period of each exchange rate. The nonlinearity tests are reported in Table 8. They show clear evidence of ESTAR nonlinearity.

Given the evidence for non linearity we found that the following "simple" ESTAR model provided parsimonious fit to the data. In particular, we estimate the following equation:

$$y_t = \alpha + \beta exp\{-\gamma(y_{t-1} - c*)^2\}y_{t-1} \tag{11}$$

---

[15]For an empirical study of transaction costs and non-linear adjustment in real exchange rates using ESTAR modelling, see Michael et al. [23]. For a description of the linearity test against LSTAR or ESTAR model, see Teräsvirta [29].

Test Statistics	$/British Pound	$/French Franc	$/Italian Lira
F_L	0.081	0.000	0.011
F_K	0.596	0.164	0.377
F_L^*	0.028	0.000	0.001

	$/Swiss Franc	$/Belgian Franc	$/Dutch Guilder
F_L	0.081	0.045	0.000
F_K	0.596	0.060	0.812
F_L^*	0.028	0.105	0.000

Table 8. Linearity Tests for Floating Periods During Inter-War: P-values of the Linearity Tests 8-10.

where y_t is the deviations from CIP during the inter-war period. In every sample we have carried the estimations under two different cases. In the first case, we restrict the parameter $c*$ to be equal to $1/2\%$ per annum as suggested by Keynes. The second case, we do not restrict the value of the $c*$ coefficient. Table 9 reports the estimates of equation 11 with corresponding p-values in brackets. There are also some residual diagnostic test reported. In particular, the Jarque and Bera (JB) test of normality; $Q(k)$ is the Ljung-Box statistic for residual autocorrelation up to order k; and $A(k)$ is the test for ARCH up to order k. An asterisk * (**) (***) denotes rejection of the null hypothesis at 10% (5%) (1%) significance level. We also present the graphs (Figures 7-12) in which the transition function $(1 - \exp\{-\gamma(y_{t-1} - c*)^2\})$ is plotted against y_{t-d} for every currency and sample periods considered above. The estimates appear to be broadly consistent with the conjecture of Keynes and Einzig.

	$/British Pound		$/French Franc		$/Italian Lira	
	Restricted	Unrestricted	Restricted	Unrestricted	Restricted	Unrestricted
α	-0.02 (0.09)	0	0.03 (0.49)	0	-0.12 (0.06)	-0.27 (0.77)
β	0.78 (0.00)	0.84 (0.00)	1.00 (0.00)	0.73 (0.00)	0.90 (0.00)	0.90 (0.00)
γ	1.01 (0.09)	2.80 (0.03)	0.36 (0.01)	0.022 (0.10)	0.091 (0.02)	0.11 (0.06)
c^*	—	0.18 (0.08)	—	0.29 (0.88)	—	0.60 (0.22)
R^2	0.50	0.50	0.85	0.86	0.74	0.75
Standard error	0.11	0.12	0.42	0.40	0.46	0.45
Durbin–Watson	2.24	2.26	2.00	1.77	2.13	2.15
JB	2.75	3.00	66.6***	25.9***	64.12***	71.91***
Q(4)	3.89	3.12	2.43	0.15	4.84	2.38
Q(12)	5.65	5.19	6.86	7.71	6.51	5.31
A(1)	0.97	1.17	0.005	0.14	0.78	0.27
A(4)	5.29	3.41	0.87	3.09	2.41	2.00

	$/Swiss Franc		$/Belgian Franc		$/Dutch Guilder	
	Restricted	Unrestricted	Restricted	Unrestricted	Restricted	Unrestricted
α	-0.0013 (0.75)	-0.01 (0.86)	-0.24 (0.00)	-0.05 (0.61)	0	0
β	0.83 (0.00)	0.84 (0.00)	0.48 (0.02)	0.81 (0.00)	1.00 (0.00)	1.00 (0.00)
γ	0.89 (0.28)	0.98 (0.30)	0.18 (0.49)	1.09 (0.45)	0.11 (0.00)	0.28 (0.00)
c^*	—	0.07 (0.80)	—	0.75 (0.00)	—	0.99 (0.00)
R^2	0.40	0.40	0.50	0.54	0.86	0.87
Standard error	0.25	0.26	0.44	0.43	0.30	0.29
Durbin–Watson	1.66	1.64	2.02	2.23	2.25	2.23
JB	13.33***	13.06***	412***	300***	53.7***	34.48***
Q(4)	1.17	1.23	6.37	7.37	3.06	5.21
Q(12)	6.88	6.81	7.17	8.05	5.17	8.23
A(1)	0.16	0.08	0.78	1.79	7.09***	3.90*
A(4)	2.77	2.67	0.79	2.42	9.31*	11.55**

Table 9. ESTAR Model: Equation. Floating periods during inter-war.

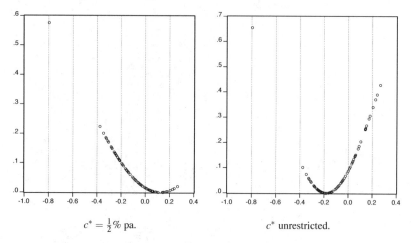

$c^* = \frac{1}{2}\%$ pa. c^* unrestricted.

Fig. 7. $/British Pound.

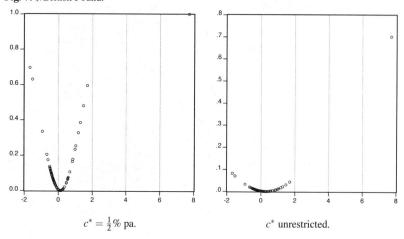

$c^* = \frac{1}{2}\%$ pa. c^* unrestricted.

Fig. 8. $/French Franc.

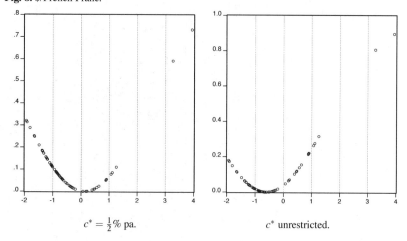

$c^* = \frac{1}{2}\%$ pa. c^* unrestricted.

Fig. 9. $/Italian Lira.

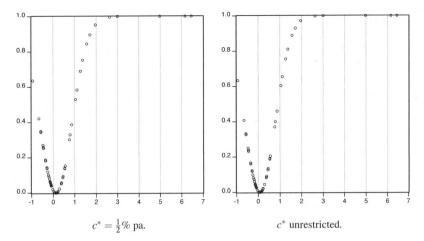

$c^* = \frac{1}{2}\%$ pa. c^* unrestricted.

Fig. 10. $/Swiss Franc.

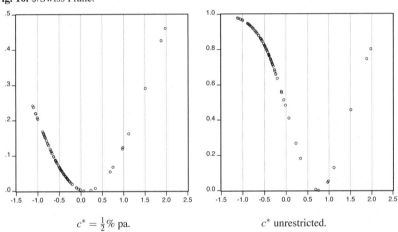

$c^* = \frac{1}{2}\%$ pa. c^* unrestricted.

Fig. 11. $/Belgian Franc.

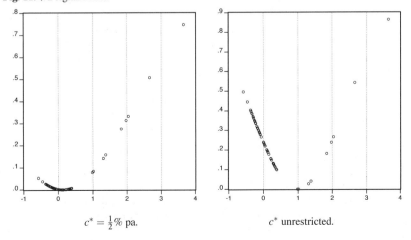

$c^* = \frac{1}{2}\%$ pa. c^* unrestricted.

Fig. 12. $/Dutch Guilder.

References

1. Baillie RT, Bollerslev T, Redfearn MR (1993) Bear squeezes, volatility spillovers and speculative attacks in the 1920s foreign exchange. Journal of International Money and Finance 12: 511-521
2. Byers JD, Peel DA (1991) Some evidence on the efficiency of the sterling-dollar and sterling-franc forward exchange rates in the interwar period. Economics Letters 35: 317-322
3. Cavaglia S, Verschoor WF, Wolff CP (1993) Further evidence on exchange rate expectations. Journal of International Money and Finance 12: 78-98
4. Cumby RE (1988) Is it risk? Explaining deviations from Uncovered Interest Parity. Journal of Monetary Economics 22: 279-299
5. Cumby RE, Obstfeld M (1984) International interest rate and price level linkages under floating exchange rates: A review of recent evidence. In Bilson JFO, Marston R (eds), Exchange rate theory and practice. University of Chicago Press for the National Bureau of Economic Research, Chicago
6. Einzig P (1937) The theory of forward exchange. London: Macmillan.
7. Einzig P (1962) The history of foreign exchange. London, Macmillan
8. Engel CM (1984) Testing for the absence of expected real profits from forward market speculation. Journal of International Economics 17: 299-308
9. Engel CM (1996) The forward discount anomaly and the risk premium: A survey of recent evidence. Journal of Empirical Finance 3: 123-192
10. Fama E (1984) Forward and spot exchange rates. Journal of Monetary Economics 14: 319-338
11. Frankel JA, Froot K (1987) Using survey data to test some standard propositions regarding exchange rate expectations. American Economic Review 77: 133-153
12. Frenkel J, Razin A (1980) Stochastic prices and test of efficiency of foreign exchange markets. Economic Letters 6: 165-170
13. Fraser P, Taylor MP (1990) Modelling risk in the interwar foreign exchange market. Scottish Journal of Political Economy 37: 241-258.
14. Hansen LP, Hodrick RJ (1980) Forward exchange rates as optimal predictors of future spot rates: An econometric analysis. Journal of Political Economy 88: 829-853
15. Hodrick RJ, Srivastava S (1984) An investigation of risk and return in forward foreign exchange. Journal of International Money and Finance 3: 5-29
16. Kaminsky G, Peruga R (1990) Can a time-varying risk-premium explain excess returns in the forward market for foreign exchange? Journal of International Economics 28: 47-70
17. Keynes JM (1923) A Tract on monetary reform. London: Macmillan
18. Lewis KK (1995) Puzzles in international financial markets. In Grossman GM, Rogoff K (eds) Handbook of International Economics, Vol. 3, North-Holland.
19. Lucas RE (1982) Interest rates and currency prices in a two-country world. Journal of Monetary Economics 10: 335-360
20. MacDonald R (1990) Are foreign exchange market forecasters "rational"? Some survey-based test. The Manchester School 58: 229-241
21. MacDonald R, Torrance TS (1989) Some survey-based tests of uncovered interest parity. In MacDonald R, Taylor MP (eds) Exchange rates and open economy macroeconomics, Blackwell, Oxford
22. MacKinnon JG (1991) Critical values for cointegration tests. In Engle R, Granger CWJ (eds) Long-run Economic Relationships, Oxford University Press
23. Michael P, Nobay AR, Peel DA (1997) Transaction costs and non-linear adjustment in real exchange rates: An empirical investigation. Journal of Political Economy 105: 862-879

24. Newey W, West K (1987) A simple positive semi-definite, heteroskedasticity and auto-correlation consistent covariance matrix. Econometrica 55: 703-708

25. Peel DA, Taylor MP (2002) Covered interest rate arbitrage in the inter-war period and the Keynes-Einzig conjecture. Journal of Money Credit and Banking ?: 51-85

26. Perron P (1989) The great crash, the oil price shock, and the unit root hypothesis. Econometrica 57: 1361-1401

27. Sarno L, Taylor MP (2002) The Economics of exchange rates. Cambridge University Press

28. Taylor MP, McMahon PC (1988) Long-run purchasing power parity in the 1920s. European Economic Review 32: 179-197

29. Teräsvirta T (1994) Specification, estimation, and evaluation of smooth transition autoregressive models. Journal American Statistics Association 89: 208-218

Testing for Fractional Cointegration: The Relationship between Government Popularity and Economic Performance in the UK*

James Davidson

University of Exeter, School of Business and Economics, Streatham Court, Rennes Drive, Exeter EX4 4PU, UK. james.davidson@exeter.ac.uk

Summary. This paper investigates the relationship between the quarterly opinion poll lead of UK governments over the period 1955-1996, and a set of economic indicators. The hypothesis of a causal link between these variables is often debated, but there is a difficulty in testing the link by conventional econometric methods. These require either stationarity or the I(1) property, but there is strong evidence from a number of different studies that opinion poll series are fractionally integrated, being nonstationary but also mean-reverting.

This paper tests the hypothesis of fractional cointegration using bootstrap methods. It first discusses the problem of defining a cointegrating relationship between series that may not have the same order of integration, and suggests a generalized cointegration model that might account for this case. Bootstrap tests of the regular and generalized (non-)cointegration hypotheses are performed, as well as tests of the null hypothesis that cointegration of either type exists. Both the regular and double bootstrap statistics are calculated, the latter method providing a correction to the finite sample size distortion to the estimation of unknown parameters.

The tests reveal little or no evidence of a link between the political and economic cycles, a conclusion that reinforces the results of earlier work suggesting that the political cycle is generated by the internal dynamics of the opinion formation process. The findings are reinforced by a case-specific Monte Carlo study, showing that the methods have ample power to reveal cointegrating relations, if they exist.

1 Introduction

A substantial literature has accumulated over recent decades, seeking theoretical and econometric links between economic conditions and the popularity of governments. Leading contributions include Goodhart and Bhansali [17], Nordhaus [28], Frey and Schneider [16], Pissarides [29], Minford and Peel [26], Holden and Peel [20], Rogoff and Sibert [30]. The evidence from econometric studies, treating this as a conventional time series modelling problem, has been at best equivocal. For example, Pissarides [29] uses the time series techniques suggested by Davidson et. al. [12] and finds some nominally significant correlation between government popularity

---

*Research supported by the ESRC under award L138251025.

and economic indicators (growth, inflation, unemployment, the exchange rate and tax rate). However, his equation does not have much predictive power. While plenty of anecdotal evidence can be cited in support of either view, whether government popularity follows the economic cycle remains an unresolved question.

More recent research has found that for a wide range of countries and democratic political systems, party support is a fractionally integrated process. See for example Byers, Davidson and Peel [6, 7, 8], Box-Steffensmeier and Smith [4] and Dolado, Gonzalo and Mayoral [13]. Byers et al. [6], henceforth referred to as BDP, show that for the UK, the monthly Gallup series for Conservative and Labour support can be well modelled as ARFIMA(0,d,0) with d around 0.75. In other words, the series is covariance nonstationary, but also not a random walk, tending to return from excursions away from the median[2]. In their paper, BDP propose a model to account for these findings based on the aggregation of heterogeneous poll responses, appealing to a well-known result of Granger [18]. The model accounts for the magnitude and duration of swings in aggregate opinion as due to the particular mix of committed and floating voters in the population. The innovations in the process are assumed to be news, of both the economic and non-economic variety. The BDP model therefore accounts for the cyclical behaviour of opinion by the internal dynamics of the aggregate opinion-formation process.

This explanation contradicts the view that swings in support follow economic indicators over the cycle. BDP explain this finding by noting that opinion polls aggregate the heterogeneous opinions of voters who perceive economic circumstances differently, so that issues on whose significance voters are divided, even if important, may have little effect on support. Thus, borrowers and depositors take a different view of the interest and inflation rates. Likewise, the unemployment rate can mean different things to different people, witness the so-called 'North-South divide' and the contrasting fortunes of manufacturing and service industries, in the UK.

However, a formal test of the relationship remains wanting. Two statistical approaches to testing for time series relationships are in common use, the correlation approach and the cointegration approach. Neither of these is valid when the data in question are fractionally integrated. Since the party support series are nonstationary, ordinary tests of significance are subject to the well-known 'spurious correlation' critique. On the other hand, cointegration analysis relies on tabulations of the distribution of certain functionals of Brownian motion, and accordingly are based on the assumption that the time series have variances diverging at the rate n. In the case of a fractionally integrated or I(d) process ($d > 1/2$) this rate is n^{2d-1}, and the limit processes are not Brownian motion but fractional Brownian motion. The Brownian

---

[2]Since support measures are confined to the unit interval, the random walk is not, of course, a feasible model of the raw data. BDP model the series for $\log[\bar{X}_t/(1 - \bar{X}_t)]$ where $100\bar{X}_t$ is the sample average support. Since this process is defined on $(-\infty, +\infty)$ a random walk is a logically feasible representation. This would be manifested in the raw data by a tendency for support to cluster near either 100% or 0%, a phenomenon not commonly observed in democratic countries. In practice, note that the range of variation of the $\bar{X}_t$ series is such that the logistic transformation is nearly linear, and the same model explains either series equally well.

functionals that define the limit distributions depend on d, and the usual cointegration tests are inappropriate.

The present paper reports some tests of the cointegration hypothesis using the bootstrap, to overcome the problems with conventional tests. The theory of these tests is discussed at length in Davidson [9, 10]. Section 2 of the paper presents the data set to be analyzed. Section 3 considers some issues in the modelling of relationships in such data. Section 4 describes and reports bootstrap tests where the null hypothesis is noncointegration. Several variants of the null hypotheses are considered, including one in which the distribution of the bootstrap data under the null is based on the BDP model, allowing some data features to be captured that cannot be represented by a simple linear data generation process. On the other hand, Section 5 reports bootstrap tests where the null hypothesis is of cointegration. The consensus of the findings is that there is no discernible evidence against noncointegration, and only the most equivocal evidence in favour of cointegration. Section 6 gives the results of some Monte Carlo experiments designed to evaluate the power of these tests. Finally, Section 7 briefly reports a short-run correlation analysis, and Section 8 summarises the findings, and concludes.

2 The Data Set

The data for the present study are quarterly observations for the period 1955:2 to 1996:4. The party support data are taken from the monthly Gallup poll series. The variable 'Lead' is measured as the end-of-quarter difference between Conservative and Labour percentage support in periods of Conservative government, and the difference between Labour and Conservative in periods of Labour government. This series is plotted in the first panel of Figure 1.

A set of dummy variables is used to represent the so-called "election cycle" discussed in BDP. It has been observed that the popularity of governments, other things equal, depends on the proximity of the most recent and forthcoming elections, largely because of a tendency for voters to register a "protest vote" in mid-term. In BDP, this effect is modelled as a quadratic function of the current government's elapsed term, and the effects were found to differ depending on whether Conservative or Labour is the party in power. To capture these effects, dummies are constructed as follows: (i) a zero-one "Labour in power" dummy ("LabGovt"); (ii) the number of quarters elapsed since the last election ("Elapsed"); (iii) the square of (ii); (iv) the product of (i) and (ii); (v) the product of (i) and (iii). The second panel of Figure 1 shows the Lead series as residuals from the election cycle, fitted to the five dummies by least squares.

Six economic indicators, plotted in Figure 2, have been chosen as possible explanations of Lead. A valid test of the cointegration hypothesis requires the data be purged of deterministic trends, and a linear trend dummy is therefore included in the test equation. As an aid to intuition the 'detrended' variables (residuals from least squares regressions on constant and trend) are shown in Figure 3. These series all appear covariance nonstationary (see Table 2). After partialing out the various dummies, we posit the 'political business cycle' hypothesis as, in effect, the existence of a cointegrating relationship between the second series in Figure 1, and those in Figure 3. The null hypothesis of non-cointegration, by contrast, would imply either that some unmeasured 'non-economic' factors drive the variations in Lead, or (more plausibly) some variant of the BDP hypothesis.[3]

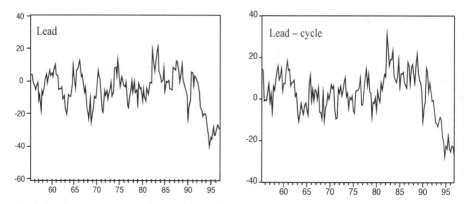

Fig. 1. Lead, before and after Removing the Election Cycle.

The results of running the full regression are shown in Table 1, and graphically in Figure 4.[4] The signs of several coefficients, such as unemployment and real earnings, are the opposite of what would be naively expected, although if the relationship turned out to be statistically significant these findings might need to be accounted for, rather than simply dismissed as spurious. Note that the residual Phillips-Perron statistic in Table 1, assuming six regressors and trend, 'rejects' nominally at the 5% level according to MacKinnon's [24] Tables. However the presence of the extra dummy variables are only the least of the complicating factors, in the correct interpretation this result.

---

[3]The possibility of a short term relationship in the differences also exists, and this is tested in Section 7.

[4]The usual standard errors and t statistics are reproduced for descriptive purposes, but of course their distribution is non-standard even asymptotically, so they cannot be used for purposes of inference.

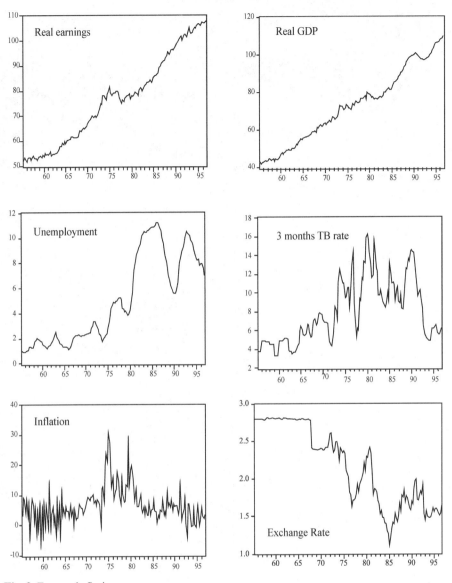

Fig. 2. Economic Series.

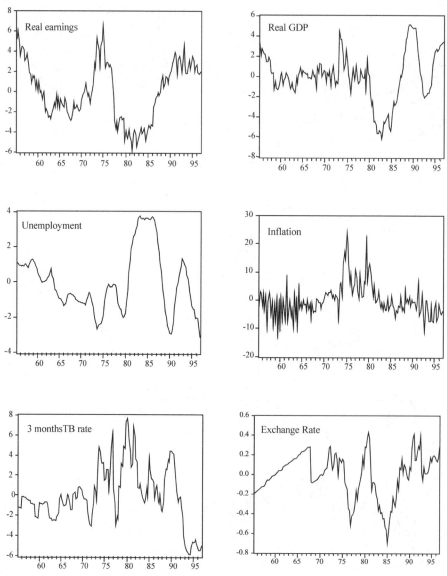

Fig. 3. Series as Deviations from Trend.

	Coefficient	Std. Error	t-Statistic
Real Earnings	−0.509	0.335	−1.55
Real GDP	1.14	0.503	2.27
Unemployment	4.07	0.830	4.90
TB Rate	1.61	0.274	5.88
Inflation	−0.050	0.134	−0.375
Exch. Rate($/£)	1.53	4.537	0.337
LabGovt	12.31	3.53	3.48
Elapsed	−2.66	0.500	−5.32
Elapsed^2	0.141	0.027	5.06
LabGovt×Elapsed	−2.23	1.02	−2.17
LabGovt×Elapsed^2	0.086	0.060	1.41
Trend	−0.626	0.196	−3.19
Constant	−26.37	26.17	−1.00

Dependent Variable: Lead   Sample: 1955:2 1996:4

R-squared	0.563	Adjusted R-squared	0.529
Durbin-Watson	0.789	F-statistic (all)	16.58
Residual PP	−6.381	F-statistic (econs)	19.12

Table 1. Regression of Lead on Economic Indicators

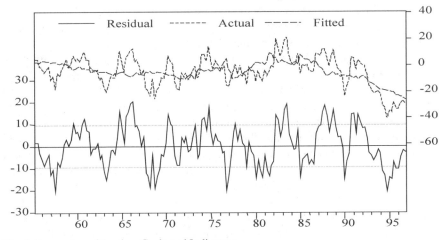

Fig. 4. Regression of Lead on Cycle and Indicators.

Consider next the results of the univariate time series modelling exercises reported in Table 2. This table shows ARFIMA(p,d,q) models for each series in the data set,[5] chosen to optimise the Schwarz [32] selection criterion, subject to the side condition that residual autocorrelation is insignificant by the Box-Pierce Q test for 12

[5]The ARFIMA estimates were computed by maximizing the Whittle likelihood, using the Ox package currently available as Time Series Modelling 4.0; see Davidson [11], Doornik [14]. The data are differenced to satisfy the stationarity/invertibility condition $|d| < 0.5$, and

	Lead	RE	GDP	Unempl	TBR	Infl.	ExchR
d	0.765	0.920	0.978	1.169	0.626	0.664	0.991
	(0.066)	(0.079)	(0.060)	(0.150)	(0.107)	(0.092)	(0.108)
p	0	0	0	2	2	1	0
q	0	0	0	0	1	0	0
ARMA Coefficients:	-	-	-	0.518	0.397	0.473	-
				(0.16)	(0.105)	(0.135)	
	-	-	-	0.208	0.466	-	-
				(0.107)	(0.094)		
	-	-	-	-	0.814	-	-
					(0.038)		
Constant	0.084	46.59	38.98	-0.22	4.924	5.942	2.23
Trend	-0.061	0.353	0.401	0.062	0.037	0.007	-0.008
$Q(12)$ - levels	12.09	12.92	17.58	17.76	12.32	19.90	11.24
$Q(12)$ - squares	11.40	12.71	9.85	19.80	9.20	17.61	11.87

Table 2. Best ARFIMA(p,d,q) models of the data set (std. errors in parentheses)

lags. The second Box-Pierce statistic provides evidence of possible ARCH-type non-linear dependence (McLeod and Li [25]), which of course the ARFIMA framework cannot account for. However, these models are generally adequate and parsimonious.

The Lead variable, in particular, is well represented by the ARFIMA$(0,d,0)$ model, with d significantly exceeding 0.5, indicating the series to be nonstationary, but also significantly less than unity. This result may be compared with those obtained by BDP, who estimated the d coefficients for Conservative and Labour support separately, in monthly and quarterly data, and obtained values close to 0.7 in both cases.[6] Those authors also found that the estimated value was not sensitive to the removal of the election cycle. The difference of two I(d) processes is also I(d) in general, although we note that this series has the additional feature of being subject to occasional switches of sign. This occurs at election dates where government and opposition change places so that, in particular, Lead is negative at the relevant dates. Such switches occurred four times during the present sample period, in 1964.4, 1970.2, 1974.1 and 1979.2. Inspection of the chart in Figure 1 does not reveal very obvious jumps at these dates, but the fact that the generation process has these non-linear features should not be overlooked. We return to this question in Section 4.2.

3 Models of Fractional Cointegration

The findings in Table 2 pose some unexpected problems for the formulation and valid testing of the putative relationship. While unemployment, the interest and exchange

---

then 1 is added to the estimate of d so obtained. For the exchange rate model, the sample period excludes the fixed parity period 1955.2 to 1971.3.

[6]Fractional processes are asymptotically self-similar, so that the value of d does not depend on the frequency of the observations. The similar values obtained in monthly and quarterly support data accord with this interpretation.

rates and earnings all have estimated d insignificantly different from unity, this is not true of either Lead, or the interest and inflation rates. These variables are significantly mean-reverting, although nonstationary ($1/2 < d < 1$). Is it possible that variables with different orders of integration can be cointegrated?

To answer this question, consider the fractional vector ECM model given in Davidson (2002). Let this take the form

$$\left[\mathbf{B}(L) + \alpha\beta'(\mathbf{K}(L)^{-1} - I)\right]\Delta(L)(\mathbf{x}_t + \Phi\mathbf{D}_t) = \varepsilon_t \tag{1}$$

where

$$\Delta(L) = \mathrm{diag}\{(1-L)^{d_1}, \ldots, (1-L)^{d_N}\} \tag{2}$$

$$\mathbf{K}(L) = \mathrm{diag}\{(1-L)^{b_1}, \ldots, (1-L)^{b_N}\} \tag{3}$$

where $d_1, \ldots, d_N$ are any nonnegative reals (assume $d_1 \geq \cdots \geq d_N$ without loss of generality), $0 \leq b_i \leq d_i$, $\mathbf{B}(L)$ is a $N \times N$ polynomial matrix whose characteristic roots are strictly outside the unit circle. In the usual way, α and β are $N \times r$ matrices with rank r. The model is modified here to include dummy variables $\mathbf{D}_t$ ($S \times 1$), which in the present set-up include the time trend and the election cycle, with Φ a constant $N \times S$ coefficient matrix. This system generates N series integrated to orders $d_1, \ldots, d_N$, such that

$$\Delta(L)(\mathbf{x}_t + \Phi\mathbf{D}_t) = \mathbf{w}_t \sim I(0) \tag{4}$$

(defining $\mathbf{w}_t$). If $\alpha = \beta = \mathbf{0}$ these are noncointegrated, but if $r > 0$ it is required, to balance the equation, that

$$\beta'\mathbf{K}(L)^{-1}\mathbf{w}_t \sim I(0). \tag{5}$$

If $b_i > 0$ for one or more i, this implies cointegration. This set-up encompasses a wide range of possible models. If $b_i = b$ and $d_i = d$ for all i it corresponds to the system proposed in Granger [19], and if $b = d = 1$ then it reduces to the Johansen [21, 22] style VECM. More generally, we can pick out a number of other cases yielding a possible modelling framework.

The first of these is where $d_i - b_i = a \geq 0$ for each i, which implies that

$$\beta'(\mathbf{x}_t + \Phi\mathbf{D}_t) \sim I(a). \tag{6}$$

If $a > 0$, this is the case often called fractional cointegration, in which the cointegrating residual is long memory and possibly even nonstationary, but has a lower order of integration than its constituent variables. It is clear that with $b_i > 0$, this model cannot have property (6) except subject to additional restrictions. As discussed in Davidson [9], either $d_1 = d_2$ or the top row of β must be equal to $\mathbf{0}$, so that x_{1t} is not cointegrated with the other variables. It is possible that this set-up could describe the present case, since the data set contains three (plausibly) I(1) series. In other words, the trends in GDP, unemployment and real earnings cannot individually drive the trend in Lead, but a combination of these could, at least in principle, do so. We do not yet consider whether such a model would be behaviourally plausible, merely note the possibility.

A second case where model (1) could generate cointegrated series is $b_i = b \leq \min_{1 \leq i \leq N} d_i$ for all i, which, to ensure the equation balances, implies that

$$[(1-L)^{-b} - 1]\beta'\mathbf{w}_t \sim I(0). \tag{7}$$

This model has the peculiarity that the cointegrated series are not the elements of $\mathbf{x}_t$ themselves, but the fractional differences of orders $d_i - b$.[7] This case will be referred to as *generalised cointegration*, to make the distinction with simple cointegration in which linear combinations of the measured variables have a lower order of integration, as in (6). This set-up imposes no restrictions on β to ensure cointegration. It allows cointegration to be defined between arbitrary sets of $I(d)$ variables, and so resolves the main limitation of the fractional model as an econometric modelling device.

Again, whether this is economically and behaviourally plausible is a matter for consideration. There is nothing unusual in having the simple difference of a variable appear in an economic relationship. For example, the (log-) price level contains (at least) the same information as the level of inflation, but the latter variable is customarily assumed relevant to agents' decisions. While economic models do not normally assign the same role to fractional differences, this is simply because such a modelling strategy has never been entertained. There seems to be no inherent reason why they should not do so. Just as the price level is relevant to some decisions and its rate of change to others, in a representative-agent framework, so may the fractional difference of a trending variable contain the relevant information for a decision involving a particular planning horizon. In turn, this could be reflected in the degree of persistence of the target variable. The question of primary interest must be whether such relationships are discoverable in the data.

The result of running the regression on the present data after semi-differencing is shown in Table 3. The variables marked with a * have been semi-differenced[8] to have a d of 0.765, based on the models in Table 2.[9] The filtered (and also detrended) series are shown, with the originals for comparison, in Figure 5.

---

[7]Note that the orders of integration of the cointegrated series are indeterminate unless we impose that the linear combination is $I(0)$.

[8]This means that the series have been transformed by the filter $(1-L)^{d-0.765}$ where d is the estimated fractional integration parameter for the series in question. Note that the calculations are performed by truncating the expansions at lag t, for $t = 1, 2, \dots$ See Davidson [9] for details.

[9]This model is actually a mixed case, in which the starred variables are assumed to make a generalized cointegrating relation with Lead for some $b \leq 0.765$, and then the unstarred variables further cointegrate with this set in the regular way to yield an $I(a)$ residual, for $a < b$. With $a = 0.101$, this would be equivalent to the pure generalized cointegration model with $b = 0.664 = \min_i d_i$, but it also admits the stronger hypothesis in which $a = 0$. It's convenient for obvious reasons to keep Lead in its original form, and the bootstrap test has power to detect either case.

Table 3. The generalized cointegration model

Dependent Variable: Lead   Sample: 1955:2 1996:4

	Coefficient	Std. Error	t-Statistic
Real Earnings*	−.0821	0.505	−1.62
Real GDP*	0.788	0.836	0.942
Unemployment*	4.00	2.03	1.96
TB Rate	1.53	0.294	5.21
Inflation	−0.265	0.144	−1.83
Exch. Rate($/£)*	−11.4	5.28	−2.16
LabGovt	8.82	3.91	2.25
Elapsed	−2.85	0.562	−5.07
Elapsed^2	0.145	0.031	4.59
LabGovt×Elapsed	−2.57	1.17	−2.20
LabGovt×Elapsed^2	0.103	0.069	1.50
Trend	−0.156	0.054	−2.86
Constant	35.52	16.38	2.16

R-squared	0.420	Adjusted R-squared	0.375
Durbin-Watson	0.694	F-statistic (all)	9.31
Residual PP	−5.81	F-statistic (econs)	10.36

On the conventional criteria, this regression is somewhat inferior to the original in Table 1, and offers little support for the generalized cointegration approach in the present context.

4 Tests of Noncointegration

4.1 The Basic Procedure

The bootstrap tests applied here are described in detail in Davidson [9, 10]. The basic procedure is to draw bootstrap replications of the model in (1) under H_0, and so generate the null distributions of two regression-based test statistics. The actual statistics yielded by the regression in Table 1 are located in these empirical distributions to yield asymptotically valid p-values.

One of these statistics is the usual F statistic for the joint significance of the economic variables. This is not a conventional statistic to test for cointegration, but its consistency as a test for cointegration in the bootstrap context is proved in Davidson [9]. Since it compares the sums of squared regression residuals with and without the test regressors included, which should have different orders of magnitude when the hypothesis of noncointegration is false, it should have some power to detect a relationship. The second statistic is the Durbin Watson statistic, which represents the more usual approach, of testing whether the regression residuals have significantly shorter memory than the variables constituting them. These therefore represent a

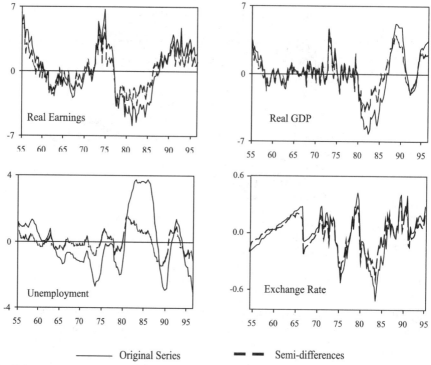

Fig. 5. Semi-Differenced Series, $d = 0.765$.

two-pronged attack on the test problem, by looking at two different features of the fitted model. Being regression based, these tests may appear directly comparable with the Engle-Granger or Phillips-Perron residual-based tests, and this is true in the sense they can only test for the null of zero cointegrating rank.[10] However as we explain below, the tests may entail structural modelling of the short-run dynamics, and in this sense have much in common with system-based tests such as Johansen's eigenvalue tests.

The test statistics are not asymptotically pivotal, meaning that they depend on nuisance parameters under H_0, specifically, the values of d and the autocovariances of the data increments. Therefore, no conventional asymptotic tests can be based on them. However, this is also true of the more conventional tests. While there exist well known fixes to correct for such nuisance parameters in tests for conventional I(1)/I(0) cointegration — of which the 'augmentation' of the Dickey-Fuller statistic

---

[10]Strictly speaking, the null hypothesis that is opposed to the regular cointegration alternative is that β contains no column in which Lead has a non-zero element. We have already noted that fractional cointegration amongst the I(1) regressors must be a feature of the alternative. Although the theory developed in Davidson [9] deals with the simplest case of $\beta = \mathbf{0}$, this generalization is perfectly valid provided the test regression is normalized on Lead.

is the best-known — there are no such fixes that can generate statistics not depending on the d values, so that a bootstrapping approach is unavoidable. [11]

The bootstrap draws are conditioned on the actual sample values of the regressors, which is computationally efficient and should also be less prone to specification error, because the generation processes of these variables do not need to be simulated[12]. This method also yields potentially more powerful tests than would bootstrapping the complete data set, noting that the conditional test distributions must have smaller dispersion than the unconditional ones.

Two versions of the null hypothesis can be distinguished, depending whether the matrix $\mathbf{B}(L)$ in (1) is assumed to be block-diagonal with respect to Lead (x_{1t}, say)[13] and the economic variables $\mathbf{x}_{2t}$, where $\mathbf{x}_t = (x_{1t}, \mathbf{x}'_{2t})'$. If it is, then the null under test is essentially that of independence between the series, which we call the strong null hypothesis. The bootstrap distribution of Lead would be simply obtained by using the univariate ARFIMA model from Table 2. In the case where this restriction is not imposed, which we call the weak null hypothesis, the short-run dynamics under H_0 have to be modelled to create the bootstrap distribution. Let $\mathbf{w}_t$ be the I(0) vector defined in (4). Because $\mathbf{x}_{2t}$ is to be held conditionally fixed, it is necessary to estimate a dynamic equation for w_{1t} containing both $w_{1,t-1}, \ldots$ and $\ldots, \mathbf{w}_{2,t+1}, \mathbf{w}_{2t}, \mathbf{w}_{2,t-1}, \ldots$, where the ellipses represent lags of total length to be specified. The inclusion of the leads as well as lags is to allow for the fact that w_{1t} could Granger-cause $\mathbf{w}_{2t}$, which is not ruled out, whether or not the regressors are weakly exogenous. With this structure, with leads/lags suitably chosen, the residuals from the regression should be asymptotically both serially uncorrelated, and orthogonal to the regressors at all orders. Resampling from the empirical distribution of these residuals, and then passing them back through the same filter in reverse, should accordingly yield a bootstrap sample having (asymptotically) the same correlation structure under H_0 as the original series. The resulting test distributions should therefore depend on the nuisance parameters in just the right way.

There is one caveat to be observed in this procedure. The test as described, in which the best-fitting dynamic equation is chosen by the usual consistent model selection criteria, should be correctly sized asymptotically, because if H_0 is true the correct model is chosen with probability 1 in the limit. However, such a test would have limited power, because when cointegration does exist, this long-run relation will contaminate the short-run dynamics, and the best model must inevitably contain a large number of leads and lags. This problem is avoided only by choosing a deliberately parsimonious model, with short leads and lags, which should capture the weak dependence under H_0 but avoid contamination under the alternative. In

---

[11]Breitung and Hassler [5] show how to construct an asymptotically pivotal test of cointegrating rank by fractionally differencing the data, but their approach would be difficult to adapt to the present problem.

[12]ARFIMA models have been fitted to them in Table 2, but only for the purpose of modelling the short-run correlations of their increments with those of Lead, so that these can be incorporated into the conditional bootstrap model.

[13]Here we are ordering and partitioning the variables differently from equations (1), where the ordering was by size of d parameter.

practice, there is a trade-off of advantages between size and power. The simulations reported in Davidson (2004a) may throw a degree of light on the nature of this trade-off.

4.2 Modelling Lead

The simplest method of implementing the tests is to take the estimated value of d from the first column of Table 2, and use this to generate an $I(d)$ series representing Lead, less the election cycle. The bootstrap series are non-cointegrated with the regressors by construction, but their increments reproduce the observed correlation structure with those of the regressors, under H_0, as described above. The use of this approach is supported in the present case by the fact that the Lead series is well described by a simple $I(d)$ model, as is evident from Table 2.

However, this method has the drawback that it adopts at best a crude simulation of the process that is believed to generate the sample data under H_0. Note first that Lead must exhibit occasional jumps, corresponding to the sign change when governing and opposing parties change places. The marginal distribution of the innovations can be correctly simulated by bootstrap resampling on the actual model residuals, but this method cannot represent the state-dependence of the large deviations (the dates of elections are not randomly drawn) nor can it avoid the paradox of having 'Lead' remain negative both before and following an election. In other words, important nonlinear features of the data generation process have been lost. Moreover, by treating the election cycle as conditionally fixed, it ignores the fact that elections and 'Lead' are generated jointly. In the British political system, an election can be called by the governing party at any time up to the limit of the five-year term, and parliamentary terms of around four years are the norm, although they can be much shorter. The probability of an election being called ahead of time obviously depends on Lead itself, and is the less likely as Lead becomes negative.

An alternative approach is to construct the bootstrap distribution of Lead to embody these features. This has been done using the estimated BDP model as a basis, notwithstanding that this is a monthly model fitted to a different, though largely overlapping, sample period. The procedure is as follows. First, monthly series for the log-odds of Conservative and Labour support, net of the election cycle, are generated by applying the appropriate fractional filter to the resampled BDP residuals. After adding the respective cycles from the BDP model to each series and converting to percentage form, the difference of the two series is constructed, signed according to the party in power, and finally, a quarterly series obtained by taking the figure for the last month in every quarter.

Within this setup, elections are modelled as random events whose probability depends on the number of unexpired periods of the current term, and also whether Lead is currently positive. This probability must in all events approach unity as the number of unexpired periods approaches zero. A simple scheme with the required properties is

$$P(\text{election in month } t) = \exp\{(\alpha - \beta \min(\text{Lead}, 0))(t - T)\}$$

where T denotes the last possible date of the current term. The parameters α and β are chosen by trial and error so that the number of elections, and changes of government, are typically close to those of the sample historical period. With $\alpha = 0.15$ and $\beta = 0.1$ the averages in 1000 replications were respectively 11.5 elections and 3.7 changes of government, which is close enough for the purposes of the exercise to the historical values of 11 and 4, respectively. Note that with this model, the dummy election cycle variables have to be resampled randomly, in each bootstrap replication.

This approach to doing the test has one drawback, that we cannot model the correlation between the increments of Lead and the economic indicators. In other words we are testing the 'strong' form of the noncointegration hypothesis, which is subject to the risk of spurious rejection, assuming we are only interested in the existence of a cointegrating relationship. There are three reasons why this is seen as an acceptable limitation; first, the strong hypothesis is in any case of independent interest, by throwing light on the short run; second, the evidence indicates that the amount of short-run correlation is small; and third, correcting the omission could not change the test outcome actually obtained.

4.3 Results

Table 4 shows the results of bootstrap tests for the four cases described above, in other words, the bootstrap models described respectively in Sections 4.1 and 4.2, applied to the regular cointegration model and the generalized cointegration model. The univariate ARFIMA models reported in Table 2 are used to provide estimates of the d parameters. To perform the generalized cointegration test the series for unemployment, real GDP and real earnings were semi-differenced as in Figure 5.

	F		DW	
Null Hypothesis	Regular	Double	Regular	Double
Regular (non-)cointegration:				
$\mathrm{I}(d)$, weak null	0.26	0.19	0.63	0.49
$\mathrm{I}(d)$, semi-weak null	0.31	0.27	0.59	0.42
BDP, strong null	0.12	-	0.69	-
Generalized (non-)cointegration:				
$\mathrm{I}(d)$, weak null	0.42	0.49	0.69	0.48
$\mathrm{I}(d)$, semi-weak null	0.46	0.38	0.65	0.50
BDP, strong null	0.26	-	0.76	-

Table 4. Noncointegration Tests: p-values

In the tests of the weak null hypothesis, based on the simple $\mathrm{I}(d)$ representation of Lead, its dth differences were modelled by regression on the lags of the regressors of lag orders -2 through $+2$, as well as 2 own-lags. This distribution was resampled, and passed back through the same filter in reverse. In the 'semi-weak null' the (not unreasonable) restriction that there is no feedback from Lead to the economic variables is imposed. In this case, future values of the differenced regressors are excluded from the dynamic model.

The bootstrap tests were performed with 1000 replications, although note that this number does not influence the precision of the estimated p-value. The tests are asymptotic and the approximation depends on sample size, with $T = 167$ in this case. It does however render the sampling error small enough to ignore, so that the tests are directly comparable with conventional asymptotic tests.

In the case of the weak and semi-weak null hypotheses, the reported p-values have been computed by the regular bootstrap and the double bootstrap. The double bootstrap has been suggested by Beran [2] as a method of minimizing size distortions. These are due to the fact that the bootstrap distribution differs from that of the sample data because it depends on estimated parameters. Such distortions are known to be worse when the statistics are not asymptotically pivotal, as in the present case. The method entails using the bootstrap p-value itself as the test statistic, since its asymptotic distribution under the null hypothesis is known (uniform on $[0,1]$). This is done by bootstrapping the bootstrap, a computationally intensive procedure that can, however, be made much more efficient by applying stopping rules, as proposed by Nankervis [27].

The double bootstrap cannot compensate for errors of specification (as opposed to estimation) in the bootstrap model, which in this case means, pre-eminently, the incorrect choice of leads/lags in the weak-null specification. However, it has been noted that increasing the lag length must tend to reduce the probability of rejection in the event the null hypothesis is false. If the hypothesis is not rejected with the chosen model, as in the present case, increasing the lag length is not likely to change the decision. In the case of the BDP simulation the bootstrap parameters are extraneously estimated, so the double bootstrap is not available. However, note here that the parameters are computed from a much larger sample (monthly data) and moreover, the assumptions of the strong null are imposed so that no parameters estimated from the present sample are utilised. Since even this test fails to reject the null at the 5% level, it is difficult to see how changing the bootstrap specification could result in a reversal of the reported results.

In all these tests the p-values exceed 10%, so on this basis there is not even slender evidence of a cointegrating relationship. The set of economic indicators chosen may be incomplete, and for example the tax rate indicator used by Pissarides [29] has not been considered here. However, the variables included should on any basis be regarded as important. One would expect at least some mild evidence of a relationship, if in fact it existed. While alternative models are clearly open to test on the same lines, this evidence clearly favours either the dominance of purely non-economic factors, in explaining the trend, or an explanation on the lines proposed by BDP.

5 Tests of Cointegration

Failure to reject the hypothesis of noncointegration at conventional significance levels may simply tell us something about the power of the tests. A natural next step is to interchange the null and alternative hypotheses, and see whether a rejection is obtained in this case. This can be done applying Shin's [33] test for the null hypothesis of cointegration. Specifically, this is a test of the hypothesis that the residuals from the putative cointegrating regression are I(0), and while Shin derives it for the usual case of I(1) data, it can be adapted in the bootstrap context to the case of I(d) data, as shown in Davidson [10].

The test is based on the KPSS statistic (Kwiatkowski et. al. [71]) from the cointegrating regression residuals that have been obtained using Saikkonen's [31] efficient estimation procedure. The problem for adapting this test to the bootstrap context is to find a way of simulating the null hypothesis. In Davidson [10] this is done in two ways. The "ECM" method is to fit an error correction model to the data. The bootstrap series for the dependent variable is then solved from this model with an inequality restriction on the error correction parameter. This restriction should be satisfied in the data if the null hypothesis is true, but in all cases will force the bootstrap data to be cointegrated, if the null is false. For the tests reported here, the upper bound on the ECM parameter has been set to the minimum of the estimated value and one of two bounding values, either -0.5, or -1. This choice represents a potential size-power trade-off, since making the bound smaller distorts the null distribution but must raise the probability of rejection when the null is false.

The second method of implementing the test is simply to regress the model residuals onto the fractionally differenced data, such that all the explanatory variables are I(0). Use of this model to construct the bootstrap series from resampled residuals again ensures that the null hypothesis holds for the series, although at the cost of some distortion of its distribution. For further details of these procedures, and formulae, see Davidson [10].

	ECM ($\mu \leq -0.5$)		ECM ($\mu \leq -1$)		I(0) Regression	
Null Hypothesis	Regular	Double	Regular	Double	Regular	Double
Regular cointegration	0.018	0.076	0	0.005	0	0.001
Generalized cointegration	0.046	0.147	0	0	0	0.003

Table 5. Shin Test: p-values

The results of these tests are shown in Table 5, where μ refers to the ECM parameter. The first columns show that the double bootstrap test with $\mu \leq -0.5$ cannot reject the null at the 5% level, although the other variants have no difficulty in doing so. However, the more relaxed bound must reduce the power of the test, in the interests of fixing the size more accurately. If the fitted value of μ in the sample data is much less that 0, this test cannot have much power, and this is a plausible occurrence even under the alternative, when the data are themselves fractionally integrated with

$d < 1$, and the lag structure is potentially overfitted. In the present case the fitted value of μ is, respectively, -0.408 in the regular cointegration model, and -0.420 in the generalized cointegration model, whereas we know that these null hypotheses cannot both be true. The results of the next section also provide some grounds for placing most reliance on the other variants of the test.

6 Power Evaluation

6.1 Noncointegration Tests

One of the virtues of the bootstrap approach is that a power evaluation can be undertaken, relevant to the specific model under test. Consider first the tests of non-cointegration. Simulations have been used to estimate the power of the test of the weak and semi-weak nulls described in Section 4.1. Note that the "BDP strong null" cannot be evaluated in this way, simply because there is no way to construct a dummy alternative hypothesis.

The first part of the simulation procedure is to construct an artificial process representing a 'cointegrating residual', which is done using the fitted dynamic equation described in Section 4.1, so that the correlation structure of the differences in the observed data is preserved. Optionally, this series is fractionally integrated, using an experimental d value. Finally, the fitted part of the regression in either Table 1 or Table 3 (to simulate regular or generalized cointegration, respectively) is added to the series, to produce an artificial regressand. When the experimental value of d is equal to 0, this method generates a fully cointegrated data set, while for cases $0 < d < 0.765$ the data may be called fractionally cointegrated.

An artificial 'null hypothesis' is created, in this framework, by integrating using the value $d = 0.765$ from Table 2, and then adding only the dummy components of the fitted model. This null model was simulated 3000 times to tabulate the true sizes of the tests. In each replication, the simulated test involves estimating the d value by maximum likelihood for the experimental dependent variable (the ARFIMA$(0,d,0)$ specification is used) as well as the parameters of the short-run dynamics. The empirical distribution functions of the p-values so obtained are shown in Figure 6. The EDFs of correctly sized tests, for which the p-values are $U(0,1)$ by construction, should lie on the diagonals, shown by the dotted lines. These tabulations can be used to compute size-corrected p-values, a procedure that is effectively equivalent to the double bootstrap; see Davidson [10] for details.

The test procedure was simulated 1000 times, for each of five values of the experimental d. The proportion of rejections at the 5% level are shown in Table 6. The two columns relating to each test show, respectively, the nominal powers, and the size-corrected powers, obtained by adjusting the p-values using the tabulations in Figure 6. The final column of the table shows the average of the 1000 R^2s obtained in the test regressions, to show how the rejection of non-cointegration relates to goodness of fit. Remember, in this connection, that the dummy variables for the election cycle account for a large proportion of the observed variation.

6.2 Shin Tests

For the power analysis of the Shin test, it is necessary to simulate the data under the null hypothesis of cointegration, to generate the EDFs for size correction. To do this the cointegrating residuals were generated using the data-fitted error correction model, modified by setting the ECM coefficient to the lesser of its sample value, and -1.

		d	F		DW		R^2
			Nominal	Corrected	Nominal	Corrected	
		0.8	0.15	0.13	0.015	0.13	0.88
	Weak	0.6	0.36	0.33	0.043	0.25	0.93
	Null	0.4	0.65	0.63	0.18	0.54	0.95
		0.2	0.86	0.85	0.47	0.84	0.95
Regular		0	0.94	0.93	0.76	0.99	0.95
Cointegration		0.8	0.19	0.12	0.03	0.11	0.88
	Semi-	0.6	0.39	0.27	0.07	0.19	0.93
	Weak	0.4	0.64	0.52	0.19	0.45	0.95
	Null	0.2	0.85	0.77	0.50	0.79	0.95
		0	0.93	0.89	0.77	0.95	0.95
		0.8	0.08	0.15	0.007	0.12	0.80
	Weak	0.6	0.21	0.33	0.02	0.18	0.89
	Null	0.4	0.42	0.56	0.06	0.35	0.92
		0.2	0.69	0.80	0.19	0.68	0.92
Generalized		0	0.83	0.90	0.37	0.88	0.92
Cointegration		0.8	0.09	0.12	0.01	0.07	0.81
	Semi-	0.6	0.20	0.25	0.02	0.10	0.89
	Weak	0.4	0.44	0.49	0.07	0.21	0.92
	Null	0.2	0.71	0.74	0.20	0.44	0.92
		0	0.84	0.87	0.41	0.74	0.92

Table 6. Powers: Tests of noncointegration

The fitted part of the regressions in Tables 1 or 3 is then added to the generated residual to produce the artificial regressand. The resulting tabulations are shown in Figure 7.

There are two approaches to simulating an alternative hypothesis. The first is to generate the residuals as under the null, but then to fractionally integrate these using a spread of experimental d values (0.2, 0.4, 0.6, 0.8 and 1 are used) before adding the fitted components. The second, denoted UR in Table 7, is simply to replace the

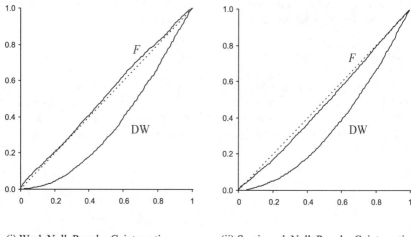

(i) Weak Null, Regular Cointegration   (ii) Semi-weak Null, Regular Cointegration

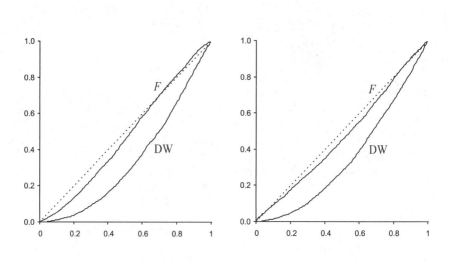

(iii) Weak Null, Generalized Cointegration   (iv) Semi-weak Null, Generalized Cointegration

Fig. 6. Empirical Distribution Functions of p-values for Tests of Non-Cointegration.

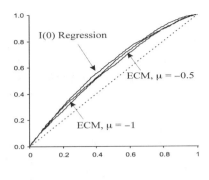

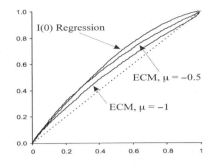

(i) Regular Cointegration   (ii) Generalized Cointegration

Fig. 7. Empirical Distribution Functions of p-values for Shin Tests of Cointegration.

ECM coefficient by 0, so that the residual process contains a unit root. The former procedure is somewhat contrived, but it allows us to evaluate the power of the test of "full" cointegration (with I(0) cointegrating residuals) against fractionally integrated alternatives.

	d	ECM, $\mu \leq -0.5$		ECM, $\mu \leq -1$		I(0) Regression		R^2
		Nominal	Corrected	Nominal	Corrected	Nominal	Corrected	
	0.2	0.19	0.14	0.20	0.14	0.35	0.24	0.94
Regular	0.4	0.33	0.24	0.45	0.37	0.72	0.61	0.94
Cointegration	0.6	0.56	0.47	0.76	0.70	0.93	0.88	0.91
	0.8	0.80	0.74	0.93	0.91	0.99	0.98	0.82
	1	0.93	0.91	0.99	0.98	1	0.99	0.76
	UR	0.78	0.73	0.97	0.96	0.98	0.97	0.82
	0.2	0.13	0.06	0.14	0.09	0.31	0.20	0.91
Generalized	0.4	0.29	0.17	0.38	0.30	0.69	0.55	0.89
Cointegration	0.6	0.52	0.38	0.66	0.59	0.93	0.87	0.82
	0.8	0.77	0.65	0.91	0.86	0.99	0.98	0.68
	1	0.90	0.82	0.99	0.98	1	0.99	0.72
	UR	0.78	0.66	0.97	0.94	0.99	0.98	0.68

Table 7. Powers: Shin Tests of Cointegration

6.3 Results

A number of considerations need to be borne in mind in reviewing these results. First, they are of course entirely specific to the data set and sample size in question. The actual data are used to represent the regressors in the simulations. While they should be generalized only with caution, the point is that, in principle, the same type of evaluation can be performed on a case-by-case basis. Second, note that the simulations of generalized cointegration do not tell us anything about the plausibility or otherwise of that particular model, but merely about the ability of the tests to detect (non)cointegration in fractionally integrated processes, where the common d is 0.765. In the Shin test, the cointegrated dependent variable under H_0 is I(1.169) (to match the largest regressor d) by construction. Hence, this evaluation is relevant to that state of the world in which the d for Lead has been mismeasured. The main contrast sought between these experiments is between the different orders of integration of the cointegrated variables.

Subject to these caveats, there is evidently reasonable power to detect both cointegration and non-cointegration, in this setting. The Durbin Watson-based test is shown in Figure 6 to under-reject quite seriously, but the F test is pretty well sized. The three variants of the Shin test all over-reject to a small degree, but the case with $\mu \leq 0.5$ appears not to be significantly better sized than the other two, even though there is a fairly substantial cost in terms of power. This finding allows us to be cautiously confident in relying on the clear rejections of the null, by the other two variants of the Shin test.

7 Tests for Short-run Correlation

There remains one further hypothesis that can be tested, that of a "short term" relationship between the fractional differences. This is a possibility additional to, and distinct from, cointegration. BDP carry out a short-run analysis in monthly data by regressing the fractional differences of party support on innovations in a number of economic series, with generally negative results (see their Table 7). We have the opportunity here to carry out an analogue of the BDP tests in quarterly data, using the fractional differences of Lead as the dependent variable, instead of party support.

Two regressions were run. The first is on the I(0) series obtained by applying the operators $(1 - L)^d$ where d is the estimated differencing parameter from the relevant column of Table 2. In the second, the residuals from the ARFIMA(p, d, q) models were used, in those cases (Unemployment, TB Rate and Inflation) where there is a fitted ARMA component. In each case, the regressor set was chosen by optimising the Schwarz [32] model selection criterion with respect to the number of included lags. In both regressions, zero lags (current values only) optimised the criterion. In the interests of space, just the F statistics for overall significance of the regressions are reported, together with the associated p-values; see Table 8, which also gives residual autocorrelation statistics.[14] The largest (absolutely) of the individual t values in these regressions is -2.19, on GDP, but note the perverse negative sign. These findings are quite closely comparable to the ones obtained in monthly data by BDP.

---

[14]The full regression results are available from the author on request.

	Significance of the Regression F(6,161) [Prob > F]	LM(4) Test for Autocorrelation F(4, 159) [Prob > F]
Fractional Differences	1.602 [0.149]	0.511 [0.727]
ARFIMA Residuals	1.552 [0.164]	0.552 [0.697]

Table 8. Tests for short-run correlation

8 Conclusion

This paper has employed a variety of novel testing techniques to look for evidence of a connection between the popularity of UK governments and economic indicators over the business cycle, and has failed to find any. Since negative findings of any sort can leave readers in doubt about the quality of the evidence, it is as well to spell out what conclusions can be drawn here.

First, in addition to the evidence on the 'short run' in Table 8, also note that the so-called 'strong' noncointegration hypothesis is effectively a test of statistical independence. Although these tests are not consistent against noncointegrating alternatives, the statistics will in general have their distributions shifted to the right in the presence of correlation between the process increments, even in the absence of cointegration.[15] Even in these cases, neither of the noncointegration tests reject, even at the 10% level, according to Table 4.

Second, while these may not be exact tests in finite samples, exact tests of level α can be constructed by rejecting only if the largest possible p-value, by choice of the unknown nuisance parameters, is less than α (see Dufour [15]). Clearly, no such test can reject the non-cointegration hypothesis, and we can therefore treat these results as exact, such that the rejection probability under the null is known not to exceed the nominal level.

Third, the most hopeful result from the viewpoint of establishing the existence of a relationship is the nonrejection of generalized cointegration by the most conservative of the Shin test variants. However, this finding is at odds with the regressions reported in Tables 1 and 3, which reverse the ranking of the two models on the basis of goodness of fit. This anomaly points to the likelihood of a 'Type 2 error' in this case. The simulation evidence also gives us grounds to give credit to the more powerful test variants, which reject the null even after size-correction.

Fourth, while the set of economic series chosen for the test may omit some important ones, those included are undeniably important. The Monte Carlo evidence shows that the noncointegration tests have some power even against alternatives where the residuals are long-memory, and even nonstationary. The implication is that omission of important factors ought not, in general, to mask an existing relationship. If the important economic trend factors have been omitted, we are forced to the conclusion

---

[15]This property is demonstrated in Davidson [9].

that these must be orthogonal to those included, and it is not at all obvious what these factors might be.

Fifth, in focusing on the formalities of cointegration testing we have not commented at length on the numerical magnitudes of the regression coefficients in Tables 1 and 3, but obviously these have dubious implications. Of the coefficients with large t values, the positive relationship between unemployment and popularity appears bizarre, although we can account for it anecdotally by pointing to, for example, the catastrophic collapse of the 1992-97 Conservative government's popularity, in step with recovery from recession. Historians of the period will explain this decline in terms of misbehaviour by politicians, internal divisions, and a loss of confidence following the exit from the Exchange Rate Mechanism. We know that such intangible factors matter. What the present results show is that objective economic conditions have an insignificant role by comparison.

In summary, this study can be claimed to provide, if anything, evidence in support of the BDP hypothesis, that local trends in popularity have quite different causes relating to the aggregation of sampled opinions. Economic events send different messages to different individual voters, and aggregating their reactions to them has unpredictable effects. Minor events are important if voters agree about them, major events may be appear to be ignored in the aggregate if voters disagree. Whatever the actual mechanism of opinion filtering, the effect is to scramble the original message so effectively that it is undetectable in statistical tests The message for governments may be that while the economy is undoubtedly important, the constituencies of winners and losers under any change of policy have to be offset against one another, and the effects are hard to disentangle.

References

1. Baillie R T (1996) Long memory processes and fractional integration in econometrics. Journal of Econometrics 73: 5-59
2. Beran R (1988) Prepivoting test statistics: a bootstrap view of asymptotic refinements. Journal of the American Statistical Association 83: 687-697
3. Box GEP, Pierce DA (1970) The distribution of residual autocorrelations in autoregressive-integrated moving average time series models. Journal of the American Statistical Association 65: 1509-26
4. Box-Steffensmeier JM, Smith RM (1996) The Dynamics of Aggregate Partisanship. American Political Science Review 90: 567-580
5. Breitung J, Hassler U (2002) Inference on the cointegration rank in fractionally integrated processes. Journal of Econometrics 110: 167.185.
6. Byers D, Davidson J, Peel DA (1997) Modelling Political Popularity: An Analysis of Long-range Dependence in Opinion Poll Series. Journal of the Royal Statistical Society, Series A 160: 471-490
7. Byers D, Davidson J, Peel DA (2000) The dynamics of aggregate political popularity: Evidence from eight countries. Electoral Studies 19: 49-62
8. Byers D, Davidson J, Peel DA (2002) Modelling political popularity: A correction. Journal of the Royal Statistical Society, Series A 165: 187-189

9. Davidson J (2002) A model of fractional cointegration, and tests for cointegration using the bootstrap. Journal of Econometrics 110: 187-212

10. Davidson J (2004) Alternative bootstrap procedures for testing cointegration in fractionally integrated processes. Journal of Econometrics (forthcoming), also at http://www.cf.ac.uk/carbs/davidsonje

11. Davidson J (2004) Time series modelling, Version 4.0, at http://www.timeseriesmodelling.com/

12. Davidson J, Hendry DF, Srba F, Yeo S (1978) Econometric modelling of the aggregate time-series relationship between consumers' expenditure and income in the United Kingdom. Economic Journal 88: 661-92

13. Dolado JJ, Gonzalo J, Mayoral L (2003) Long range dependence in Spanish political opinion poll series. Journal of Applied Econometrics 18: 137-1552

14. Doornik JA (1999) Object-oriented matrix programming using Ox, 3rd edition, London: Timberlake Consultants Press and Oxford: http://www.nuff.ox.ac.uk/Users/Doornik

15. Dufour J-M (2000) Monte Carlo tests with nuisance parameters: a general approach to finite sample inference and nonstandard asymptotics. Mimeo, Department of Economic Science, University of Montreal

16. Frey B S, Schneider F (1978) A politico-economic model of the United Kingdom. Economic Journal 88: 243-253

17. Goodhart CAE, Bhansali RJ (1970) Political economy. Political Studies 18: 265-279

18. Granger CWJ (1980) Long memory relationships and the aggregation of dynamic models. Journal of Econometrics 14: 227-238

19. Granger CWJ (1986) Developments in the study of cointegrated economic variables. Oxford Bulletin of Economics and Statistics 48: 213-228

20. Holden K, Peel D (1985) An alternative approach to explaining political popularity. Electoral Studies 4: 231-239

21. Johansen S (1988) Statistical Analysis of Cointegration Vectors. Journal of Economic Dynamics and Control 12: 231-54

22. Johansen S (1991) Estimation and hypothesis testing of cointegration vectors in Gaussian vector autoregressive models. Econometrica 59: 1551-80

23. Kwiatkowski D, Phillips PCB, Schmidt P, Shin Y (1992) Testing the null hypothesis of stationarity against the alternative of a unit root. Journal of Econometrics 54: 159-78

24. MacKinnon JG (1991) Critical values for cointegration tests. In Engle R, Granger CWJ (eds) Long-run Economic Relationships, Oxford University Press

25. McLeod AI, Li WK (1983) Diagnostic checking ARMA time series models using squared-residual autocorrelations. Journal of Time Series Analysis 4: 269-273

26. Minford APL, Peel DA (1982) The political theory of the business cycle. European Economic Review 17: 253-270

27. Nankervis JC (2001) Stopping rules for double bootstrap tests. Working paper, University of Surrey

28. Nordhaus (1975) Political Business Cycle. Review of Economic Studies 42 (2)

29. Pissarides C (1980) British Government Popularity and Economic Performance. Economic Journal 90: 569-581

30. Rogoff K, Sibert A (1989) Equilibrium political business cycles. Review of Economic Studies 55 1-16

31. Saikkonen P (1991) Asymptotically efficient estimation of cointegration regressions. Econometric Theory 7: 1-21

32. Schwarz G (1978) Estimating the Dimension of a Model. Annals of Statistics 6: 461-4

33. Shin Y (1994) A residual-based test of the null of cointegration against the alternative of no cointegration. Econometric Theory 10: 91-115

Non-stationarity Tests in Macroeconomic Time Series

Olivier Darné[1] and Claude Diebolt[2]

[1] CERESUR, University of La Réunion, Faculty of Law and Economics, 15 Avenue René Cassin, BP 7151, 97715 Saint Denis Mess cedex 9, France.
olivier.darne@univ-reunion.fr
[2] BETA-CNRS, University Louis Pasteur of Strasbourg, Faculty of Economics and Management, 61 avenue de la Forêt Noire, 67085 Strasbourg Cedex, France.
cdiebolt@cournot.u-strasbg.fr

Summary. This paper presents a selective survey of the literature on non-stationarity tests, namely standard and efficient unit root tests and stationarity tests, with or without structural changes. We also present the direct relation between non-stationarity tests and four economic theories, such as business cycles, hysteresis, purchasing power parity and convergence.

Key words: Unit root tests, Stationarity tests, Breaks, Business cycles, Hysteresis, Purchasing power parity, Convergence.

JEL Classification: C12, C22

1 Introduction

Since the influential paper of Nelson and Plosser [99], much attention has been devoted to studying the non-stationarity of macroeconomic time series. The literature observes two types of non-stationary processes: (i) trend-stationary [TS] processes (or processes that are stationary around a trend) where non-stationarity is deterministic, and (ii) difference-stationary [DS] processes (or processes that are stationary in first-differences) where non-stationarity is stochastic (presence of unit roots). In the existence of a unit root, the underlying trend is stochastic, which implies that the series has a long memory, and shocks have persistent effects. As a result, the series does not return to its former path following a random disturbance, and the level of the series shifts permanently. On the other hand, if the series does not contain a unit root, the underlying trend is deterministic and the series has a short memory. In this case, a shock has no permanent impact and the series returns to its steady trend after the shock.

The distinction between the two classes of non-stationary processes is important from the viewpoint of statistical inference because stationarity is achieved from different methods: by removing a time trend (*detrending*, i.e. regressing on time trend) for a TS process and by differencing for a DS process. There have been several studies that have investigated the effects that arise when stationarity is achieved from inappropriate method (Chan et al. [34]; Nelson and Kang [97, 98]). If the time series is DS and we treat it as TS, this is a case of under-differencing and implies the creation of short cyclical movements and, inversely, we have a case of over-differencing[3] and creation of long cyclical movements. These two forms of non-stationarity have radically different implications for forecasting time series: forecast-error variances grow linearly in the forecast horizon for the DS process, but are bounded for the TS process (Clements and Hendry [38]).

As suggested by Stock [145], there are four main areas for testing univariate nonstationarity in economic time series: (1) data description; (2) medium- and long-term forecasting; (3) a guide for subsequent multivariate modelling; and (4) information on the degree of persistence in a time series and, in particular, on its order of integration can help to guide the construction or testing of economic theories. Here we focus on the fourth area by establishing the direct relation between non-stationarity tests and some economic theories such as business cycles, hysteresis, purchasing power parity and convergence.

The nature of the trend or the non-stationarity (deterministic or stochastic) is generally studied from the unit root tests[4]. Following the seminal work of Fuller [57] and Dickey and Fuller [43], numerous procedures have been developed for testing the hypothesis that a univariate time series contains a unit root against the alternative hypothesis that it is level or trend stationary, called *"standard unit root tests"*. However, the power of these unit root tests has been questioned. Evidence has been provided indicating that these unit root tests have size distorsions and low power against meaningful stationary alternatives. Therefore, some useful modifications of these tests have been suggested to solve these problems. Moreover, these standard unit root tests have a common feature of including a constant and/or a deterministic trend in their test regression. However, some studies showed that elimination of deterministic components may bring an efficiency gain to the unit root tests, and this type of tests is called *"efficient unit root tests"*. Nevertheless, the tests mentioned above are all based on the null hypothesis of a unit root, which assures that the hypothesis will be accepted (at conventional significance level of 5%) unless there is strong evidence against it. As a result, *"stationarity tests"* have been proposed for which the null hypothesis is level or trend stationary against the unit root alternative. Besides, some studies have shown that the presence of breaks in the time series can also bias the unit root and stationarity tests. Therefore, some tests taking into account structural breaks have been developed: *"unit root tests with structural changes"* and *"stationarity tests with structural changes"*.

The outline of the paper is as follows. In Section 2, we briefly describe the different types of non-stationarity tests as mentioned above. The direct relation between

---

[3]There has been some debate in the literature on the over-differencing versus under-differencing issue, arguing that the former is a less serious error than the latter.

[4]This paper focus only on univariate time series.

non-stationarity tests and four economic theories (business cycles, hysteresis, purchasing power parity and convergence) is presented in Section 3. Section 4 concludes.

2 Non-stationarity Tests

2.1 Standard Unit Root Tests

The standard Dickey-Fuller test [43] [DF] was developed around three univariate order-one autoregressive models:

$$\text{No drift case:} \qquad y_t = \rho y_{t-1} + \varepsilon_t \qquad (1)$$

$$\text{Drift case:} \qquad y_t = \alpha + \rho y_{t-1} + \varepsilon_t \qquad (2)$$

$$\text{Trend case:} \qquad y_t = \alpha + \delta t + \rho y_{t-1} + \varepsilon_t \qquad (3)$$

where $\{\varepsilon_t\}$ is a sequence of independent normal random variables with mean zero and variance σ^2, i.e. $\varepsilon_t \sim IN(0, \sigma^2)$.

The ρ's parameters of the three models are estimated from the ordinary least squares (OLS) method for testing the hypothesis of the presence of a unit root, i.e. the null hypothesis[5] $H_0 : \rho = 1$, against the alternative $H_1 : |\rho| < 1$. There are two possible tests based on either the least squares estimator of ρ, $T(\hat{\rho} - 1)$, or the t-ratio associated with that estimator, $t_{\hat{\rho}}$, defined by

$$T(\hat{\rho} - 1) = \frac{T^{-1} \sum_{t=1}^{T} y_{t-1} \varepsilon_t}{T^{-2} \sum_{t=1}^{T} y_{t-1}^2} \qquad (4)$$

$$t_{\hat{\rho}} = \frac{T(\hat{\rho} - 1)}{\sigma_{\hat{\rho}}} \qquad (5)$$

where $\sigma_{\hat{\rho}}$ is the standard error of $\hat{\rho}$.

The standard Dickey-Fuller [DF] test is based on independently and identically distributed (*i.i.d.*) errors. When the errors are correlated, there is a need to either change the estimation method (adopt another regression model) or modify the statistics to obtain consistent estimators and statistics. Dickey and Fuller [44] use the first approach of changing the estimating regressions using the parametric approach whereas Phillips [124] and Phillips and Perron [125] follow the second approach of modifying the statistics using a nonparametric approach.

Dickey and Fuller [44] extended the standard DF test by developing the Augmented Dickey-Fuller [ADF] test by estimating an autoregression of Δy_t on its own lags and y_{t-1} using OLS (for the model without constant and linear trend)

---

[5]The unit root hypothesis implies that the coefficient ρ is unity, and random shocks have a permanent effect on the series. If this coefficient was less than unity, the series would be stationary (mean reverting) and random shocks would dissipate over time.

$$\Delta y_t = \rho y_{t-1} + \sum_{j=1}^{k} \beta_j \Delta y_{t-j} + \varepsilon_t \tag{6}$$

where k is the number of lags.

In the presence of moving-average errors (the presence of the serial correlation in errors), the ADF tests incorporate the additional regressors (Δy_{t-k}) into the model to correct the serial correlations in the errors. It has been observed that the size and power properties of the ADF tests are sensitive to the number of lagged terms used (Schwert [137]; Agiakoglou and Newbold [1, 2]). Several guidelines have been suggested for the choice of k. See Ng and Perron [102].

ADF test results are very responsive to the presence of intercept and trend terms. In general, including too many deterministic regressors results in lost power, whereas not including enough of them increases the probability of not rejection the unit root null.

Phillips [124] and Phillips and Perron [125] [PP] proposed a non-parametric approach to correct residual autocorrelation by modifying the test statistics

$$Z_\rho = T(\hat{\rho} - 1) - (1/2)(s_{Tl}^2 - s_\varepsilon^2)\left(T^{-2}\sum_{t=1}^{T} X_{t-1}^2\right)^{-1} \tag{7}$$

$$Z_\tau = (s_\varepsilon/s_{Tl})t_{\hat{\rho}} - (1/2)(s_{Tl}^2 - s_\varepsilon^2)\left(s_{Tl}^2 T^{-2}\sum_{t=1}^{T} X_{t-1}^2\right)^{-1/2}$$

s_ε^2 and s_{Tl}^2 are consistent estimators of the short-run (σ_ε^2) and long-run (σ^2) variances[6] of the estimated residuals $\hat{\varepsilon}_t$. They are defined as

$$s_\varepsilon^2 = T^{-1}\sum_{t=1}^{T} \hat{\varepsilon}_t^2$$

$$s_{wa}^2 = s_\varepsilon^2 + 2T^{-1}\sum_{t=1}^{l} w(s,l)\sum_{t=i+1}^{T} (\hat{\varepsilon}_t\hat{\varepsilon}_{t-i})$$

where $w(s,l)$ is an optimal weighting function corresponding to the choice of a spectral window. Newey and West [100] suggested the Bartlett window, $w(l,s) = 1 - s/(l+1)$. Perron [110] provide some guidelines for the selection of l[7]. Note that the PP tests are less sensitive to the choice of l than the ADF test to the choice of k.

One of the major problems of the standard unit root tests based on AR models has been that they have size distorsions and low power against meaningful stationary alternatives in the presence of large MA components (Schwert [136, 137]; Dejong et al. [42]). There have several solutions to the problems of size distortion and low power of the ADF and PP tests.

The modifications of ADF tests are unit root tests in ARMA models (Said and Dickey [132, 133]) and unit root tests based on instrumental variable regressions (Hall [59];

---

[6]The variances are defined as $\sigma_\varepsilon^2 = \lim_{T\to\infty} T^{-1}\sum_{t=1}^{T} E(\varepsilon_t^2)$ (variance of errors) and $\sigma^2 = \lim_{T\to\infty} T^{-1}E(S_T^2)$ (variance of the sum of errors), where $S_T = \sum_{t=1}^{T} \varepsilon_t$.

[7]Generally, the value $l = T^{1/4}$ is chosen.

Pantula and Hall [107]). Several news have been suggested such as unit root tests based on weighted symmetric estimators (Park and Fuller [109]; Fuller [58]), tests based on conditional (Dickey and Gonzalez-Farias [45]; Yap and Reinsel [153]) or unconditional maximum likelihood estimation (Shin and Fuller [139]), and tests based on reverse and forward regressions (Leybourne [81]).

The PP tests suffer from serious size distortions when there are negative MA errors[8]. Perron and Ng [115] suggest modifications of the PP tests to correct this problem using methods proposed by Stock [144].

2.2 Efficient Unit Root Tests

The standard unit root tests have a common feature of including a constant and/or a deterministic trend in the test regression. However, some studies showed that elimination of deterministic components may bring an efficiency gain to the unit root tests, i.e. increasing power of tests (Schmidt and Phillips [135]).

Elliott, Rothenberg and Stock [50] [ERS] developed a unit root test based on a quasi-difference detrending of the series. They suggested the Dickey-Fuller generalized least squares (DF-GLS) test using the following regression

$$\Delta y_t^d = \beta_0 y_{t-1}^d + \sum_{j=1}^{k} \beta_j \Delta y_{t-j}^d + \varepsilon_t \tag{8}$$

where y_t^d is the locally detrended series y_t. The DF-GLS t-test is performed by testing the null hypothesis $\beta_0 = 0$ against the alternative $\beta_0 < 0$. The local detrending series is defined by

$$y_t^d = y_t - \hat{\psi}' z_t$$

where z_t equals to 1 for the constant mean case, and $(1,t)$ for the linear trend case, and $\hat{\psi}$ is the GLS estimator obtained by regressing $\bar{y}$ on $\bar{z}$ where

$$\bar{y} = (y_1, (1 - \bar{\alpha}B)y_2, \ldots, (1 - \bar{\alpha}B)y_T)'$$
$$\bar{z} = (z_1, (1 - \bar{\alpha}B)z_2, \ldots, (1 - \bar{\alpha}B)z_T)'$$

and $\bar{\alpha} = 1 + \bar{c}/T$. ERS advise $\bar{c} = -7$ for the constant mean case and $\bar{c} = -13.5$ for the linear trend case[9].

Ayat and Burridge [6] extended the ERS test to the quadratic trend case (with $\bar{c} = -18.5$) and Xiao and Phillips [152] to the ARMA models.

Dufour and King [47] also proposed a test analogous to that of ERS with a point optimal invariant test[10]. Hwang and Schmidt [66] suggested another type of GLS

---

[8]The DF tests do not have such serious size distortions but it is less powerful than the PP tests.

[9]Elliott [49] extended the ERS test to the case where the initial observation is drawn from its unconditional distribution under the alternative rather than the more usual assumption of a fixed initial observation (see Burridge and Taylor [23]).

[10]See King [69] for a detailed discussion on point optimal invariant tests.

tests by detrending the series for the Bhargava [19], Schmidt and Phillips [135] and Dufour and King [47] tests. Recently, Ng and Perron [103][11] considered the Perron and Ng [115] tests under GLS detrending.

Another type of efficient unit root tests have been developed based on recursive demeaning (Shin and So [141, 142]) and detrending (Taylor [147]) of the data.

2.3 Stationarity Tests

There have been several tests for stationarity as null, although these are not as numerous as tests using unit AR root as null. Some of these are: Kwiatkowski, Phillips, Schmidt and Shin [71] and Leybourne and McCabe [82], among others.

Kwiatkowski et al. [71] [KPSS] developed a stationary test which takes into account the possible residual autocorrelations in the time series. This procedure tests the null hypothesis of level or trend stationarity against the unit root alternative. The KPSS test starts with the model

$$y_t = \beta t + r_t + \varepsilon_t$$

where ε_t is a stationary process, and r_t is a random walk given by $r_t = r_{t-1} + u_t$ with $u_t \sim N(0, \sigma_u^2)$. The initial value r_0 is treated as fixed and serves the role of an intercept. The stationarity hypothesis is $\sigma_u^2 = 0$ (or r_t is a constant). Under the null hypothesis if $\beta \neq 0$ then y_t is trend-stationary, and if $\beta = 0$ then y_t is level-stationary (i.e. stationary around a level r_0). KPSS suggest to use a Lagrange multiplier test for the null hypothesis of stationarity. The test statistic is defined by

$$\eta = T^{-2} \frac{\sum_{t=1}^{T} \hat{S}_t^2}{s_{Tl}^2}$$

where $\hat{S}_t$ is the partial sum of the residuals $\hat{e}_t$ from the regression of y_t on either a constant or a constant and a time trend defined by

$$\hat{S}_t = \sum_{i=1}^{t} \hat{e}_i \qquad \text{for } t = (1, ..., T)$$

and s_{Tl}^2 is the long-run variance of the residuals $\hat{e}_t$, as used by Phillips and Perron [125]. As parameter l is to be determined, KPSS suggest $l = int[12(T/100)^{1/4}]$ where $int[.]$ is the enter part.

Hobijn, Franses and Ooms [65] generalized the KPSS tests in two directions: First, they advise use of the automatic selection procedure in the estimation of the long-run variance introduced by Newey and West [101]; second, they test the null hypothesis of trend stationarity, level stationarity and zero mean stationarity.

---

[11] Moreover, Ng and Perron [103] suggested use of a class of Modified Information Criteria (MIC) which performs better in selecting appropriate values of k (the number of lags).

Leybourne and McCabe [82] [LMC][12] suggested a similar test for stationarity that differs from the KPSS test in its treatment of autocorrelation based on additional lagged autoregressions (as in the ADF test).

The test is based on a generalization of the local level model (Harvey [10]) defined by

$$\Phi(L)y_t = \alpha_t + \beta t + \varepsilon_t$$
$$\alpha_t = \alpha_{t-1} + v_t, \qquad \alpha_0 = \alpha, \qquad t = 1, \dots, T$$

where $\Phi(L) = 1 - \phi_1 L - \phi_2 L^2 - \cdots - \phi_p L^p$ is a pth order AR polynomial with the roots outside the unit circle, $\varepsilon_t \sim$ iid $(0,\sigma_\varepsilon^2)$ and $v_t \sim$ iid $(0,\sigma_v^2)$, and ε_t and v_t are independent. This model can be shown to be equivalent to the ARIMA(p,1,1) process

$$\Phi(L)(1-L)y_t = \beta + (1-\theta)\xi_t \qquad 0 < \theta \le 1$$

with $\xi_t \sim$ i.i.d. $(0,\sigma_\xi^2)$, $\sigma_\xi^2 = \sigma_\varepsilon^2 \theta^{-1}$, and θ is related to σ_v^2 by the relation $\theta = (r + 2 - (r^2 + 4r)^{1/2})/2$, r being the signal/noise ratio $r = \sigma_v^2 / \sigma_\varepsilon^2$. Here, $\sigma_v^2 = 0$ implies that $\theta = 1$ and $\sigma_v^2 > 0$ involves that $0 < \theta < 1$. Therefore, the null hypothesis of stationarity is $H_0 : \sigma_v^2 = 0$, i.e. y_t is a stationary ARIMA(p,0,0) process, and the alternative is $H_1 : \sigma_v^2 > 0$, i.e. y_t is an ARIMA(p,1,1) with a positive MA(1) coefficient.

The LMC test procedure consists of the following steps:

1. Estimate the ARIMA(p,1,1) model by the maximum likelihood method $\Delta y_t = \beta + \sum_{i=1}^{p} \phi_i \Delta y_{t-i} + \xi_t - \theta \xi_{t-1}$ to get $\hat{\phi}_i$
2. Construct y_t^* as $y_t^* = y_t - \sum_{i=1}^{p} \hat{\phi}_i y_{t-i}$
3. Regress y_t^* on either an intercept or an intercept and a time trend to get the residuals $\hat{\varepsilon}_t$.

Then the test statistic is

$$\hat{s} = T^{-2} \frac{\sum_{t=1}^{T} \hat{S}_t^{*2}}{\hat{\sigma}_\varepsilon^2}$$

where $\hat{\sigma}_\varepsilon^2 = \hat{\varepsilon}'\hat{\varepsilon}/T$ is a consistent estimator of σ_ε^2, and $\hat{S}_t^*$ is the partial sum of the residuals $\hat{S}_t^* = \sum_{t=1}^{T} \hat{\varepsilon}_t$. Leybourne and McCabe [82] show that the asymptotic distribution of the test statistics are the same as the corresponding statistics derived by KPSS and thus one can use the critical values tabulated by KPSS.

Leybourne and McCabe [83] extended the LMC test by proposing an optimal method of selecting the order of the AR component in the fitted ARIMA model.

Caner et Kilian [26] showed the size distorsions of KPSS and LMC tests if the model under the null hypothesis is stationary but highly persistent. Lanne and Saikkonen [80] proposed modifications of the parametric tests of Saikkonen and Luukkonen [134] and Leybourne and McCabe [82] to solve this problem.

---

[12]The LMC test can be viewed as an analogue of the ADF test whereas the KPSS test is an analogue of the Phillips-Perron test.

Others stationarity tests have been developed, for example Tanaka [146], Saikkonen and Luukkonen [134] and Arellano and Pantula [5] presented analogy between tests for an MA unit root and tests for stationarity as null, Choi [36] proposed a test based on the residuals whereas that of Xiao [151] is based on fluctuation tests.

3 Non-stationarity Tests with Structural Changes

3.1 Unit Root Tests with Structural Changes

One major drawback of unit root tests is that, in all of them, the implicit assumption is that the deterministic trend is correctly specified. Perron [111] and Rappoport and Reichlin [127] showed that the unit root tests can be biased toward the non-rejection of the unit root null hypothesis when the time series is stationary around a structural break in the deterministic trend (see also Hendry and Neale [64]; Montañés and Reyes [96]; Leybourne and Newbold [85]). Leybourne, Mills and Newbold [84] showed the converse phenomenon that the presence of a break in a time series generated by a difference-stationary process can lead to spurious rejections of the unit root null hypothesis. Perron [111] proposed a unit root test with structural break based on the assumption that the break point is known *a priori*.

Given a known structural break which is assumed to be given exogenously, Perron [111] has proposed a modified DF test for a unit root in the noise function with three different types of deterministic trend function. The time of a structural change is referred to as T_B, with $1 < T_B < T$. The models are

$$\text{Model A:} \quad DT_t = \mu_0 + \mu_1 DU_t + \delta t$$
$$\text{Model B:} \quad DT_t = \mu + \delta_0 t + \delta_1 DT_t$$
$$\text{Model C:} \quad DT_t = \mu_0 + \mu_1 DU_t + \delta_0 t + \delta_1 DT_t^*$$

where $DU_t = 1$ if $t > T_B$, 0 otherwise; $DT_t = t - T_B$ if $t > T_B$, 0 otherwise; $DT_t^* = t$ if $t > T_B$, 0 otherwise. Model A, the *crash* model, allows for a one-time change in the intercept of the trend function, Model B, the *changing growth* model, allows for a change in the slope of the trend function without any change in the level at the break time, and Model C, the *mixed* model, allows both effects.

The null hypothesis assumes a unit root with exogenous structural break since the deterministic trend function includes dummy variables (DU_t, DT_t, DT_t^*), and the alternative is a *segmented-* or *broken-trend* stationary system which also incorporates the same dummy variables. Perron [111] extended the Dickey-Fuller testing strategy to ensure a consistent testing procedure against shifting trend functions, using the t-statistics $t_{\hat{\rho}}(\lambda)$ which depend on the location of the break point $\lambda = T_B/T$ with $\lambda \in [0, 1]$. Perron tabulated critical values for fixed values of λ.

Others unit root tests with a break at a known point in time have been developed. Perron [112, 113]) and Perron and Vogelsang [119] extended the Perron test for a break in mean, whereas Amsler and Lee [4] modified the Schmidt-Phillips [135] test in the presence of a structural change[13].

Perron's procedure is a conditional test given a known break point. This assumption of a known break date (treated as an exogenous event) raised the problem of pre-testing and data-mining regarding the choice of the break data (Christiano [37]). Kim et al. [67] showed that that the Perron [111] tests are biased in the presence of an erroneous location of the break point[14].

After Perron [111], several methods have been developed for endogenizing the choice of a break point into testing procedures in which the date of the break point is *a priori* unknown and determined from the data. One of these is the Zivot and Andrews [155] test. They developed unit root tests with an endogenous structural break. The test procedure specifies the null hypothesis as an integrated process without exogenous structural break, and the alternative assumes a trend-stationary process with a one-time break in the trend occurring at an unknown time. The goal is to estimate the breakpoint that gives the most weight to the trend-stationary alternative. The time of break is selected by choosing the value of T_B for which the Dickey-Fuller t-statistic $t_{\hat{\rho}}$ is minimized:

$$\tilde{t}_{\hat{\rho},i} = \inf_{\lambda \in \wedge} t_{\hat{\rho},i}(\lambda) \qquad\qquad i = \text{A,B,C}$$

where $\wedge$ is a closed subset of $(0,1)$ and $\lambda = T_B/T$.

Nunes, Newbold and Kuan [104, 105], Vogelsang and Perron [150], and Lee and Strazicich [78] criticized the Zivot-Andrews test in two ways: first, assuming no break under the null hypothesis[15] and second, using a minimum sequential Dickey-Fuller test. There have several solutions to these problems. Lee and Strazicich [77] and Perron and Rodriguez [116] proposed endogenous break unit root tests based on Schmidt-Phillips [135] test, and ERS [50] and Ng-Perron [103] tests, respectively, rather than Dickey-Fuller test. Perron and Vogelsang [118] and Perron [114] suggested an alternative method to select the break date by choosing it such that the absolute value of the t-statistic on the coefficient of the break is maximized[16]. Banerjee, Lumsdaine and Stock [13] applied variety of recursive and sequential tests endogenizing the break point.

Moreover, Lee and Strazicich [78] showed that the Zivot-Andrews [155] and Perron [114] endogenous break unit root tests tend to determine the break point incorrectly at $T_B - 1$ instead of at the true break T_B, and more so as the magnitude of the break increases (results are similar under the null and alternative hypotheses).

---

[13]See Lanne and Lütkepohl [73] for a comparison of different unit root tests with a break at a known point in time.

[14]Hecq and Urbain [62] and Montañés [95] obtained similar results in the context of the Perron [112] tests.

[15]Nunes et al. [105] and Lee and Strazicich [78] provide evidence that assuming no break under the null in endogenous break test lead to significant rejection of the unit root null when the data generating process is a unit root with break.

[16]Perron and Rodriguez [116] showed that this method can yield tests with less power.

This previous literature consider endogenizing only one break point but do not consider the possibility of two break points. Kim, Leybourne and Newbold [67] showed that the Perron [111] and Zivot-Andrews tests may be biased when a second break is present but not taken into account. Therefore, Lumsdaine and Papell [91], Clemente et al. [39], and Lee and Strazicich [80] developed endogenous two-break unit root tests by extending the Zivo-Andrews [155], Perron-Vogelsang [118] and Lee-Strazicich [77] tests, respectively. However, no endogenous break unit root tests have been proposed to more than two breaks[17].

It can also be observed that these tests generally propose three models according to the form of break but do not select them. This gives different results depending on the model chosen. The conclusions thus depend on the choice of model. Furthermore, Sen [138] showed that serious power distorsions occur if the form of break is misspecified.

The breaks considered were breaks in trends, mostly one break and in a few cases multiple breaks. However, the non-stationarity tests can be biased by another type of points: the outliers. Furthermore, Balke and Fomby [12], Bradley and Jansen [22] and Darné and Dieblot [41] showed that these outliers exist in most macroeconomics series and most of them correspond to major economic events. Generally, four main types of outliers are considered: the additive outliers (AO), the innovative outliers (IO), the level shifts (LS) and the temporary changes (TC)[18]. The structural breaks considered above correspond to one type of outliers[19] (see Maddala and Kim [92]). It has been noted in several papers that outliers lead to size distortions in unit root tests. The type of distortion depends on the type of outliers. For example, Franses and Haldrup [52] and Shin et al. [140] showed that the presence of additive outliers induces in the errors a negative moving-average component which causes the unit root tests to exhibit substantial size distorsions towards rejecting the null hypothesis too often (Vogelsang [149]). To solve this problem, Franses and Haldrup [52] and Shin et al. [140], Vogelsang [149] and Perron and Rodriguez [117] proposed procedures for testing unit roots in the presence of AOs. Another approach to dealing with AOs is to apply the Ng and Perron [103] tests that are robust to negative MA errors (which is a consequence of additive outliers). See Yin and Maddala [154] for the effects of the other types of outliers.

3.2 Stationarity Tests with Structural Changes

Following the studies on the unit root tests, Lee et al. [76], Carrion et al. [29] and Badillo et al. [7] showed that the stationarity tests of KPSS [71] and LMC [82] can be biased toward rejecting the null hypothesis of stationarity in favor of the false

---

[17]Moreover, Bai [8, 9], Bai and Perron [10, 11] and Altissimo and Corradi [3], among others, developed procedures for detecting the number of structural breaks in a time series.

[18]See Tsay [148] and Chen and Liu [35] for a detailed discussion on the outliers.

[19]As suggested by Harvey, Leybourne and Newbold [61] and Lee and Strazicich [80], a structural break under the unit root null hypothesis can be interpreted as a large permanent shock or outlier.

alternative unit root hypothesis when the series contains structural breaks. Therefore, Lee and Strazicich [79] proposed a test for stationarity in the presence of a structural break, where the unknown break point is endogenously determined. They consider two models:

$$\text{Model A:} \qquad y_t = \alpha + \delta_1 D_t + e_t$$
$$\text{Model B:} \qquad y_t = \alpha + \gamma t + \delta_1 D_t + \delta_2 DT_t^* + e_t$$

where $D_t = 1$ and $DT_t^* = t - T_B$ for $t > T_B$ and zero otherwise, with T_B being the break point. Model A describes a stationary process with a one-time shift in the level, and Model B allows for a sudden change in the level followed by a change in the slope of the trend function.

Lee and Strazicich [79] select the break point by minimizing the test statistic analogous to that of KPSS [71]:

$$\tilde{\eta}_i = \inf_{\lambda \in \Lambda} \eta_i(\lambda) \qquad\qquad i = A, B$$
$$\text{with} \qquad \eta_i = T^{-2} \frac{\sum_{t=1}^{T} \hat{S}_t^2}{s_{Tl}^2}$$

where Λ is a closed subset of $(0, 1)$ and $\lambda = T_B/T$.

Busetti and Harvey [24] and Kurozumi [70] also extended the KPSS test to take into account the presence of one structural break[20], whereas Carrion et al. [30] deal with two structural breaks. Moreover, Carrion et al. [29] generalized that of LMC [82].

Recently, Carrion [28] showed that the KPSS test that allows for a level shift diverges when the breaking date is erroneously positioned. Therefore, the drawbacks attributed to the unit root tests with structural breaks can be also attributed to the stationarity tests with structural breaks, namely the presence of multiple breaks (more than two breaks), the specification of break form, and the presence of outliers[21].

4 Non-stationarity and Macroeconomic Theory

4.1 Business Cycles

Real Gross National Product [GNP] is a particularly important series to investigate in this regard because the evidence for or against the existence of a unit root in GNP

---

[20]Moreover, Busetti and Taylor [25] showed that stationarity tests can be biased in the presence of variance shifts. They generalized the Busetti-Harvey [24] approach to develop tests that are invariant to breaks in slope/level and variance. Kim et al. [68] obtained the same results for the ADF tests and suggested modifications of the ADF tests to allow structural break in the variance.

[21]Recently, Darné [40] showed that the KPSS tests are very robust to AOs whereas the LMC test exhibits size distorsions and loss of power.

provides support for the validity of competing macroeconomic theories. If GNP can be characterized by stationary movements around a deterministic trend, this supports monetary theories of the business cycle (Friedman [55]; and Lucas [89, 90]). In this case, monetary shocks are the main source of output fluctuation, but have a temporary effect. Therefore, the output returns to its "natural rate", representing the long run path of the economy. Conversely, if GNP has a unit root, and is therefore characterized by a random walk (possibly with a drift), this provides support for real business cycle [RBC] models (Kydland and Prescott [72]; Long and Plosser [86]). The RBC models postulates that the long run path of the economy is mainly guided by real factors such as technological changes. Otherwise, the permanent productivity shocks resulting from technological changes are the main source of economic fluctuations. Therefore, the GNP can be characterized by permanent shocks that are assumed to be randomly generated every observation period.

For the analysis of current economic conditions, if the non-stationarity is deterministic, the shocks driving the fluctuations have no effect on the long term. The output series is then decomposed into a secular component, i.e. a long run deterministic trend (growth), and a cyclical component, i.e. a stationary short run fluctuations around trend. The variations of the current economic conditions are only due to innovations affecting the cyclical component. We have independence between growth and economic fluctuations.

On the contrary, if the non-stationarity is stochastic the output consists of a non-stationary growth component plus a stationary cyclical component, and the fluctuations can be attributed to the both components. In this case, the movements in output are persistent: since the cyclical component is assumed to be stationary, the output fluctuations are mostly associated with the secular component.

4.2 Hysteresis

Theorical investigations consistent with a unit root in unemployment have been undertaken (see, for example, Blanchard and Summers [20]; Lindbeck and Snower [88]). Time series results have played an important role in the controversy over the natural rate and hysteresis hypotheses[22].

The[23] high and persistent levels of unemployment experienced by European countries since the mid-1970s have led to a major reconsideration of the natural rate paradigm of Phelps [121, 122] and Friedman [55]. Theories that describe fluctuations in unemployment as movements around the natural rate have been challenged by hysteresis theories, which model extreme persistence in unemployment, and structuralist theories, which describe fluctuations in unemployment as both movements around and shifts of the natural rate.

---

[22]See Røed [129] and Mikhail, Eberwein and Handa [94] for a review on persistence and hysteresis in unemployment.

[23]See Papell, Murray and Ghiblawi [108].

Traditional theories describe movements of unemployment as fluctuations around the natural rate[24], which is generally defined as the equilibrium (correct expectations) unemployment rate (Phelps [121, 122]; Friedman [55]). They argue that the rise in unemployment rates is caused by adjustment to an underlying long-run equilibrium natural rate of unemployment which has increased in response to changes in structural characteristics of the labour market. The unemployment rate is then assumed to converge to an exogenously determined constant natural rate. Since the natural rate of unemployment is attained when employment is on its normal trend path, shocks to the economy have a temporary effect on unemployment. Therefore, traditional theories imply that unemployment is either level stationary or trend stationary.

Recently, structuralist theories of unemployment (Layard, Nickell and Jackman [75]; Phelps [123]) propose to endogenize the natural unemployment rate in terms of structural characteristics of the economy. They assume that the structural factors in the economy affect the natural unemployment rate[25]. The most of shocks cause temporary movements of unemployment around the natural rate, but occasional shocks cause permanent changes in the natural rate itself. In this case, the unemployment would be stationary around a process that is subject to structural breaks.

Theories incorporating hysteresis have become the most popular explanation for the increase in unemployment in Europe. Hysteresis arises when the medium-term equilibrium rate of unemployment is path dependent, i.e. its depends on the history of unemployment. Otherwise, the current level of unemployment will depend on its own history (Blanchard and Summers [20, 21]). Formally, hysteresis means that temporary shocks have permanent effect on the level of unemployment. There are two notions of hysteresis[26]: (1) the *full* or *pure* hysteresis in which the unemployment depends on a linear combination of its own past values with coefficients summing to one (this means that unemployment should exhibit a unit root); and (2) the *partial* or *loose* hysteresis in which temporary shocks have highly persistent, but not permanent, effect on unemployment, where the sum of coefficients is close but not necessarily equal to one. Generally, the hysteresis hypothesis implies the presence of a unit root (or close to a unit root) in the literature on the time series properties of unemployment.

4.3 Purchasing Power Parity

The purchasing power parity [PPP] states that once converted to a common currency, the real exchange rate, national price levels should be equal. The basic idea is that if goods market arbitrage enforces broad parity in prices across a sufficient range of

---

[24]The concept of the natural rate of unemployment - since its introduction by Friedman [55] in an analogy to Wicksell's concept of the natural rate of interest and its formulation by Phelps [121, 122] - applies the doctrine of monetary neutrality to the unemployment level.

[25]See Papell, Murray and Ghiblawi [108] and Everaert [51] for some possibles examples of structural factors.

[26]See Blanchard and Summers [20].

individual goods (the law of one price), then there should also be a high correlation in aggregate price levels (Froot and Rogoff [56]; Rogoff [130])[27].

The PPP can be viewed as a long-run equilibrium condition for the exchange rates: the real exchange rate should tend toward PPP in the very long run. The long-run PPP is also a central building block in the monetary models of exchange rate determination (Frenkel [53, 54]; Dornbusch [46]).

Research on long-run PPP can be in the form of testing the stationarity of real exchange rates. The rationale behind such tests is simple. The real exchange rate can be expressed as a deviation from PPP (in log form). The real exchange rate[28] is defined as the nominal exchange rate deflated by a ratio of foreign and domestic price levels. In logarithmic form

$$q_t = s_t + p_t^* - p_t$$

where s_t is the logarithm of the nominal exchange rate (the home-currency price of foreign currency), and p_t and p_t^* are the logarithms of the domestic and foreign price indexes, respectively.

If the real exchange rate is stationary around a constant mean, it converges to a constant mean (the PPP value). This implies that deviations from PPP dissipate over time, and therefore PPP is said to hold in long run. There is evidence of long-run mean reversion. The deviations of the real exchange rate from its mean value are only temporary.

If the real exchange rate contains a unit root, it has no mean-reversion property, in which case all deviations from PPP are permanent. This implies that there is no tendency for PPP to hold in the long run.

If the real exchange rate is stationary but around a mean which is subject to occasional structural changes, there is reversion to a changing mean. This hypothesis is called the *quasi purchasing power parity* [QPPP] by Hegwood and Papell [63].

4.4 Convergence

The degree to which (per capita) incomes have converged across countries (or regions), over time, has been the subject of extensive research, and is connected with research in economic growth theory. Two theories have come to dominate the literature on economic growth. The traditional neoclassical growth models (Solow [143]; Cass [31])[29] predict that given the same saving rate, population growth, and technology, economies will "converge absolutely" to the same per capita income in the long-run steady-state. As such, convergence implies that countries with relatively low

---

[27]The concept of PPP is widely attributed to Cassel [32, 33]. See Officer [106] for an extensive discussion of the origins of PPP theory.

[28]Dealing with absolute rather than relative PPP (see Officer [106], and Rogoff [130]) and imposing the symmetry and proportionality conditions: (1) symmetry between domestic and foreign prices, and (2) proportionality between relative prices and the exchange rate (see Edison, Gagnon and Melick [48]).

[29]See Barro and Sala-i-Martin [15].

initial levels of income (poor countries) will grow faster than countries with relatively initial levels of income (rich countries) in order to catch-up. That is, differences in per capita income across different economies will tend to decrease or narrow over time (Baumol [16]; Barro [14]). Given persistent heterogeneous characteristics, neoclassical growth models predict that incomes will "converge conditionally" to their own steady-state or "compensating differential". In contrast endogenous growth models (Romer [131]; Rebelo [128]) can generate patterns of growth that do not exhibit any tendency towards convergence. Initially it was suggested that the presence or otherwise of convergence could form the basis of a test of the neoclassical growth model against the more recent endogenous growth models.

Most empirical work on convergence showed that there exists a negative relationship between initial log per-capita income and rates of growth. Given its dependence upon the factors determining the steady state, Mankiw, Romer and Weil [93] and Barro and Sala-i-Martin [15] refer to this form of convergence as *conditional convergence*[30].

Recently, another form of convergence examines the presence of unit root in the log of the per capita income of one country relative to that of the economy as a whole. We refer to this notion of convergence as *time series convergence*[31].

For each country i, the logarithm of the ratio of per capita income relative to the average of all countries is define as

$$RI_{i,t} = \ln \left(\frac{y_{i,t}}{\frac{1}{n} \sum_{j=1}^{n} y_{j,t}} \right) \qquad i = 1, \ldots, n$$

where $y_{i,t}$ is the per capita income for country i, and n is the number of countries of interest.

Failure to reject the unit root null hypothesis indicates evidence against income convergence. In this case, following a shock to relative income in country i there is no tendency for per capita income to return to the average; thus implying that incomes diverge.

Contrary to this, rejection of a unit root supports the alternative hypothesis that shocks to relative income are temporary, implying that incomes converge.

Carlino and Mills [27] defined *stochastic convergence* (or weak convergence) which postulates convergence if the log relative income is trend stationary whereas Li and Papell [87] proposed a stronger definition of convergence, *deterministic convergence*, where the log relative income is level stationary.

5 Conclusion

This paper presented a selective survey of the literature on non-stationarity tests. We also discussed some problems with these tests and some solutions and alterna-

---

[30]This is a cross-section notion of convergence or β-convergence.

[31]Bernard and Durlauf [17, 18] also proposed definitions of convergence from long-run forecasts. Their definitions of convergence, *catching-up* and *long-run convergence*, are closely linked to the concepts of stochastic and deterministic cointegration.

tives that have been suggested. Although often used, the Dickey-Fuller and Phillips-Perron tests lack power against meaningful alternatives and should not be employed any more in applied work. More efficient and powerful non-stationary tests are now available. We also advocate to pre-test the presence of breaks and outliers before to apply non-stationarity tests because they can imply spurious results.

References

1. Agiakoglou C, Newbold P (1992) Empirical evidence on Dickey-Fuller type tests. Journal of Time Series Analysis 6: 471-483
2. Agiakoglou C, Newbold P (1996) The balance between size and power in Dickey-Fuller tests with data-dependent rules for the choice of truncation lag. Economics Letters 52: 229-234
3. Altissimo F, Corradi V (2003) Strong rules for detecting the number of breaks in a time series. Journal of Econometrics 117: 207-244
4. Amsler C, Lee J (1995) An LM test for a unit-root in the presence of a structural change. Econometric Theory 11: 359-368
5. Arellano C, Pantula SG (1995) Testing for trend stationarity versus difference stationarity. Journal of Time Series Analysis 16: 147-164
6. Ayat L, Burridge P (2000) Unit root tests in the presence of uncertainty about the non-stochastic trend. Journal of Econometrics 95: 71-96
7. Badillo R, Belaire-Franch J, Contreras D (2002) Spurious rejection of the stationarity hypothesis in the presence of a break point. Applied Economics 34: 1917-1923
8. Bai J (1997) Estimating multiple breaks one at the time. Econometric Theory 13: 315-352
9. Bai J (1999) Likelihood ratio tests for multiple structural changes. Journal of Econometrics 91: 299-323
10. Bai J, Perron P (1998) Estimating and testing linear models with multiple structural changes. Econometrica 66: 47-78
11. Bai J, Perron P (2003) Computation and analysis of multiple structural change models. Journal of Applied Econometrics 18: 1-22
12. Balke NS, Fomby TB (1994) Large shocks, small shocks, and economic fluctuations: Outliers in macroeconomic time series. Journal of Applied Econometrics 9: 181-200
13. Banerjee A, Lumsdaine RL, Stock JH (1992) Recursive and sequential tests of the unit-root and trend-break hypotheses: theory and international evidence. Journal of Business and Economic Statistics 10: 271-287
14. Barro RJ (1991) Economic growth in a cross section of countries. Quarterly Journal of Economics 106: 407-443
15. Barro RJ, Sala-i-Martin X (1992) Convergence. Journal of Political Economy 100: 223-251
16. Baumol WJ (1986) Productivity growth, convergence, and welfare: What the long-run data show. American Economic Review 76: 1072-1085
17. Bernard AB, Durlauf SN (1995) Convergence in international output. Journal of Applied Econometrics 10: 97-108
18. Bernard AB, Durlauf SN (1996) Interpreting tests of the convergence hypothesis. Journal of Econometrics 71: 161-173
19. Bhargava A (1986) On the theory of testing for unit roots in observed time series. Review of Economic Studies 53: 369-384

20. Blanchard O, Summers L (1986) Hysteresis and the European unemployment problem. In Fischer (ed) NBER macroeconomic annual MIT Press, Cambridge
21. Blanchard O, Summers L (1987) Hysteresis in unemployment. European Economic Review 31: 288-295
22. Bradley MD, Jansen DW (1995) Unit roots and infrequent large shocks: New international evidence on output growth. Journal of Money, Credit, and Banking 27: 876-893
23. Burridge P, Taylor AMR (2000) On the power of GLS-type unit root tests. Oxford Bulletin of Economics and Statistics 62: 633-645
24. Busetti F, Harvey AC (2001) Testing for the presence of a random walk in series with structural breaks. Journal of Time Series Analysis 22: 127-150
25. Busetti F, Taylor AMR (2003) Variance shifts, structural breaks, and stationarity tests. Journal of Business and Economic Statistics 21: 510-531
26. Caner M, Kilian L (2001) Size distortions of tests of the null hypothesis of stationarity: evidence and implications for the PPP debate. Journal of International Money and Finance 20: 639-657
27. Carlino G, Mills L (1993) Are US regional economies converging? A time series analysis. Journal of Monetary Economics 32: 335-346
28. Carrion JL (2003) Breaking date misspecification error for the level shift KPSS test. Economics Letters 81: 365-371
29. Carrion JL, Sansó A, Artís M (1998) Stationarity tests in the presence of structural breaks. Working Paper DOCT 98R04, Department of Econometrics, Statistics and Spanish Economy, University of Barcelona
30. Carrion JL, Sansó A, Artís M (2003) The KPSS test with two structural breaks. Technical Report, Department of Econometrics, Statistics and Spanish Economy, University of Barcelona
31. Cass DM (1965) Optimum growth in an aggregate model of capital accumulation. Review of Economic Studies 32: 233-240
32. Cassel G (1916) The present situation of the foreign exchanges. Economic Journal 26: 62-65
33. Cassel G (1918) Abnormal deviations in international exchange. Economic Journal 28: 413-415
34. Chan KH, Hayya JC, Ord JK (1977) A note on trend removal methods: the case of polynomial regression versus variate differencing. Econometrica 45: 737-744
35. Chen C, Liu LM (1993) Joint estimation of model parameters and outlier effects in time series. Journal of the American Statistical Association 88: 284-297
36. Choi I (1994) Residual based tests for the null of stationary with applications to U.S. macroeconomic time series. Econometric Theory 10: 720-746
37. Christiano LJ (1992) Searching for a break in GNP. Journal of Business and Economic Statistics 10: 271-287
38. Clements MP, Hendry DF (2001) Forecasting with difference-stationary and trend-stationary models. Econometrics Journal 4: 1-9
39. Clemente J, Montañés A, Reyes M (1998) Testing for a unit root in variables with a double change in the mean. Economics Letters 59: 175-182
40. Darné O (2004) The effects of additive outliers on stationarity tests: A Monte Carlo study. Economics Bulletin 3: 1-8
41. Darné O, Diebolt C (2004) Unit roots and infrequent large shocks: New international evidence on output. Journal of Monetary Economics 51: 1449-1465
42. DeJong DN, Nankervis JC, Savin NE, Whiteman CH (1992) The power problems of unit root tests in time series with autoregressive errors. Journal of Econometrics 53: 323-343

43. Dickey DA, Fuller WA (1979) Distribution of the estimators for autoregressive time series with unit root. Journal of the American Statistical Association 74: 427-481
44. Dickey DA, Fuller WA (1981) Likelihood ratio statistics for autoregressive time series with unit root. Econometrica 49: 1057-1072
45. Dickey DA, Gonzalez-Farias G (1992) A new maximum likelihood approach to testing for unit roots. Proceedings of the Business and Economic Statistics Section, American Statistical Association
46. Dornbusch R (1976) Expectations and exchange rate dynamics. Journal of Political Economy 84: 1161-1176
47. Dufour JM, King M (1991) Optimal invariant tests for the autocorrelation coefficient in linear regressions with stationary and nonstationary errors. Journal of Econometrics 47: 115-143
48. Edison HJ, Gagnon JE, Melick WR (1996) Understanding the empirical literature on purchasing power parity: The Post-Bretton Woods era. Journal of International Money and Finance 16: 1-17
49. Elliott G (1999) Efficient tests for a unit root when the initial observation is drawn from its unconditional distribution. International Economic Review 40: 767-783
50. Elliott G, Rothenberg TJ, Stock JH (1996) Efficient tests for an autoregressive unit root. Econometrica 64: 813-836
51. Everaert G (2001) Infrequent large shocks to unemployment: New evidence on alternative persistence perspectives. Labour 15: 555-577
52. Franses PH, Haldrup N (1994) The effects of additive outliers on tests for unit roots and cointegration. Journal of Business and Economic Statistics 12: 471-478
53. Frenkel JA (1976) A monetary approach to the exchange rate: Doctrinal aspects and empirical evidence. Scandinavian Journal of Economics 78: 200-224
54. Frenkel JA (1978) Purchasing power parity: Doctrinal perspective and evidence from the 1920s. Journal of International Economics 8: 169-191
55. Friedman M (1968) The role of monetary policy. American Economic Review 58: 1-17
56. Froot KA, Rogoff K (1995) Perspectives on PPP and long-run real exchange rates. In Grossman and Rogoff (eds) Handbook of international economics, North-Holland, Amsterdam
57. Fuller WA (1976) Introduction to statistical time series. John Wiley, New York.
58. Fuller WA (1996) Introduction to statistical time series. Second Edition, John Wiley, New York
59. Hall A (1989) Testing for a unit root in the presence of moving average errors. Biometrika 76: 49-56
60. Harvey AC (1989) Forecasting, structural time series models and the Kalman filter. Cambridge University Press
61. Harvey DI, Leybourne SJ, Newbold P (2001) Innovational outlier unit root tests with an endogenously determined break in level. Oxfor Bulletin of Economics and Statistics 63: 559-575
62. Hecq A, Urbain J-P (1993) Misspecification tests, unit roots and level shifts. Economics Letters 43: 129-135
63. Hegwood ND, Papell DH (1998) Quasi purchasing power parity. International Journal of Finance and Economics 3: 279-289
64. Hendry DF, Neale AF (1991) A Monte Carlo study of the effects of structural breaks for unit roots. In Hackl P, Westlund AH (eds) Economic structural change, analysis and forecasting, Springer, Berlin
65. Hobijn B, Franses PH, Ooms M (1998) Generalizations of the KPSS-test for stationarity. Econometric Institute Report No. 9802/A, Erasmus University Rotterdam

66. Hwang J, Schmidt P (1996) Alternatives methods of detrending and the power of unit root tests. Journal of Econometrics 71: 227-248
67. Kim T-H, Leybourne SJ, Newbold P (2000) Spurious rejections by Perron tests in the presence of a break. Oxford Bulletin of Economics and Statistics 62: 433-444
68. Kim T-H, Leybourne SJ, Newbold P (2002) Unit root tests with a break in innovation variance . Journal of Econometrics 109: 365-387
69. King ML (1988) Towards a theory of point optimal testing. Econometric Reviews 6: 169-218
70. Kurozumi E (2002) Testing for stationarity with a break. Journal of Econometrics 108: 63-99
71. Kwiatkowski D, Phillips P, Schmidt P, Shin Y (1992) Testing the null hypothesis of stationary against the alternative of a unit root: how sure are we that economic time series have a unit root? Journal of Econometrics 54: 159-178
72. Kydland FE, Prescott EC (1982) Time to build and aggregate fluctuations. Econometrica 50: 1345-1370
73. Lanne M, Lütkepohl H (2002) Unit root tests for time series with level shifts: A comparison of different proposals. Economics Letters 75: 109-114
74. Lanne M, Saikkonen P (2003) Reducing size distorsions of parametric stationarity tests. Journal of Time Series Analysis 24: 423-439
75. Layard R, Nickell S, Jackman R (1991) Unemployment: Macroeconomic performance and the labour market. Oxford University Press, Oxford.
76. Lee J, Huang CJ, Shin Y (1997) On stationary tests in the presence of structural breaks. Economics Letters 55: 165-172
77. Lee J, Strazicich M (1999) Minimum LM unit root tests. Mimeo, Department of Economics, University of Central Florida
78. Lee J, Strazicich M (2001) Break point estimation and spurious rejections with endogenous unit root tests. Oxford Bulletin of Economics and Statistics 68: 535-558
79. Lee J, Strazicich M (2001) Testing the null of stationarity in the presence of a structural break. Applied Economics Letters 8: 377-382
80. Lee J, Strazicich M (2003) Minimum LM unit root tests with two structural breaks. Review of Economics and Statistics 85: 1082-1089
81. Leybourne SJ (1995) Testing for unit roots using forward and reverse Dickey-Fuller regressions. Oxford Bulletin of Economics and Statistics 57: 559-571
82. Leybourne SJ, McCabe BPM (1994) A consistent test for a unit root. Journal of Business and Economic Statistics 12: 157-166
83. Leybourne SJ, McCabe BPM (1999) Modified stationarity tests with data-dependent model-selection rules. Journal of Business and Economic Statistics 17: 264-270
84. Leybourne SJ, Mills TC, Newbold P (1998) Spurious rejections by Dickey-Fuller tests in the presence of a break under the null. Journal of Econometrics 87: 191-203
85. Leybourne SJ, Newbold P (2000) Behaviour of Dickey-Fuller t-tests when there is a break under the alternatives hypothesis. Econometric Theory 16: 779-789
86. Long JB, Plosser CI (1983) Real business cycle. Journal of Political Economy 91: 39-69
87. Li Q, Papell D (1999) Convergence of international output: Time series evidence for 16 OECD countries. International Review of Economics and Finance 8: 267-280
88. Lindbeck A, Snower DJ (1989) The insider-outsider theory of employment and unemployment. MIT Press, Cambridge
89. Lucas RE (1972) Expectations and neutrality of money. Journal of Economic Theory 4: 103-124
90. Lucas RE (1974) Some international evidence on output inflation tradeoffs. American Economic Review 63: 326-334

91. Lumsdaine R, Papell D (1997) Multiple trend breaks and the unit-root hypothesis. Review of Economics and Statistics 79: 212-218
92. Maddala GS, Kim I-M (2000) Unit roots, cointegration and structural change. Cambridge University Press, Cambridge
93. Mankiw NG, Romer D, Weil DN (1992) A contribution to the empirics of economic growth. Quarterly Journal of Economics 107: 407-438
94. Mikhail O, Eberwein CJ, Handa J (2003) The measurement of persistence and hysteresis in aggregate unemployment. Working Paper, Department of Economics, University of Central Florida
95. Montañés A (1997) Level shifts, unit roots and misspecification of the breaking date. Economics Letters 54: 7-13
96. Montañés A, Reyes M (1998) Effect of a shift in the trend function on Dickey-Fuller unit root tests. Econometric Theory 14: 355-363
97. Nelson CR, Kang H (1981) Spurious periodicity in inappropriately detrended time series. Econometrica 49: 741-751
98. Nelson CR, Kang H (1984) Pitfalls in the use of time as an explonatory variable in regression. Journal of Business and Economic Statistics 2: 73-82
99. Nelson CR, Plosser CI (1982) Trends and random walks in macroeconomic time series. Journal of Monetary Economics 10: 139-162
100. Newey W, West K (1987) A simple positive semi-definite heteroskedasticity and autocorrelation-consistent covariance matrix. Econometrica 55: 703-708
101. Newey W, West K (1994) Automatic lag selection and covariance matrix estimation. Review of Economic Studies 61: 631-653
102. Ng S, Perron P (1995) Unit root tests in ARMA models with data dependent methods for the selection of the truncation lag. Journal of the American Statistical Association 90: 268-281
103. Ng S, Perron P (2001) Lag length selection and the construction of unit root tests with good size and power. Econometrica 69: 1519-1554
104. Nunes L, Newbold P, Kuan C (1996) Spurious number of breaks. Economics Letters 50: 175-178
105. Nunes L, Newbold P, Kuan C (1997) Testing for unit roots with breaks: Evidence on the great crash and the unit root hypothesis reconsidered. Oxford Bulletin of Economics and Statistics 59: 435-448
106. Officer LH (1982) Purchasing power parity and exchange rate: Theory, evidence and relevance. JAI Press, Greenwich
107. Pantula SG, Hall A (1991) Testing for unit roots in autoregressive moving average models. Journal of Econometrics 48: 325-353
108. Papell DH, Murray CJ, Ghiblawi H (2000) The structure of unemployment. The Review of Economics and Statistics 82: 309-315
109. Park HJ, Fuller WA (1995) Alternatives estimators and unit root tests for the autoregressive process. Journal of Time Series Analysis 16: 415-429
110. Perron P (1988) Trends and random walks in macroeconomic time series: Further evidence from a new approach. Journal of Economic Dynamics and Control 12: 297-332
111. Perron P (1989) The great crash, the oil price shock, and the unit root hypothesis. Econometrica 57: 1361-1401
112. Perron P. (1990), "Testing for a unit root in a time series with a changing mean", *Journal of Business and Economic Statistics*, 8, 153-162.
113. Perron P (1993) The great crash, the oil price shock, and the unit root hypothesis: Erratum. Econometrica 61: 248-249

114. Perron P (1997) Further evidence on breaking trend functions in macroeconomic variables. Journal of Econometrics 80: 355-385
115. Perron P, Ng S (1996) Useful modifications to unit root tests with dependent errors and their local asymptotic properties. Review of Economic Studies 63: 435-465
116. Perron P, Rodriguez G (2003) GLS detrending, efficient unit root tests and structural change. Journal of Econometrics 115: 1-27
117. Perron P, Rodriguez G (2003) Searching for additive outliers in nonstationary time series. Journal of Time Series Analysis 24: 193-220
118. Perron P, Vogelsang TJ (1992) Nonstationarity and level shifts with an application to purchasing power parity. Journal of Business and Economic Statistics 10: 301-320
119. Perron P, Vogelsang TJ (1992) Testing for a unit root in a time series with a changing mean: corrections and extensions. Journal of Business and Economic Statistics 10: 467-470
120. Perron P, Vogelsang TJ (1993) A note on the asymptotic distributions of unit root tests in the additive outlier model with breaks. Revista de Econometria 13: 181-201
121. Phelps E (1967) Phillips curves, expectations of inflation and optimal unemployment over time. Economica 34: 254-281
122. Phelps E (1968) Money wage dynamics and labor market equilibrium. Journal of Political Economy 76: 678-711
123. Phelps E (1994) Structural slumps: The modern equilibrium theory of unemployment, interest, and assets. Harvard University Press, Cambridge.
124. Phillips P.C.B. (1987), "Time series regression with a unit root", Econometrica, 55, 277-301.
125. Phillips PCB, Perron P (1988) Testing for unit root in time series regression. Biometrika 75: 347-353
126. Phillips PCB, Xiao Z (1998) A primer on unit root testing. Journal of Economic Surveys 12: 1-51
127. Rappoport P, Reichlin L (1989) Segmented trends and non-stationary time series. Economic Journal 99: 168-177
128. Rebelo S (1991) Long-run policy analysis and long-run growth. Journal of Political Economy 99: 500-521
129. Røed K (1997) Hysteresis in unemployment. Journal of Economic Surveys 11: 389-418
130. Rogoff K (1996) The purchasing power parity puzzle. Journal of Economic Literature 34: 647-668
131. Romer PM (1986) Increasing returns and long-run growth. Journal of Political Economy 94: 1002-1037
132. Said SE, Dickey DA (1984) Testing for unit roots in autoregressive moving average models of unknown order. Biometrika 71: 599-607
133. Said SE, Dickey DA (1985) Hypothesis testing in ARIMA(p,1,q) models. Journal of the American Statistical Association 80: 369-374
134. Saikkonen P, Luukkonen R (1993) Testing for a moving average unit root in autoregressive integrated moving average models. Journal of the American Statistical Association 88: 596-601
135. Schmidt P, Phillips PCB (1992) LM tests for a unit root in the presence of deterministic trends. Oxford Bulletin of Economics and Statistics 54: 257-289
136. Schwert GW (1987) Effects of model specification on tests for unit roots in macroeconomic data. Journal of Monetary Economics 20: 73-103
137. Schwert GW (1989) Tests for unit roots: A Monte Carlo investigation. Journal of Business and Economic Statistics 7: 147-160

138. Sen A (2003) On unit-root tests when the alternative is a trend-break stationary process. Journal of Business and Economic Statistics 21: 174-184

139. Shin DW, Fuller WA (1998) Unit root tests based on unconditional maximum likelihood estimation for the autoregressive moving average. Journal of Time Series Analysis 19: 591-599

140. Shin DW, Sarkar S, Lee JH (1996) Unit root tests for time series with outliers. Statistics and Probability Letters 30: 189-197

141. Shin DW, So BS (2001) Recursive mean adjustment and tests for unit roots. Journal of Time Series Analysis 22: 595-612

142. Shin DW, So BS (2002) Recursive mean adjustment and tests for nonstationarities. Economics Letters 75: 203-208

143. Solow RM (1956) A contribution of the theory of economic growth. The Quarterly Journal of Economics 70: 65-94

144. Stock JH (1990) A class of tests for integration and cointegration. Manuscript, Harvard University

145. Stock JH (1994) Unit roots, structural breaks and trends. In Engle, McFadden (eds) Handbook of econometrics, Vol. 4, North-Holland

146. Tanaka K (1990) Testing for a moving average unit root. Econometric Theory 6: 433-444

147. Taylor AMR (2002) Regression-based unit root tests with recursive mean adjustment for seasonal and nonseasonal time series. Journal of Business and Economic Statistics 20: 269-281

148. Tsay RS (1988) Outliers, level shifts, and variance changes in time series. Journal of Forecasting 7: 1-20

149. Vogelsang TJ (1999) Two simple procedures for testing for a unit root when there are additive outliers. Journal of Time Series Analysis 20: 237-252

150. Vogelsang TJ, Perron P (1998) Additional tests for a unit root allowing the possibility of breaks in the trend function. International Economic Review 39: 1073-1100

151. Xiao Z (2001) Testing the null hypothesis of stationarity against an autoregressive unit root alternative. Journal of Time Series Analysis 22: 87-105

152. Xiao Z, Phillips PCB (1998) An ADF coefficient test for a unit root in ARMA models of unknown order with empirical applications to the US economy. The Econometrics Journal 1: 27-43

153. Yap SF, Reinsel GC (1995) Results on estimation and testing for unit roots in the nonstationary autoregressive moving-average model. Journal of Time Series Analysis 16: 339-353

154. Yin Y, Maddala GS (1997) The effects of different types of outliers on unit root tests. In Fomby, Hill (eds), Advances in econometrics, Vol. 13, JAI Press, Greenwich, Conn

155. Zivot E, Andrews DWK (1992) Further evidence on the great crash, the oil price shock and the unit root hypothesis. Journal of Business and Economic Statistics 10: 251-270

Seasonality, Nonstationarity and the Structural Forecasting of the Index of Industrial Production[*]

Eugene Kouassi[1] and Walter C. Labys[2]

[1] University of Abidjan - Cocody, Department of Economics, P.O. Box V, Abidjan 43, Ivory Coast. Eugene_kouassi@hotmail.com

[2] West Virginia University, Regional Research Institute, Natural Resource Economics Program, 2034 Agricultural Sciences Building, PO Box 6108, Morgantown, WV 26506-6108. wlabys@wvu.edu

Summary. In this paper we focus on two STS models suitable for forecasting the index of industrial production. The first model requires that the index be transformed with a first and seasonal difference filters. The second model considers the index in its second difference filter, while seasonality is modeled with a constant and seasonal dummy variables. Tests designed to discriminate empirically between these two models are also conducted. Our results prefer the performance of the second model, particularly when the conventional ML estimation procedure is replaced by the ALS procedure. This process together with appropriate seasonal adjustment advances the possibility of using the suggested index forecasts to help to predict business cycle turning points.

Key words: : Index of industrial production, Forecasting, Structural time series models.

JEL classification: C22, E23, E27

1 Introduction and Motivation

The analysis and forecasting of indexes of industrial production, both in aggregate and for individual sectors, continues to capture interest, because of their pertinence as measures of economic performance and international cross-performance comparisons. Despite this notable role, consensus has not yet been reached as to which

---

[*]The authors express their gratitude to Professors A. C. Harvey (University of Cambridge, UK), S. J. Koopman (Tilburg University, The Netherlands), J. Goldstein (Bowdoin College, USA), D. Bolduc (University of Laval, Canada), Dr. C. C. A. Winder (De Nederlandsche Bank NV, Amsterdam, The Netherlands), and all the participants to the 39th Canadian Economic Association Meeting in 1999 in Hull (Quebec, Canada) for helpful discussions and suggestions. They also wish to acknowledge the helpful comments and detailed and valuable reports on an earlier version of this paper by two anonymous referees and an editor. The usual disclaimer applies.

appropriate modeling and forecasting strategy to adopt. In this paper we consider two structural models as possibilities for forecasting the index of industrial production. The first is the well-known basic structural time series (STS) model advocated by Harvey and Durbin [13], which requires that the series under consideration be transformed by first and seasonal difference filters (e.g., see Harvey [10, 11]) respectively to achieve stationary. The second is the STS model that makes use of a second difference filter and assumes that the sum of the seasonal components in twelve consecutive periods equals zero and hence the seasonal pattern can be described with a constant and seasonal dummy variables (e.g., see Harvey [10, 11]).

The rationale and primary motive of the present study is the observation that the forecasts for the index of industrial production from the first model, following Harvey and Todd [12], Harvey and Durbin [13] and Harvey [10, 11], fluctuate too widely. This might indicate that the model is mis-specified; and that the second would be more appropriate.

This paper continues as follows. In Section 2, the two competing forecasting models are introduced and their theoretical backgrounds discussed. In Section 3, a brief account is given of a method to test for (seasonal) unit roots in monthly data, as a procedure to choose between the models. Section 4 introduces and extends the asymptotic least squares (ALS) estimation method for the case of monthly data, as an alternative to the classic and well-known maximum likelihood (ML) estimation method of STS models developed by Harvey and Peters (1990). In Section 5, an ALS method is applied to estimate both STS seasonal models, while in Section 6 forecasting schemes are applied to the industrial production series under investigation. From an extensive predictive performance analysis the appropriate model for forecasting the index of industrial production emerges. Finally, in Section 7, some concluding remarks and suggestions for future research are given.

2 Model Specification

Consider y_t a time series to be modeled and which can be decomposed as:

$$y_t = \mu_t + \gamma_t + \vartheta_t, \qquad t = 1, \ldots, T \qquad (1)$$

where μ_t is the trend component, γ_t is the seasonal component, and ϑ_t is the irregular component.

In the STS methodology described by Harvey [10, 11], the process generating the trend is regarded as a local approximation to a linear trend, i.e.,

$$\mu_t = \mu_{t-1} + \beta_{t-1} + \eta_t, \qquad t = 1, \ldots, T \qquad (2)$$

and

$$\beta_t = \beta_{t-1} + \varsigma_t, \qquad t = 1, \ldots, T \qquad (3)$$

where, β_t is the slope and η_t and ς_t are distributed independently of each other and over time with means zero and variances σ_η^2 and σ_ς^2, respectively.

The process generating the seasonal component, γ_t, (in the case of monthly data), is

$$\gamma_t = -\sum_{j=1}^{11} \gamma_{t-j} + \omega_t, \qquad t = 1, \ldots, T \qquad (4)$$

where ω is an independently distributed term with mean zero and variance σ_ω^2. Here, we assume that the seasonal pattern is slowly changing, but by a mechanism which ensures that the sum of the seasonal components over any s consecutive time periods has an expected value of zero and a variance which remains constant over time (e.g., see Harvey [10]).

Unlike the trend and the seasonal component, the irregular component is assumed to be stationary. In the basic model it is a white-noise disturbance term with mean zero and variance, σ_ϑ^2.

2.1 Model 1

Substitution of the processes for the trend and seasonal component in equation (1) leads to the first competing STS forecasting model which is:

$$\Delta\Delta_{12}y_t = (1 + L + L^2 + L^3 + L^4 + L^5 + L^6 + L^7 + L^8 + L^9 + L^{10} \qquad (5)$$
$$+ L^{11})\varsigma_{t-1} + \Delta_{12}\eta_t + \Delta^2\omega_t + \Delta\Delta_{12}\vartheta_t, \qquad t = 14, \ldots, T$$

with L the lag operator, $\Delta = 1 - L$ and $\Delta_{12} = 1 - L^{12}$, and thus $\Delta\Delta_{12}y_t \sim$ a MA(13) process[3], but with a number of non-linear restrictions on the parameters (e.g., see Harvey [10]). In equation (5), $\Delta\Delta_{12}y_t$ is stationary since it has been obtained by a first and seasonal difference filters, respectively, and hence has thirteen roots (solving for the equations $1 - L = 0$ and $1 - L^{12} = 0$ in $\forall$, the vector space of complex numbers), a double unit root, $L = 1$, and eleven seasonal unit roots which are.

$$-1; \pm i; -\frac{1}{2}\left(1 \pm i\sqrt{3}\right); \frac{1}{2}\left(1 \pm i\sqrt{3}\right); -\frac{1}{2}\left(\sqrt{3} \pm i\right); -\frac{1}{2}\left(\sqrt{3} \pm i\right) \qquad (6)$$

where $i^2 = -1$. The seasonal roots correspond to 6, 3, 9, 8, 4, 2, 10, 7, 5, 1, and 11 cycles per year, respectively. The frequencies of these roots are π, $\pm\pi/2$, $\pm 2\pi/3$, $\pm\pi/3$, $\pm 5\pi/6$ and $\pm\pi/6$, respectively.

2.2 Model 2

One may also assume that seasonal pattern is not stochastic but constant over time. In terms of the basic STS model, we have $\sigma_\omega^2 = 0$. For the observed y_t it follows that:

$$\Delta^2 y_t = \varsigma_{t-1} + \Delta\eta_t + \Delta^2\gamma_t + \Delta^2\vartheta_t, \qquad t = 14, \ldots, T \qquad (7)$$

---

[3]More generally the autocovariance function of the basic STS model $\Delta\Delta_s y_t$ based on seasonal dummies indicates that the reduced form is such that $\Delta\Delta_s y_t \sim$ MA(s + 1). The unrestricted reduced form therefore contains more parameters than the structural form, namely s+2 as opposed to s (e.g. Harvey [10], pp. 69, 75 and 511).

The assumption that the sum of the seasonal components in twelve consecutive periods equals zero implies $\gamma_t = \gamma_{t-12}$ - (and therefore $\Delta^2\gamma_t = \Delta^2\gamma_{t-12}$) - and hence the seasonal pattern can be described with seasonal dummy variables (e.g., see Winder [21], p. 99). According to equation (7), $\Delta^2\gamma_t \sim$ a MA(10) process[4] with deterministic seasonal components (e.g., see Harvey [10], p. 69), γ_t has, therefore, only 10 unit roots (e.g., see Harvey [10], pp. 69, 75 and 511).

2.3 Problems of Mis-specification

These two structural forecasting competing models and, more generally, the class of STS models are often used in modeling exercises (e.g., see Harvey [10, 11]). A practical problem which often occurs in empirical studies is that this class of models may produce forecasts that are either very low or very high. This may be caused by the fact that the appropriate model for y_t is equation (5) while using equation (7), or vice versa. This results in over-differencing and mis-specification. Transforming a series with the $\Delta\Delta_{12}$ filter assumes the presence of 13 roots on the unit circle, two of which are at the zero frequency. Hence, in the case which only the Δ filter (or more generally the Δ^k filter applied k times ($k \in R\backslash\{0\}$) is sufficient to remove non-stationarity, the incorrect assumption of the presence of the other roots implies over-differencing. The mis-specification also can originate from treating deterministic seasonality incorrectly, as being stochastic or vice versa. Osborn [19] and Franses [6] empirically demonstrate that this type of mis-specification often occurs.

Since over-differencing and mis-specification are serious dangers in modeling, we will examine the time series structure of the index of industrial production for the countries under investigation without any predisposition regarding the nature of seasonality and/or the non-stationarity they may have.

3 Testing for (Seasonal) Unit Roots

To determine what might be the most appropriate STS specification for a particular data series, we first must understand the underlying data generating process. Indexes of industrial production for (i) Canada, (ii) Germany, (iii) Japan, and (iv) the United States are considered in the present study. The data are from the OECD (1998) historical series "Main Economic Indicators" covering the period January 1960 until April 1998[5]. In the empirical analysis that follows, we consider the log-transformed series.

A preliminary step in industrial production modeling strategy is to examine the seasonality and/ or non-stationarity issues related to these series. Therefore, we tested all indexes of industrial production for the presence of (seasonal) unit roots. Since

---

[4]In fact $S(L)\gamma_t \sim$ MA $(s-2)$, (e.g., see Harvey [10], pp. 69, 75 and 511).

[5]The data for Canada start in January 1961 while that of Germany are available only on the period March 1990 to April 1998 because of the reunification of the western and eastern parts.

the differencing operator L^{12} assumes the presence of 12 roots on the unit circle, this becomes clear by observing that:

$$\left(1-B^{12}\right) = (1-B)(1+B)(1-iB)(1+iB) \tag{8}$$

$$\left[1+\left(\sqrt{3}+i\right)B/2\right]\left[1+\left(\sqrt{3}-i\right)B/2\right]$$

$$\left[1-\left(\sqrt{3}-i\right)B/2\right]\left[1-\left(\sqrt{3}+i\right)B/2\right]$$

$$\left[1+\left(i\sqrt{3}+1\right)B/2\right]\left[1-\left(i\sqrt{3}-1\right)B/2\right]$$

$$\left[1-\left(i\sqrt{3}+1\right)B/2\right]\left[1+\left(i\sqrt{3}-1\right)B/2\right]$$

where all terms other than $(1-B)$ correspond to seasonal unit roots.

Following the methodology developed by Franses [6], the presence of (seasonal) unit roots can be tested using the auxiliary regression which is given by:

$$\Psi(B)y_{8,t} = \varphi_1 y_{1,t-1} + \varphi_2 y_{2,t-1} + \varphi_3 y_{3,t-1} + \varphi_4 y_{3,t-2} + \varphi_5 y_{4,t-1} +$$
$$\varphi_6 y_{4,t-2} + \varphi_7 y_{5,t-1} + \varphi_8 y_{5,t-2} + \varphi_9 y_{6,t-1} + \varphi_{10} y_{6,t-2} +$$
$$\varphi_{11} y_{7,t-1} + \varphi_{12} y_{7,t-2} + \zeta + \zeta_t \tag{9}$$

The $y_{i,t}$ variables are constructed from the original series, y_t, as follows:

$$y_{1,t} = (1+B)\left(1+B^2\right)\left(1+B^4+B^8\right)y_t$$
$$y_{2,t} = -(1-B)\left(1+B^2\right)\left(1+B^4+B^8\right)y_t$$
$$y_{3,t} = -\left(1-B^2\right)\left(1+B^4+B^8\right)y_t$$
$$y_{4,t} = -\left(1-B^4\right)\left(1-\sqrt{3}B+B^2\right)\left(1+B^2+B^4\right)y_t$$
$$y_{5,t} = -\left(1-B^4\right)\left(1+\sqrt{3}B+B^2\right)\left(1+B^2+B^4\right)y_t$$
$$y_{6,t} = -\left(1-B^4\right)\left(1-B^2+B^4\right)\left(1-B+B^2\right)y_t$$
$$y_{7,t} = -\left(1-B^4\right)\left(1-B^2+B^4\right)\left(1+B+B^2\right)y_t$$
$$y_{8,t} = \left(1-B^{12}\right)y_t$$

where B is the backshift operator given by $(1-B^i)y_t = y_t - y_{t-i}$ and all the industrial production index series are in natural logarithms. Lagged values of the dependent variables $y_{8,t}$ are included as right-hand-side variables in the regression to account for a possible ARMA error process where the lagged dependent variables enter the regression through the $\Psi(B)$ lagged polynomial term (e.g., see Joutz et al. [15]). The number of lagged dependent variables is chosen by minimizing the Akaike FPE and the Bayesian Schwartz Criterion. Following the guidelines above, the ζ term includes a constant, eleven seasonal dummies, and a trend. For comparison purposes, we also test for unit roots in an equation where the ζ includes a constant with eleven seasonal dummies, but no trend.

Applying ordinary least squares (OLS) to equation (9) gives estimates of the φ_i. In case there are (seasonal) unit roots, the corresponding φ_i are zero. Due to the fact that pairs of complex unit roots are conjugates, it should be noted that these roots are only present when pairs of φ_i's are equal to zero simultaneously. For example, the roots i and $-$i are only present when φ_3 and φ_4 are equal to zero. There will be no seasonal unit roots if φ_2 through φ_{12} are significantly different from zero. If $\varphi_1 = 0$ then the presence of root 1 can not be rejected. When $\varphi_1 = 0$, and when φ_2 through φ_{12} are significantly different from zero, this implies the presence of a unit root but no seasonal unit root. Therefore, a first difference seasonal dummy variable model is appropriate. However, $\varphi_i = 0$ for $i = 1, 2, \ldots, 12$ implies the presence of both a unit root and eleven seasonal roots. In this case a multiplicative seasonal difference model of the form $(1 - B)(1 - B^{12}$ would be the model of choice.

The general result of testing the null hypothesis that $\varphi_i = 0$ for $i = 1, 2, \ldots, 12$ is that seasonality and non-stationarity in the series of industrial production can be appropriately modeled with a STS model with a constant and seasonal dummy variables (e.g., see Tables 1 and 2). Therefore the regularly and commonly applied Δ_{12} not to mention the $\Delta\Delta_{12}$ filter, is inappropriate for the data under investigation. This latter conclusion is consistent with Beaulieu and Miron [3], Osborn [19], Franses [6] and Joutz et al. [15] who argue in favor of seasonal dummies rather than seasonal differencing.

4 Asymptotic Least Squares Estimation Procedure

There are a number of estimation techniques in the econometric literature that can be used to estimate STS models including the traditional ML (e.g., see Harvey [10]; Harvey and Peters [14]) estimation procedure. ML estimation of the parameters of unobserved components models is generally carried out with the Kalman filter. The review of the Harvey and Peters [14] indicates, however, that this can be quite complex, even if relatively simple STS models are considered; not to mention non-convergence and/or non-optimality issues often encountered in applied econometric studies with the Kalman filter. Various studies have therefore examined frequency domain estimation as an alternative. Young et al. [22], for instance, apply the sequential spectral decomposition approach which enabled them to carry out the estimation process in completely recursive terms, albeit at the cost of strict optimality in ML sense.

In this paper, however, we consider the ALS procedure[6] suggested by Gourieroux, Monfort and Trognon [8], Kodde et al. [16], and Monfort and Rabemananjara [18]. ALS is a two-stage estimation procedure and explores the relationships between univariate ARIMA models and STS models. In the first stage an ARIMA model is estimated and in the second a non-linear optimization problem subject to inequality constraints is solved. This approach yields estimators which are asymptotically efficient and ALS is therefore an alternative for ML estimation via the Kalman filter.

---

[6]ALS estimation technique is very attractive and easy to implement, although it has some limitations (e.g., see Dagenais and Dufour [5]; Hansen et al. [9]).

	Canada	Germany	Japan	USA
t-statistics				
φ_1	0.0210	-0.0602	0.0008	0.0609^a
φ_2	-0.1010^a	0.0373	0.0070	-0.1242^a
φ_3	-0.0298^c	0.1633^b	0.0085	-0.0498^b
φ_4	-0.0121	-0.1899^a	-0.0490^b	-0.0572^b
φ_5	-0.0529^c	-0.1348	-0.0846^a	-0.1027^b
φ_6	0.0035	-0.2261^a	-0.0889^a	0.0065
φ_7	0.0011	0.2281^a	0.0332	0.0136
φ_8	-0.0403	-0.3588^a	-0.1046^a	-0.0723^b
φ_9	-0.0605	0.0254	-0.0428	-0.1884^a
φ_{10}	0.0098	-0.1745	-0.0578	0.0472
φ_{11}	0.0041	0.0703	0.0459	-0.0044
φ_{12}	-0.0072^b	-0.2418^b	-0.1739^a	-0.1180^a
F-statistics				
φ_3, φ_4	1.8104	4.2160^a	2.6494^c	8.6111^a
φ_5, φ_6	4.5489^a	3.2171^b	4.2730^a	8.4041^a
φ_7, φ_8	11.3400^a	12.3412^a	27.1688^a	16.3382^a
φ_9, φ_{10}	1.4224	1.8846	1.0239	6.1451^a
$\varphi_{11}, \varphi_{12}$	5.6636^a	3.7671^b	13.8730^a	13.0988^a
$\varphi_3, \ldots, \varphi_{12}$	5.7823^a	4.3591^a	8.9659^a	11.0993^a

Notes: (i) The auxiliary regression contains constant, trend and seasonal dummies, while $\varphi(B)$ is $(1 - \varphi B^{12})$ and the number of observations for each series equals 447. (ii) a, b and c denote statistical significance at 1, 5, and 10% levels, respectively.

Table 1. Testing for Seasonal Unit Roots (Constant, Trend and Seasonal Dummies).

In its most simple form, the ALS procedure first estimates an ARIMA model and then performs a GLS regression.

4.1 Description of the ALS Procedure

The basic idea of ALS estimation is to use a general specification which is easy to estimate containing the model of interest as a special case. The correspondence between the general and specific model is described by a set of relationships between the parameters of the general model and those of the specific one. ALS estimation is carried out in two stages. In the first stage the parameters of the general model are estimated. Given these estimates and the set of relationships between the parameters of the general and specific model, the ALS estimators of interest are determined in the second stage. This approach yields estimators which are asymptotically equivalent to ML, if the parameters of the general model have been estimated with ML.

Equation (5) implies a restricted MA (13) process for $\Delta\Delta_{12}y_t$. For the general model, which is easy to estimate, an unrestricted MA (13) process is chosen:

	Canada	Germany	Japan	USA
t-statistics				
φ_1	0.0206	-0.0027	0.0004	0.0599^a
φ_2	$-.1028^a$	0.0454	0.0067	-0.1337^a
φ_3	-0.0288	0.1200	0.0088	-0.0489^b
φ_4	-0.0088	-0.2350^a	-0.0483^b	-0.0437^c
φ_5	-0.0502	-0.1766^b	-0.0840^a	-0.0961^b
φ_6	0.0061	-0.2534^b	-0.0883^a	0.0162
φ_7	-0.0026	0.1977^b	0.0329	0.0034
φ_8	-0.0376	-0.3348	-0.1042^a	-0.0637^b
φ_9	-0.057	-0.0361	-0.0420	-0.1758^a
φ_{10}	0.0138	-0.2085^b	-0.0568	0.0677
φ_{11}	0.0020	0.0597	0.0453	-0.0153
φ_{12}	-0.0701	-0.2600^b	-0.1733^a	-0.1058^a
F-statistics				
φ_3, φ_4	1.5637	4.2054^a	2.5955^c	6.4298^a
φ_5, φ_6	4.3684^a	3.3550^b	4.2333^a	8.1403^a
φ_7, φ_8	11.9587^a	10.0507^a	27.2199^a	16.9767^a
φ_9, φ_{10}	1.3569	1.6944	0.9941	5.9401^a
$\varphi_{11}, \varphi_{12}$	5.7489^a	3.9862^a	13.8455^a	12.2980^a
$\varphi_3, \ldots, \varphi_{12}$	5.9927^a	3.6329^b	8.9839^a	10.9079^a

Notes: (i) The auxiliary regression contains constant and seasonal dummies, while $\varphi(B)$ is $(1 - \varphi B^{12})$ and the number of observations for each series equals 447. (ii) a, b and c denote statistical significance at 1, 5, and 10% levels, respectively.

Table 2. Testing for Seasonal Unit Roots (Constant and Seasonal Dummies).

$$\Delta\Delta_{12}y_t = (1 + \theta_1 L + \theta_2 L^2 + \theta_3 L^3 + \theta_4 L^4 + \theta_5 L^5 + \theta_6 L^6 \tag{10}$$
$$+ \theta_7 L^7 + \theta_8 L^8 + \theta_9 L^9 + \theta_{10} L^{10} + \theta_{11} L^{11} + \theta_{12} L^{12}$$
$$+ \theta_{13} L^{13}) \varsigma_t \qquad \varsigma_t \sim \text{NID}(0, \sigma_\varsigma^2)$$

The relationships between the parameters in equations (5) and (7) can be established with the autocovariance of $\Delta\Delta_{12}y_t$, yielding:

$$(1 + \theta_1^2 + \theta_2^2 + \theta_3^2 + \theta_4^2 + \theta_5^2 + \theta_6^2 + \theta_7^2 + \theta_8^2 + \theta_9^2 + \theta_{10}^2 + \theta_{11}^2 + \theta_{12}^2 + \theta_{13}^2)\sigma_\varsigma^2 =$$
$$12\sigma_\varsigma^2 + 2\sigma_\eta^2 + 6\sigma_\omega^2 + 4\sigma_\vartheta^2$$

$$(\theta_1 + \theta_2\theta_1 + \theta_3\theta_2 + \theta_4\theta_3\theta_5\theta_4 + \theta_6\theta_5 + \theta_7\theta_6 + \theta_8\theta_7 + \theta_9\theta_8 + \theta_{10}\theta_9 + \theta_{11}\theta_{10} +$$
$$\theta_{12}\theta_{11} + \theta_{13}\theta_{12})\sigma_\varsigma^2 = 11\sigma_\varsigma^2 - 4\sigma_\omega^2 - 2\sigma_\vartheta^2$$

$$(\theta_2 + \theta_3\theta_1 + \theta_4\theta_2 + \theta_5\theta_3\theta_6\theta_4 + \theta_7\theta_5 + \theta_8\theta_6 + \theta_9\theta_7 + \theta_{10}\theta_8 + \theta_{11}\theta_9 + \theta_{12}\theta_{10} +$$
$$\theta_{13}\theta_{11})\sigma_\varsigma^2 = 10\sigma_\varsigma^2 + \sigma_\omega^2$$

$$(\theta_3 + \theta_4\theta_1 + \theta_5\theta_2 + \theta_6\theta_3\theta_7\theta_4 + \theta_8\theta_5 + \theta_9\theta_6 + \theta_{10}\theta_7 + \theta_{11}\theta_8 + \theta_{12}\theta_9 +$$
$$\theta_{13}\theta_{10})\sigma_\varsigma^2 = 9\sigma_\varsigma^2$$

$$(\theta_4 + \theta_5\theta_1 + \theta_6\theta_2 + \theta_7\theta_3\theta_8\theta_4 + \theta_9\theta_5 + \theta_{10}\theta_6 + \theta_{11}\theta_7 + \theta_{12}\theta_8 + \theta_{13}\theta_9)\sigma_\varsigma^2 =$$
$$8\sigma_\varsigma^2$$

$$(\theta_5 + \theta_6\theta_1 + \theta_7\theta_2 + \theta_8\theta_3\theta_9\theta_4 + \theta_{10}\theta_5 + \theta_{11}\theta_6 + \theta_{12}\theta_7 + \theta_{13}\theta_8)\sigma_\varsigma^2 = 7\sigma_\varsigma^2$$

$$(\theta_6 + \theta_7\theta_1 + \theta_8\theta_2 + \theta_9\theta_3\theta_{10}\theta_4 + \theta_{11}\theta_5 + \theta_{12}\theta_6 + \theta_{13}\theta_7)\sigma_\varsigma^2 = 6\sigma_\varsigma^2$$

$$(\theta_7 + \theta_8\theta_1 + \theta_9\theta_2 + \theta_{10}\theta_3\theta_{11}\theta_4 + \theta_{12}\theta_5 + \theta_{13}\theta_6)\sigma_\varsigma^2 = 5\sigma_\varsigma^2$$

$$(\theta_8 + \theta_9\theta_1 + \theta_{10}\theta_2 + \theta_{11}\theta_3\theta_{12}\theta_4 + \theta_{13}\theta_5)\sigma_\varsigma^2 = 4\sigma_\varsigma^2$$

$$(\theta_9 + \theta_{10}\theta_1 + \theta_{11}\theta_2 + \theta_{12}\theta_3\theta_{13}\theta_4)\sigma_\varsigma^2 = 3\sigma_\varsigma^2$$

$$(\theta_{10} + \theta_{11}\theta_1 + \theta_{12}\theta_2 + \theta_{13}\theta_3)\sigma_\varsigma^2 = 2\sigma_\varsigma^2$$

$$(\theta_{11} + \theta_{12}\theta_1 + \theta_{13}\theta_2)\sigma_\varsigma^2 = \sigma_\varsigma^2 + \sigma_\vartheta^2$$

$$(\theta_{12} + \theta_{13}\theta_1)\sigma_\varsigma^2 = -\sigma_\varsigma^2 - 2\sigma_\vartheta^2$$

$$(\theta_{13})\sigma_\varsigma^2 = \sigma_\vartheta^2$$

or in matrix notation

$$g(\delta) = A\rho \tag{11}$$

with g a vector of functions in $\delta = (\theta_1, \theta_2, \theta_3, \theta_4, \theta_5, \theta_6, \theta_8, \theta_9, \theta_{10}, \theta_{11}, \theta_{12}, \theta_{13}, \sigma_\vartheta^2)'$, $\rho = (\sigma_\varsigma^2, \sigma_\eta^2, \sigma_\omega^2, \sigma_\vartheta^2)'$ and therefore:

$$
A_{StochasticSeasonality} = \begin{pmatrix}
12 & 2 & 6 & 4 \\
11 & 0 & -4 & -2 \\
10 & 0 & 1 & 0 \\
9 & 0 & 0 & 0 \\
8 & 0 & 0 & 0 \\
7 & 0 & 0 & 0 \\
6 & 0 & 0 & 0 \\
5 & 0 & 0 & 0 \\
4 & 0 & 0 & 0 \\
3 & 0 & 0 & 0 \\
2 & 0 & 0 & 0 \\
1 & 0 & 0 & 1 \\
0 & -1 & 0 & -2 \\
0 & 0 & 0 & 1
\end{pmatrix}
$$

Further details of this solution are provided in Appendix 1.

Accounting for the restriction imposed in Section (fixed seasonality), we have a special case of matrix $A_{StochasticSeasonality}$:

$$
A_{FixedSeasonality} = \begin{pmatrix}
1 & 2 & 6 & 6 \\
0 & -1 & -4 & -6 \\
0 & 0 & 1 & 1
\end{pmatrix}
$$

see Appendix 2 for more details

Turning to the general case, given the first-stage estimate of δ, $\hat{\delta}$ ALS minimizes the distances of $g(\hat{\delta}) - A\rho$ in the metric of the matrix

$$
S^{-1} = \left[\frac{\partial g}{\partial \delta'} \Omega \frac{\partial g'}{\partial \delta} \right] \tag{12}
$$

where Ω is the covariance matrix of $\hat{\delta}$, i.e.

$$
\left[g(\hat{\delta}) - A\rho \right]' S \left[g(\hat{\delta}) - A\rho \right] \tag{13}
$$

yielding the ALS estimate

$$
\hat{\rho} = \left[A'SA \right]^{-1} A'S \left[g(\hat{\delta}) \right] \tag{14}
$$

4.2 Asymptotic Properties

If δ consistently, $\hat{\rho}$ will also be consistent. Moreover, the large sample distribution of $\hat{\rho}$ is

$$
\sqrt{T}(\hat{\rho} - \rho) \overset{L}{\Rightarrow} N\left(0, (A'SA)^{-1}\right) \tag{15}
$$

if $\hat{\rho}$ has a large sample normal distribution.

Since the variances are non-negative, an iterative algorithm minimizing the quadratic form (11) subject to inequality restrictions for the parameters is necessary. If, however, all the variance parameters are strictly positive the ALS estimator in equation (12) is equivalent to the GLS estimator in the model:

$$g(\hat{\delta}) = A\rho + u, \qquad E(u) = 0, \qquad \text{and } E(uu') = S \qquad (16)$$

The unrestricted MA (13) model (equation 5) contains fourteen parameters. Since the basic STS model has only twelve unknown parameters, two restrictions have been imposed. These restrictions are based on the Wald test. The Wald statistic has a value equal to the minimum of the objective function (11) multiplied by the number of observations.

5 Asymptotic Least Squares Estimation Results

The ALS estimation procedure is now used to estimate the above STS models. For the sake of clarity and conciseness, the econometric analysis is based upon the following steps:

5.1 Step 1: STS Model Specification

Since the basic STS model has often been applied successfully (e.g., see Harvey [10]; Harvey and Todd [12]; Harvey and Durbin [13]; Winder [21]), we adopt its specification. Also, since unit root tests strongly reject the presence of seasonal unit roots, we examine the alternative model using a deterministic seasonal specification. This model is described by equations (1)-(3) and $\sum_{j=0}^{11} \gamma_{t-j} = 0$. It has been argued above that this model implies a MA (10) process with deterministic seasonals for $\Delta^2 y_t$. This ARIMA process can be used as the general model. In this case, both the STS model and the corresponding ARIMA model have twenty-two parameters. Equation (7) is, therefore, only a reparameterization of the general model. The relationships between the parameters of interest and those of the MA (10) with seasonal dummies can be derived in an analogous way, as performed in the previous section for the basic STS model. Summarizing the two STS models, we have:

Model 1:

$$\Delta\Delta_{12} y_t = (1 + L + L^2 + L^3 + L^4 + L^5 + L^6 + L^7 + L^8 + L^9 + L^{10}$$
$$+ L^{11})\varsigma_{t-1} + \Delta_{12}\eta_t + \Delta^2\omega_t + \Delta\Delta_{12}\vartheta_t$$

Model 2:

$$\Delta^2 y_t = \varsigma_{t-1} + \Delta\eta_t + \Delta^2\gamma_t + \Delta^2\vartheta_t$$

Preliminary Tests

Before estimating these two STS models, we first investigate the underlying time series properties of the level and first differences of the data. Our results indicate an important increase in volatility occurred in the post–1970 and -1980 periods. These periods correspond to:

- 1973 – first oil price shock,
- 1979 – second oil price shock, and
- 1987 – stock market crash.

These findings have important implications for the specification of STS models (e.g., see Goldstein [7]). The heteroscedasticity and trend shifts can be theorized in one of four ways as a result of (e.g., see Goldstein [7]): (i) the normal evolution of the stochastic components of the STS model; (ii) a structural change in the data generation process; (iii) an increase in volatilities, a consequence of (significant) random shocks which increase variances and levels in an autocorrelated (damped, but persistent) manner; or (iv) in the case of increased volatility only, a simple heteroscedasticity pattern (as a continuous function of time). Each of these four perspectives supports, respectively, a different statistical specification: (i) a STS model for the entire sample; (ii) two (or more) separate STS models, one estimated prior to the structural break and the other after; (iii) an autoregressive conditional heteroscedasticity (ARCH) model integrated with a single period STS model; and (iv) a STS model for $\log (Y_t)$ rather than Y_t.

The heteroscedasticity pattern in the data and the possible trend shifts cast serious doubt on the appropriateness of a single uncorrected STS model with assumed homoscedasticity error variances for the entire sample range (e.g., see Goldstein [7]). The existence of a heteroscedasticity pattern which is a positive step-function, rather than a continuous function of time, also suggests that a log transformation may (not necessarily) improve the properties of the statistical estimates.

The ARCH and structural change models are competing perspectives on the evolution of a heteroscedasticity pattern. The former is a stochastic explanation, whereas the latter is structural/deterministic. An ARCH interpretation implies that the damping process is slow enough such that significant supply shocks in the 1970s and 1980s have resulted in increased volatility into the 1990s without a return of $\sigma^2_{\theta_t}$ to its steady state. In contrast, a structural break argument focuses on major regime shifts, circa 1970 and 1980, associated with a significantly lower rate of productivity growth, increased levels of indebtedness, the intensification of international competition, a decline in profitability, and weakness in the international monetary system. These fundamental changes in both the economic and institutional structures created a permanently more uncertain and volatile environment for macroeconomic time series and particulary for the index of industrial production; accounting for these changes is thus, crucial in the modeling process.

Based upon a model selection strategy and the structural shift arguments which are the most likely, we thus report estimation results for three distinct periods: [1960:01–1973:03], [1973:05–1987:09] and [1987:11–1998:04]. These break points have been identified in two recent and separate papers by Goldstein [7] and Badillo et al. [2]. The results reported below are robust for alternative break points between these sub-periods and the log-transformation appears to improve diagnostics and post-sample testing.

5.2 Step 2: STS Model Estimation and Results

Tables 3 and 4 present the ALS estimates for the two STS models, respectively. Because of the large amount of information, all results of estimation will not be discussed in detail. Instead, we focus on some general features and mention some salient facts. The first remarkable result is that for all of the industrial production index series, the seasonal dummy variables are significant in the $\Delta^2 \ln y_t$ STS model; this confirms the appropriateness of the inclusion of these variables in this STS model. A second important result is that for the STS models with stochastic seasonality two of the hyper-parameters equal zero, namely the variance of the seasonal disturbance term and the variance of the slope. This might suggest that seasonality is fixed or constant over time rather than stochastic and thus seasonality may be modeled by a constant and seasonal dummy variable. In the case of the STS model with seasonal dummy variables the two hyper-parameters that equal zero are the variance of the level and the slope. In addition, the hyper-parameters from the STS model with seasonal dummy variables are significant and relatively smaller than that of the basic STS model; this implies that the STS model with seasonal dummy variables ($\Delta^2 \ln y_t$ model) is more accurate than the STS model with stochastic seasonality ($\Delta\Delta_{12} \ln y_t$ model).

5.3 Step 3: Diagnostics

The appropriateness of the two STS models ($\Delta\Delta_{12} \ln y_t$ and $\Delta^2 \ln y_t$ models) is now evaluated based on goodness-of-fit statistics[7] which are reported in Tables 3 (for the $\Delta\Delta_{12} \ln y_t$ model) and 4 (for the $\Delta^2 \ln y_t$ model), respectively. The goodness-of-fit statistics considered are: the prediction error variance for one-step-ahead predictions, the Box-Ljung test for serial correlation of the residuals, Q(lag length), the Jarque-Bera test for normality of the residuals, N, a standard split sample test for heteroscedasticity, H, the percentage improvement in fit over a random walk plus drift model, R_D^2, and the percentage improvement in fit over a random walk plus drift and fixed seasonals, R_S^2. The normality statistic has under the null a $\chi^2(2)$ distribution. The statistic for heteroscedasticity ($F(25,25)$) distributed and the Ljung-Box statistic has under the null of white noise a $\chi^2(12)$ distribution. The prediction error variance for one-step-ahead predictions is globally satisfactory for all of the indexes of industrial production (e.g., see Table 4). In addition, results in Table 4 show that normality and heteroscedasticity have to be rejected for the majority of the industrial production index series when using the $\Delta\Delta_{12} \ln y_t$ model.

The R_D^2 statistics, which report the percentage improvement in fit over the random walk with drift model, range from 0.03 to 0.15 for the $\Delta\Delta_{12} \ln y_t$ model, while they

---

[7]The goodness-of-fit statistics used are based on Harvey's definitions and notations (e.g., see Harvey [10]).

range from 0.21 to 0.43 for the $\Delta^2 \ln y_t$ model. This result provides further evidence for the appropriateness of this latter specification ($\Delta^2 \ln y_t$ model) in modeling the index of industrial production.

The R_S^2 statistics, which also report the percentage improvement in fit over the random walk drift model and fixed seasonals, range from 0.05 to 0.11 for the $\Delta\Delta_{12} \ln y_t$ model and 0.15 to 0.35 for the $\Delta^2 \ln y_t$ model. This result is indeed another support for the appropriateness of this latter specification ($\Delta^2 \ln y_t$ model) in modeling the index of industrial production.

5.4 Step 4: Post-Sample Testing

To further evaluate the adequacy of the estimated models, we also assessed their post-sample predictive performance. In each case, the formal post-sample predictive test was based on the CUSUM test (e.g., see Harvey [10], pp. 257 and 272). An alternative test considered as well is the Chow test. Under the null hypothesis that the model is correctly specified, the Chow statistic is $F(14, 119)$ distributed for sub-period 1, $F(17, 145)$ distributed for sub-period 2, and $F(12, 100)$ distributed for sub-period 3; while on these same sub-periods the CUSUM statistic has a $t(119)$, $t(145)$ and $t(100)$ distribution respectively. Except in a few cases (e.g., see Table 4), the post-sample results indicate rather better prediction performance for the $\Delta^2 \ln y_t$ model than for the $\Delta\Delta_{12} \ln y_t$ model; this provides additional evidence of the appropriateness of the STS with seasonal dummies in modeling the index of industrial production.

6 Forecasting

To evaluate the $\Delta\Delta_{12} \ln y_t$ and $\Delta^2 \ln y_t$ models with respect to their forecasting performance; and following Andrews [1], forecasts for the 12 months out-of-sample are generated from each of the two models.

To investigate whether there are significant differences between the forecasts, the non-parametric sign (exact binomial), sign (normal approximation), Wilcoxon-ranks and Van der Waerden (normal scores) tests and a number of evaluating criteria are considered in Table 5. Discriminating test results do not establish a clear superiority for either of the two models. The general result with respect to the criteria mean error (ME) through root mean squared error (RMSE) and Theil's U statistic, however, seems to be that the $\Delta^2 \ln y_t$ model outperforms the $\Delta\Delta_{12} \ln y_t$ model, irrespective of country and sub-period consideration. It is also clear that the number of positive forecast errors M from using the $\Delta^2 \ln y_t$ model are closer to what might have been expected on average, while those when using a $\Delta\Delta_{12} \ln y_t$ model are higher and out of any reasonable range.

From the results of (i) PIMSE, which denotes the percentage improvement of forecasts from the $\Delta^2 \ln y_t$ model with respect to mean squared error, and of (ii) SIGNSE, which reports the number of times the squared error of $\Delta^2 \ln y_t$ model is smaller than that of $\Delta\Delta_{12} \ln y_t$ model in pairwise comparison, it clearly appears that most of the differences between the models are significant and are in favor of the $\Delta^2 \ln y_t$ model.

7 Final Remarks

In this paper, it has been shown that correctly taking account of the type of seasonality and non-stationarity in monthly data can improve forecasting performance. This is illustrated in the context of the STS models which include a number of variants (STS with trend; STS with trend and cycle; STS with trend and seasonality; STS with trend, cycle and seasonality etc.), and thus feature a high risk of increased misspecification based on inappropriate data transformations.

The major result of the paper, which is applied to the forecasting of the index of industrial production, is that the recognition of the presence of seasonal unit roots can have important implications for forecasting and model building. Recent additional arguments for not automatically and systematically applying difference or moving average filters can be found in Franses [6]. The understanding and control of the properties of these filters based on their transfer functions is a necessary, though not sufficient, condition for adequately modeling and forecasting of economic time series. Finally, we have shown that employing the ALS estimation procedure together with the STS approach can provide production index forecasts of high accuracy, making it a useful alternative to other production index forecasting approaches based on explanatory variables for forecasting turning points in the business cycle.

	Country					
	Canada	Germany	Japan		USA	
			[1960:01 - 1973:03]			
(i) Parameter Estimates						
σ_ϕ^2	1.085	—	0.980	0.019	0.908	0.0002
σ_η^2	0.001	—	0.013	0.002	0.024	0
σ_ζ^2	0	—	0	0	0	0
σ_ω^2	0	—	0	0	0	0
(ii) Diagnostics						
Prediction Error Variance	1.023	—	1.022	0.0003	0.991	0.0003
Heteroskedasticity	3.474[a]	—	0.545	0.544	1.074	1.073
Ljung-Box Q(24) statistic	8.236	—	35.508[a]		22.887[b]	
Ljung-Box Q(36) statistic	11.552	—	49.168[a]		37.423[b]	
Jarque-Bera Normality statistic	27.353[a] —	—	0.423	2.539	2.344	1.028
R_D^2	0.552	—	0.532	0.533	0.436	0.437
R_S^2	0.524	—	0.523	0.521	0.428	0.429
(iii) Post-sample Testing						
Chow F-test	3.548[a]	—	0.688		0.330	2.051[c]
CUSUM-test	0.554	—	1.047		-1.265	-1.266

Table 3. Estimation Results of Models for $\Delta_1 \Delta_{12} \ln y_t$.

Country

[1973:05 - 1987:09]

	Canada	Germany	Japan		USA	
(i) Parameter Estimates						
σ^2_ε	1.017	—	0.917	0.0004	0.635	0.0001
σ^2_η	0.006	—	0.023	0	0.117	0
σ^2_ζ	0	—	0	0	0	0
σ^2_ω	0	—	0	0	0	0
(ii) Diagnostics						
Prediction Error Variance	1.032	—	1.008	0.0004	0.913	0.0002
Heteroskedasticity	0.671	—	0.661	0.660	0.515	0.517
Ljung-Box Q(24) statistic	24.186[b]	—	29.099[a]		25.180[a]	
Ljung-Box Q(36) statistic	38.479[b]	—	40.027[b]		33.788[c]	
Jarque-Bera Normality statistic	1.900	—	11.056[b]	1.799	0.055	4.972
R^2_D	0.539	—	0.512	0.511	0.307	0.308
R^2_S	0.536	—	0.504	0.514	0.300	0.299
(iii) Post-sample Testing						
Chow F-test	3.036[a]	—	0.605	1.011	0.531	0.633
CUSUM-test	0.720	—	0.596	0.599	0.145	0.147

Table 3. Continued.

	Country				
	Canada	Germany	Italy	Japan	USA
			[1987:11 - 1998:04]		
(i) Parameter Estimates					
σ_ε^2	1.057	0.829	0.0002	0.797	0.686
σ_η^2	0.0004	0	0	0	0
σ_ς^2	0	0	0	0	0
σ_ω^2	0	0.003	0.0002	0.0001	0.0003
(ii) Diagnostics					
Prediction Error Variance	0.995	1.165	0.0007	0.772	0.729
Heteroskedasticity	0.936	1.288	1.016	1.102	0.148
Ljung-Box Q(24) statistic	9.313	10.218	—	14.949	19.888[a]
Ljung-Box Q(36) statistic	16.620	18.199	—	30.716	29.841
Jarque-Bera Normality statistic	0.023	0.237	0.019	75.531[a]	492.999[a]
R_D^2	0.585	0.555	0.583	0.643	0.628
R_S^2	0.574	0.534	0.557	0.614	0.596
(iii) Post-sample Testing					
Chow F-test	2.316[a]	1.197	2.244[a]	1.396	3.023[a]
CUSUM-test	0.091	-0.232	-0.024	-1.527	-0.548

Notes: a, b and c indicate statistical significance at 1%, 5% and 10% levels, respectively.

Table 3. Continued.

	Country [1960:01 - 1973:03]			
	Canada	Germany	Japan	USA
(i) Parameter Estimates				
γ_1	1.442^a	—	-1.928^a	0.955^a
γ_2	1.425^a	—	1.367^a	0.621^a
γ_3	0.351^a	—	-0.254^a	-0.185^c
γ_4	1.005^a	—	-2.152^a	-0.040
γ_5	0.839^a	—	0.234^b	0.259^b
γ_6	1.072^a	—	-0.017	0.586^a
γ_7	-0.555^a	—	-0.772^a	-1.743^a
γ_8	2.395^a	—	-0.848^a	2.511^a
γ_9	1.069^a	—	0.544^a	0.102
γ_{10}	0.272^b	—	-0.935^a	-0.492^a
γ_{11}	1.025^a	—	-0.557^a	-0.309^b
σ^2_ψ	4.17×10^{-6}	—	0.0006	0.002
σ^2_ζ	0	—	0	0
σ^2_η	0	—	0	0
σ^2_ε	0.031	—	0.045	0.082
(ii) Diagnostics				
Prediction Error Variance	0.030	—	0.046	0.090
Heteroskedasticity	2.640^a	—	0.594	1.266
Ljung-Box Q(24) statistic	36.313^a	—	82.996^a	20.197
Ljung-Box Q(36) statistic	39.899^a	—	94.348^a	35.288
Jarque-Bera Normality statistic	83.115^a	—	2.560	1.886
R^2_D	0.985	—	0.984	0.968
R^2_S	0.880	—	0.856	0.638
(iii) Post-sample Testing				
Chow F-test	1.162	—	0.951	2.235^a
CUSUM-test	1.006	—	1.204	-0.168

Table 4. Estimation Results of Models for $\Delta^2 \ln y_t$.

	Country [1973:05 - 1987:09]			
	Canada	Germany	Japan	USA
(i) Parameter Estimates				
Y_1	1.899^a	—	-1.605^a	0.976^a
Y_2	1.691^a	—	1.581^a	0.933^a
Y_3	0.168^c	—	0.041	-0.536^a
Y_4	0.737^a	—	-1.501^a	0.174
Y_5	1.166^a	—	-0.119	0.350^a
Y_6	1.566^a	—	0.450^a	0.933^a
Y_7	-0.799	—	-0.515^a	-1.592^a
Y_8	2.928^a	—	-1.095^a	2.192^a
Y_9	1.317^a	—	1.316^a	-0.132
Y_{10}	0.196^b	—	-1.105^a	-0.451^a
Y_{11}	1.215^a	—	-0.184	-0.061
σ^2_ζ	0.0004	—	0.006	0.013
σ^2_ψ	0	—	0	0
σ^2_η	0	—	0	0
σ^2_ξ	0	—	0	0
σ^2_ω	0.034	—	0.033	0.072
(ii) Diagnostics				
Prediction Error Variance	0.035	—	0.035	0.113
Heteroskedasticity	0.678	—	0.782	0.596
Ljung-Box Q(24) statistic	33.653^a	—	41.573^a	33.497^a
Ljung-Box Q(36) statistic	47.031^a	—	56.586^a	45.412^a
Jarque-Bera Normality statistic	2.293	—	0.273	16.541
R^2_D	0.987	—	0.987	0.961
R^2_S	0.786	—	0.812	0.685
(iii) Post-sample Testing				
Chow F-test	0.393	—	1.136	0.688
CUSUM-test	0.457	—	0.489	0.158

Table 4. Continued.

		Country		
	Canada	Germany	Japan	USA
		[1987:11 - 1998:04]		
(i) Parameter Estimates				
γ_1	2.223^a	0.538^b	-0.996^a	0.918^a
γ_2	1.707^a	1.115^a	1.223^a	-0.060
γ_3	0.229^a	1.109^a	0.311^b	-0.332
γ_4	0.852^a	-1.062^a	-1.822^a	-0.158
γ_5	1.319^a	0.739^a	0.338^b	0.277^b
γ_6	1.523^a	1.116^a	0.777^a	0.788^a
γ_7	-0.570^a	-0.489^b	-0.472^a	-1.657^a
γ_8	3.251^a	0.292	-1.024^a	1.944^a
γ_9	0.864^a	2.451^a	1.362^a	-0.946^a
γ_{10}	0.568^b	-0.759^a	-0.937^a	-0.312^b
γ_{11}	1.297^a	0.052	-0.027	-0.212^b
σ^2_ϕ	2.01×10^{-5}	0	0	0.226
σ^2_η	0	0	1.18×10^{-5}	0
σ^2_ζ	0	0.002	0	0
σ^2_ω	0.019	0.077	0.030	0.016
(ii) Diagnostics				
Prediction Error Variance	0.017	0.073	0.017	0.286
Heteroskedasticity	1.393	1.136	0.073	0.076
Ljung-Box Q(24) statistic	16.688	16.126	16.626	13.793
Ljung-Box Q(36) statistic	28.821	30.853	31.819	22.676
Jarque-Bera Normality statistic	0.221	2.076	67.373^a	1832.027^a
R^2_D	0.994	0.981	0.994	0.913
R^2_S	0.845	0.139	0.664	0.668
(iii) Post-sample Testing				
Chow F-test	3.509^a	1.707^c	0.306	0.263
CUSUM-test	0.189	-0.974	0.558	-0.429

Notes: a, b and c indicate statistical significance at 1%, 5% and 10% levels, respectively.

Table 4. Continued.

216 Eugene Kouassi and Walter C. Labys

	Canada		Germany		Japan		USA	
	$\Delta\Delta_{12}\ln y_t$	$\Delta^2\ln y_t$	$\Delta\Delta_{12}\ln y_t$	$\Delta^2\ln y_t$	$\Delta\Delta_{12}\ln y_t$	$\Delta^2\ln y_t$	$\Delta\Delta_{12}\ln y_t$	$\Delta^2\ln y_t$
			[1960:01 - 1973:03]					
ME	-0.041	0.010	—	—	-0.007	-0.003	-0.003	0.008
MAE	1.034	0.499	—	—	0.588	0.168	0.742	0.320
MAPE	675.446	47.634	—	—	132.012	72.174	222.099	46.082
RMSE	1.238	0.575	—	—	0.687	0.189	0.868	0.358
M	4	5	—	—	1	0	6	5
Theil's U Statistic	0.634	0.288	—	—	0.456	0.093	0.510	0.161
PIMSE of $\Delta^2\ln y_t$	44.250[b]	—	—	—	27.825[b]	—	41.275[b]	—
SIGNSE	8[b]	—	—	—	12[b]	—	12[b]	—
Sign (exact binomial)	74	—	—	—	76	—	81	—
Sign (normal approximation)	1.123	—	—	—	0.413	—	1.241	—
Wilcoxon Signed-Ranks Test	0.606	—	—	—	0.556	—	1.463	—
Van der Waerden Test	-0.426	—	—	—	-0.422	—	1.602[c]	—
			[1973:05 - 1987:09]					
ME	0.0005	0.003	—	—	-0.002	-0.004	0.028	-0.032
MAE	0.483	0.143	—	—	0.682	0.194	0.416	0.233
MAPE	243.227	131.848	—	—	273.899	33.013	201.264	107.741
RMSE	0.563	0.180	—	—	0.743	0.260	0.501	0.297
M	0	4	—	—	2	3	2	2
Theil's U Statistic	0.482	0.101	—	—	0.558	0.116	0.436	0.165
PIMSE of $\Delta^2\ln y_t$	52.651[b]	—	—	—	42.528[b]	—	24.025[b]	—
SIGNSE	6[b]	—	—	—	11[b]	—	7[b]	—
Sign (exact binomial)	95	—	—	—	95	—	90	—
Sign (normal approximation)	1.216	—	—	—	1.216	—	0.455	—
Wilcoxon Signed-Ranks Test	1.618[c]	—	—	—	0.985	—	0.954	—
Van der Waerden Test	-1.553	—	—	—	-0.768	—	1.092	—

Table 5. Evaluation of the 12 Months Out-of-Sample Forecasting Performance of Models.

	Canada		Germany		Japan		USA	
	$\Delta\Delta_{12}\ln y_t$	$\Delta^2\ln y_t$	$\Delta\Delta_{12}\ln y_t$	$\Delta^2\ln y_t$	$\Delta\Delta_{12}\ln y_t$	$\Delta^2\ln y_t$	$\Delta\Delta_{12}\ln y_t$	$\Delta^2\ln y_t$
			[1987:11 - 1998:04]					
ME	-0.008	-0.007	-0.150	-0.001	-0.027	-0.001	-0.029	0.001
MAE	0.802	0.199	1.009	0.249	0.623	0.282	0.312	0.185
MAPE	101.052	219.681	86.757	23.300	179.345	75.234	128.211	64.267
RMSE	0.996	0.251	1.224	0.346	0.715	0.307	0.392	0.229
M	6	3	7	4	3	3	0	0
Theil's U Statistic	0.986	0.133	0.584	0.159	0.630	0.152	0.519	0.137
PIMSE of $\Delta^2\ln y_t$	16.216[b]	–	23.500[b]	–	38.600[b]	–	58.416[b]	–
SIGNSE	12[b]	–	12[b]	–	12[b]	–	3[b]	–
Sign (exact binomial)	66	–	42	–	70	–	69	–
Sign (normal approximation)	0.536	–	0.222	–	1.158	–	0.979	–
Wilcoxon Signed-Ranks Test	0.177	–	0.706	–	1.124	–	0.545	–
Van der Waerden Test	0.124	–	0.676	–	-0.859	–	0.368	–

Notes: (i) The forecast error is defined as the true value y minus the forecasted value f. Forecast evaluation criteria are the mean error, ME, mean absolute error, MAE, mean absolute percentage error, MAPE, and root mean squared error, RMSE. M denotes the number of times y exceeds f. U is Theil's test statistic. PIMSE denotes the percentage improvement of forecasts from the Δ^2 ln y_t model with respect to mean squared error. SIGNSE refers to the sign test which reports the number of times the squared error of Δ^2 ln y_t model is smaller than that of $\Delta\Delta_{12}$ ln y_t model in y_t model with respect to mean squared error. The Binomial sign test statistic reports the value of the sample proportion above and below the true median from a binomial pairwise comparison. The Binomial sign test statistic reports the value of the sample proportion above and below the true median if the sample were drawn randomly from a normal distribution. The Normal approximation sign test statistic refers to the value of the sample proportion above and below the true median if the sample were drawn randomly from a normal distribution. The Wilcoxon signed-rank test statistic refers to the ranks of positive differences between the forecasts. The Van der Waerden test statistic is similar to the Wilcoxon signed-rank test but it is based on smoothed ranks. Definitions and asymptotic results for these non-parametric test can be found in Conover (1980) and Sheskin (1997). (ii) a, b and c indicate statistical significance at 1%, 5% and 10% levels, respectively.

Table 5. Evaluation of the 12 Months Out-of-Sample Forecasting Performance of Models (continued).

Appendix 1. Autocovariances of $\Delta\Delta_{12}y_t$

$$\begin{aligned}
\Delta\Delta_{12}y_t &= (1+L+L^2+L^3+L^4+L^5+L^6+L^7+L^8+L^9+L^{10}\\
&\quad +L^{11})\varsigma_{t-1}+\Delta_{12}\eta_t+\Delta^2\omega_t+\Delta\Delta_{12}\vartheta_t\\
&= \varsigma_{t-1}+\varsigma_{t-2}+\varsigma_{t-3}+\varsigma_{t-4}+\varsigma_{t-5}+\varsigma_{t-5}+\varsigma_{t-7}+\varsigma_{t-8}\\
&\quad +\varsigma_{t-9}+\varsigma_{t-10}+\varsigma_{t-11}+\varsigma_{t-12}+\eta_t-\eta_{t-12}+\omega_t-2\omega_{t-1}\\
&\quad +\omega_{t-2}+\vartheta_t-\vartheta_{t-1}-\vartheta_{t-12}+\vartheta_{t-13}
\end{aligned}$$

Define $X_t = \Delta\Delta_{12}y_t$, we obtain:

1. $E[X_tX_t] = 12\sigma_\varsigma^2+2\sigma_\eta^2+6\sigma_\omega^2+4\sigma_\vartheta^2$
2. $E[X_tX_{t-1}] = 11\sigma_\varsigma^2-4\sigma_\omega^2-2\sigma_\vartheta^2$
3. $E[X_tX_{t-2}] = 10\sigma_\varsigma^2+\sigma_\omega^2$
4. $E[X_tX_{t-3}] = 9\sigma_\varsigma^2$
5. $E[X_tX_{t-4}] = 8\sigma_\varsigma^2$
6. $E[X_tX_{t-5}] = 7\sigma_\varsigma^2$
7. $E[X_tX_{t-6}] = 6\sigma_\varsigma^2$
8. $E[X_tX_{t-7}] = 5\sigma_\varsigma^2$
9. $E[X_tX_{t-8}] = 4\sigma_\varsigma^2$
10. $E[X_tX_{t-9}] = 3\sigma_\varsigma^2$
11. $E[X_tX_{t-10}] = 2\sigma_\varsigma^2$
12. $E[X_tX_{t-11}] = \sigma_\varsigma^2+\sigma_\vartheta^2$
13. $E[X_tX_{t-12}] = -\sigma_\varsigma^2-2\sigma_\vartheta^2$
14. $E[X_tX_{t-13}] = \sigma_\vartheta^2$
15. $E[X_tX_{t-h}] = 0, \qquad \forall h \geq 14.$

Appendix 2. Autocovariances of $\Delta^2 y_t$

$$\begin{aligned}
\Delta^2 y_t &= \varsigma_{t-1}+\Delta\eta_t+\Delta^2\gamma_t+\Delta^2\vartheta_t\\
&= \varsigma_{t-1}+\eta_t-\eta_{t-1}+\gamma_t-2\gamma_{t-1}+\gamma_{t-2}+\vartheta_t-2\vartheta_{t-1}+\vartheta_{t-2}
\end{aligned}$$

Define $X_t = \Delta^2 y_t$, we obtain

1. $E[X_tX_t] = \sigma_\varsigma^2+2\sigma_\eta^2+6\sigma_\gamma^2+6\sigma_\vartheta^2$
2. $E[X_tX_{t-1}] = -\sigma_\eta^2-4\sigma_\gamma^2-4\sigma_\vartheta^2$
3. $E[X_tX_{t-2}] = \sigma_\gamma^2+\sigma_\vartheta^2$
4. $E[X_tX_{t-3}] = 0, \qquad \forall h \geq 3.$

Appendix 3. Discussion of ML Estimates via the Kalman Filter

In order to compare the ALS estimation results with the ML estimates obtained via the Kalman filter, the two STS models have also been estimated with the computer package STAMP, version 5 (e.g., see Koopman et al. [17]). The results of exact ML estimation in the time domain with numerical optimization carried out by a quasi-Newton algorithm can be obtained upon request from the authors.

In general results from the STS model with seasonal dummy variables based on ML estimation are fairly good and closed to those of ALS estimates discussed in the paper. The estimates of the seasonals are very similar also. The differences for the estimates of the variance parameters are somewhat larger. The t-ratios appear to be larger than those of the ALS estimates, but this result does not hold for all series.

For the results based on the basic STS model, the discrepancies between the Kalman filter estimates and those according to ALS are larger. This holds notably for the series for which two or three variance parameters were found to be zero with ALS.

The appropriateness of the models estimated by ML via the Kalman filter has been examined by the same statistical criteria as in the main text. The results for diagnostics or post-sample testing are very similar to those for the STS models estimated by ALS. This holds notably for the tests for normality and heteroscedasticity except for Canada and Germany and for the second sub-period. With respect to the Ljung-Box statistic the differences between the ALS – and Kalman filter – estimated models are somewhat larger; Ljung – Box statistic being larger for the Kalman filter – estimated models.

The results on post sample predictive testing (CUSUM and Chow test) also yield a similar picture to those for the ALS – estimated models except in the case of Canada and Japan and for the first sub-period.

Appendix 4. Forecast Summary

The following Table provides comparisons of forecast and actual values over time for the index of industrial production.

Model 1

	Canada			Germany			Japan			USA		
	Actual	Predicted	Error	Actual	Predicted	Error	Actual	Predicted	Error	Actual	Predicted	Error
1997:04	120.60	120.57	0.03	100.60	100.60	0.00	100.30	100.30	0.00	123.70	123.70	0.00
1997:05	119.00	119.01	-0.01	94.30	94.34	-0.04	98.70	98.67	0.03	123.00	123.01	-0.01
1997:06	121.70	121.70	0.00	102.90	102.84	0.06	103.40	103.39	0.01	127.10	127.05	0.05
1997:07	110.50	110.48	0.02	101.60	101.57	0.03	107.40	107.42	-0.02	124.10	124.15	-0.05
1997:08	118.50	118.51	-0.01	88.50	88.56	-0.06	94.10	94.10	0.00	129.90	129.83	0.07
1997:09	124.00	123.99	0.01	105.60	105.58	0.02	106.60	106.59	0.01	130.20	130.24	-0.04
1997:10	125.60	125.59	0.01	109.20	109.18	0.02	103.70	103.72	-0.02	129.60	129.60	0.00
1997:11	127.10	127.12	-0.02	106.70	106.71	-0.01	99.30	99.34	-0.04	128.00	128.00	0.00
1997:12	116.20	116.18	0.02	99.30	99.31	-0.01	100.60	100.59	0.01	126.80	126.79	0.01
1998:01	115.20	115.24	-0.04	96.50	96.46	0.04	93.20	93.26	-0.01	127.30	127.28	0.02
1998:02	127.40	127.37	0.03	99.80	99.79	0.01	96.40	96.41	-0.01	128.60	128.59	0.01
1998:03	128.40	128.40	0.00	113.20	113.15	0.05	108.00	108.01	-0.01	128.90	128.90	0.00
1998:04	—	—	—	105.10	105.16	-0.06	94.50	94.50	0.00	126.80	126.81	-0.01

Model 2

	Canada			Germany			Japan			USA		
	Actual	Predicted	Error	Actual	Predicted	Error	Actual	Predicted	Error	Actual	Predicted	Error
1997:04	120.60	120.55	0.05	100.60	100.60	0.00						
1997:05	119.00	119.05	-0.05	94.30	99.33	-5.03						
1997:06	121.70	121.61	0.09	102.90	102.78	0.12						
1997:07	110.50	110.62	-0.12	101.60	101.61	-0.01						
1997:08	118.50	118.35	0.15	88.50	88.68	-0.18						
1997:09	124.00	124.00	0.00	105.60	105.28	0.32						
1997:10	125.60	125.67	-0.07	109.20	109.35	-0.15						
1997:11	127.10	127.06	0.04	106.70	106.74	-0.04						
1997:12	116.20	116.28	-0.08	99.30	99.34	-0.04						
1998:01	115.20	115.15	0.05	96.50	96.42	0.08						
1998:02	127.40	127.27	0.13	99.80	99.77	0.03						
1998:03	128.40	128.50	-0.10	113.20	113.12	0.08						
1998:04	—	—	—	105.10	105.25	-0.15						

Table 6. 12 Months-out-of Sample Forecasts.

References

1. Andrews RL (1994) Forecasting performance structural of time series model. Journal of Business and Economic Statistics 12: 129-133
2. Badillo D, Labys WC, Yangru W (1999) Identifying trends and breaks in primary commodity prices. European Financial Review 5: 315-330
3. Beaulieu JJ, Miron JA (1993) Seasonal unit roots in aggregate U.S. data (with discussion). Journal of Econometrics 55: 305-331
4. Conover WJ (1980) Practical nonparametric statistics. 2nd Edition, New-York, John Wiley and Sons
5. Dagenais M, Dufour JM (1991) Invariance, Nonlinear models and asymptotic tests. Econometrica 59: 1601-1615
6. Franses PH (1991) Seasonality, non-stationarity and the forecasting of monthly time series. International Journal of Forecasting 7: 199-208
7. Goldstein J (1997) Is the endogenous business cycle dead? Southern Economic Journal 63: 962-977
8. Gourieroux C, Monfort A, Trognon A (1985) Moindres carrés asymptotiques. Annales de l'INSEE 58: 91-122
9. Hansen LP, Heaton J, Yaron A (1996) Finite sample properties of some alternative GMM estimators. Journal of Business and Economic Statistics 14: 262-280
10. Harvey AC (1989) Forecasting, structural time series models and the Kalman filter. Cambridge: Cambridge University Press
11. Harvey AC (1994) Time series models. 2nd Edition, Cambridge, MA: The MIT Press
12. Harvey AC, Todd PHJ 1983) Forecasting economic time series with structural and Box-Jenkins models (with discussion). Journal of Business and Economic Statistics 1: 299-315
13. Harvey AC, Durbin J (1986) The effects of seat belt legislation on British road casualties: A case study in structural time series modelling. Journal of the Royal Statistical Society, Series A 149: 187-227
14. Harvey AC, Peters S (1990) Estimation procedures for structural time series models. Journal of Forecasting 9: 89-108
15. Joutz FL, Maddala GS, Trost RP (1995) An integrated bayesian vector autoregression and error correction model for forecasting electricity consumption and prices. Journal of Forecasting 14: 287-310
16. Kodde D, Palm FC, Pfann GA (1990) Asymptotic least squares estimation: Efficiency considerations and applications. Journal of Applied Econometrics 3: 229-243
17. Koopman SJ, Harvey AC, Doornik J, Shephard N (1995) STAMP 5.0 - structural time series package. London: Chapman and Hall
18. Monfort A, Rabemananjara R (1990) From a VAR model to a structural model, with an application to the wage-price spiral. Journal of Applied Econometrics 5: 203-227
19. Osborn DR (1990) A survey of seasonality in U.K. macroeconomic variables. International Journal of Forecasting 6: 327-336
20. Sheskin DJ (1997) Parametric and nonparametric statistical procedures. CRC Press
21. Winder CCA (1997) Structural time-series modelling of monetary aggregates: A case study for eleven European countries. Journal of Forecasting 16: 97-123
22. Young PC, Ng CN, Lane K, Parker D (1991) Recursive forecasting, smoothing and seasonal adjustment of non-stationary environment data. Journal of Forecasting 10: 57-89

Complex Dynamics in Macroeconomics: A Novel Approach

Catherine Kyrtsou[1] and Constantinos E. Vorlow[2]

[1] University of Macedonia, Department of Economics, Egnatia str. 156, 54006, Thessaloniki, GREECE. ckyrtsou@uom.gr

[2] Durham Business School, University of Durham, Mill Hill Lane, Durham DH13LB, UK. K.E.Vorloou@durham.ac.uk

Summary. In this work we employ the Recurrence Quantification Analysis (RQA) framework, effective in discovering evidence of non-linear determinism and complex dynamics in short, noisy and irregular signals. We apply RQA to a set of US macroeconomic time series and simulated sequences in order to provide a classification based on topological aspects of their dynamics. Through RQA we can in general obtain useful information on the quality and complexity of the structure of the dynamics in an economy, as this is embedded in its macroeconomic time series.

Key words: Recurrence Plots, Recurrence Quantification Analysis, Chaos, Complex Dynamics, Macroeconomic Time Series Analysis.

1 Introduction

Deterministic chaos, usually referred to simply as "chaos", implies presence of structure and often very complex order on a global scale but absence of these characteristics on a local scale. Self-organization and emergence are also salient features of chaotic systems. In general, chaotic processes may be characterized by irregular and long-term unpredictable behavior, however this behavior is purely deterministic. Sequences that are outcomes of chaotic dynamics often exhibit some qualitative features of stochastic-random time series. Chaos can often appear as noise, as a quasi-periodic or aperiodic sequence, as a bounded oscillation with an infinite period and a broadband spectrum. Kellert [37] suggests as a working definition for chaos the aperiodic behavior in a deterministic system which exhibits sensitive dependence on initial conditions. The important point here is that complex and chaotic systems can self regulate and respond to external stimulations (such as new information, shocks and "extreme" events) more effectively and flexibly than linear or non-deterministic systems. Moreover such systems have the ability to self-organize and return to stable states only due to internal dynamics and not some exogenous influence. They are often characterized by a feedback mechanism which could be used to control or forecast their future states. Hence, although sensitive to small perturbations of initial conditions, chaotic dynamics may allow for a greater level of efficiency in short term predictions, and they can be controlled around a periodic dynamically unstable state (Ott et al. [52]). Chaos and randomness are frequently confused as there are a few similarities between them (Mayer-Kress [46]) and "traditional" statistical analysis tools may often misinterpret chaotic determinism as randomness. For this reason, the investigation of nonlinearity and complex dynamics (chaos not excluded) should rely on a more sensitive toolkit (Abarbanel [1]).

Nonlinear determinism and complexity is usually observed in various open and dissipative physiological and physical systems, with feedbacks and qualitative dynamics that occasionally resemble much those of economies or financial markets (Mandelbrot [42]; Brock [13]; Hommes [32]; Mandelbrot and Hudson [43]).[3] The possibility of the existence of non-linear determinism in financial or economic phenomena is not a novel idea. One should refer to Mirowski [49, 50] for a historic perspective on the issue and to Barnett and Chen [7], Frank and Stengos [24, 25], Frank et al [23], Scheinkman and LeBaron [58], Brock and Sayers [17], Hsieh [34], Brock et al [16], Brock and Dechert [15], Brock [14], Peters [53], Mayfield and Mizrach [47] for the earlier influential work. However, due to the limitations posed by the available theoretical background, data quality and research technology, there has been no clear answer on the issue of the existence of chaotic-complex dynamics, especially in financial markets. The search for chaos is still an area of rigorous research as the ability to determine the types of dependence and forecast the dynamics of stock prices or key economic indicators, is of paramount importance to activities such as economic planning, financial risk management and optimal design of securities.

Nonlinearity and chaos has been a area of substantial research in economics (Kesley [38]; Barnett and Chen [7]; Baumol and Benhabib [9]; Boldrin and Woodford [11]; Brock [13]; Barnett and Hinich [8]; Butler [19]; Bordignon and Lisi [12]). While there are several pieces of literature centered on the theoretical considerations of the existence of complex or chaotic dynamics in macroeconomic systems (Grandmont [28, 29, 30]; Boldrin and Woodford[11]), empirical confirmation has been difficult, mainly due to the absence of a framework applicable to small information sets such as macroeconomic time series (Frank and Stengos [25, 24]; Brock and Sayers [17]; Scheinkman and LeBaron [59]; Scheinkman [57]; Brock [14]; Brock and Dechert [15]; Brock et al. [16]; Liu et al. [41]). A large part of earlier empirical investigation evolves around the BDS test (Brock and Dechert [15]) which is based on the correlation integral. The main limitation of investigations for chaotic dynamics is the absence of a well established statistical test for chaos. There have also been serious considerations about procedures based on invariant measures, as they may produce biased results for short and noisy sequences (Theiler [62]; Osborne and Provenzale [51]; Wolff [68]; Ramsey et al. [55]; Abarbanel [1]). Hence, practical as well as theoretical issues (Ramsey [54]; Granger [31]), appear to be the main

---

[3]Hence the influence of practices in economic research from other sciences and the birth of *Econophysics* to which research on nonlinear dynamics is a large contributor.

factors contributing to an earlier relative unpopularity of the hypothesis of chaos in economics and finance. However, even in the absence of conclusive empirical evidence and support, the presence of chaos in an economic system has posed in the past serious considerations, especially for policy makers (Bullard and Butler [18]).

In this work, avoiding some of the pitfalls or ambiguities of existing research, we employ a fairly novel methodology effective in discovering evidence of nonlinear determinism and complex dynamics in short, noisy and irregular signals. *Recurrence Quantification Analysis* (RQA, Zbilut and Webber [69]) aims at revealing the details of the system's higher dimensional phase space dynamics from a single observable output. In our case and for demonstration purposes, as such an output we consider sequences of growth rates of key economic indicators from the US economy. Through RQA we can obtain a qualitative and quantitative view of periodical or nonstanionary dynamics, economic shocks, or even examine how long an economy or market remains in a period of relative calmness. Although our aim is not to strongly support the premise that key economic indicators are governed by chaotic dynamics, we entertain the idea that significant lessons can be learned by the application of RQA on economic and financial time series in general. Intuitively, a methodology such as RQA could shed more light on the quality and complexity of internal dynamics of economies such as the US. It could also be used to provide results for comparison with those of more traditional and established business cycle methodologies and to reexamine the validity of stylized facts.

The structure of this paper is as follows: In Section 2 we briefly discuss phase space reconstruction and the basics of RQA. In Section 3 we present the RQA results on a set of macroeconomic time series and simulated sequences. Finally in Section 4 we conclude providing pointers for future research.

2 Recurrence Quantification Analysis

According to embedding theorems developed by Takens and others (Takens [61]; Sauer et al. [56]), phase space dynamics can be faithfully reconstructed in a pseudo phase-space by *delay coordinate embedding* [4] from a system's single observable output. For example, in the case of modeling an economy as a complex system, as such an observable we can accept the Gross Domestic Product (GDP) or the level of unemployment. Time series embedding answers to the problem of unfolding the dynamics as received from one dimensional time series, preferably obtaining through this process a good idea of the dimensionality of the original phase-space dynamics. When the examined sequence obeys to random dynamics, the original phase space will be most probably of a very high dimension and the dynamics of the system-economy will be characterized by a very high entropy. However, if its dynamics follow chaotic laws, they are expected to be concentrated in a small area of the phase space which will be of low dimensionality.

The reconstruction of the phase-space dynamics is achieved via the determination of the embedding dimension d_E and the time delay τ. The embedding technique

---

[4] Also known as *time series embedding*.

simply generates a set of vectors which are lagged non-homogeneous sub-samples of the original series. Defining the original time-series process x as vector of N elements:

$$x_1, x_2, x_3, \ldots, x_N, \tag{1}$$

the following sequence of vectors can be generated:

$$y_1, y_2, y_3, \ldots, y_m, \tag{2}$$

where $m = N - (d_E - 1)\tau$, d_E is the embedding dimension and τ the time delay. Hence the m vectors from (2) consist of d_E elements:

$$y_k = [x_k, x_{k+\tau}, x_{k+2\tau}, \ldots, x_{k+(d_E-1)\tau}] = \mathbf{y}(k), \tag{3}$$

for $k=1,2,\ldots,m$. In the special case of $d_E=1$ we obtain a one dimensional embedding which is equivalent to no embedding at all. It is obvious that the whole embedding exercise is based on the determination of the parameters d_E and τ. Inappropriate choice of their values can either prevent the discovery of any low-dimensional dynamics or lead to false positive indications of nonlinear-deterministic structure. However, for the purpose of RQA it has been shown lately that embedding is not such a crucial issue (see Section 2.1).

Phase portraits (i.e., delay scatter plots) can be used to visualize nonlinear dynamics. However, they can be realized in two or three dimensional representations and can sometimes provide mixed or unclear information. Another effective way to visualize phase space dynamics from a reconstruction as in equations (2-3), are recurrence plots introduced by Eckmann et al. [21]. Thresholded recurrence plots (also called "recurrence matrices") are simply the graphical representation of a matrix computed according to the following equation:

$$\mathbf{R}_{i,j} = \Theta(\varepsilon - \|\mathbf{y}(i) - \mathbf{y}(j)\|), \quad i, j = 1, \cdots, m, \tag{4}$$

where $\mathbf{y}$ denotes the vectors obtained from an embedding, $\Theta(\bullet)$ is the Heaviside function and ε is a predefined threshold (also called "resolution"), and measured usually in units of the standard deviation of the time series x. By construction of the recurrence matrix, the probability of a recurrence occurring at a point with coordinates (i,j) $(i, j \leq m)$ is given by the correlation integral for the time series, which measures the probability that two points are within a certain distance ε from one another:

$$C(\varepsilon) = \frac{2}{m(m-1)} \sum_{i=1}^{m} \sum_{j=1}^{i-1} \Theta(\varepsilon - \|\mathbf{y}(i) - \mathbf{y}(j)\|). \tag{5}$$

Recurrence matrices may be very dense or relatively sparse, depending on the dynamics observed. They are square symmetrical $m \times m$ grids of 1 and 0 values denoting closeness or distance of the embedded vectors, according to the Heaviside function. Usually black color is assigned to close points when graphically representing thresholded recurrence matrices. A black dot simply shows that the system returns to the ε-neighborhood of the corresponding point in phase space, hence the term "recurrence" (see Figure 2). Due to construction, the upper and lower triangular areas of the plots are symmetrical as the distance $\|\mathbf{y}(i) - \mathbf{y}(j)\|$ is the same as $\|\mathbf{y}(j) - \mathbf{y}(i)\|$. All the 45 degree angle (lower) diagonal elements are darkened as every vector is close to itself. If we omit the Heaviside function in eq. (4), we obtain what is loosely termed as a global recurrence plot, a colored version of the thresholded one, where a predefined set of colors measures the range of distances between all embedded vectors(Figure 1). In thresholded plots, strong recurrent and deterministic dynamics will appear as repeating patterns and parallel line segments to the lower diagonal. Random dynamics lead usually to unstructured recurrence plots with homogeneously distributed points all over the diagram (refer to Antoniou and Vorlow [2] and Casdagli [20] for examples). Usually a change in the density of recurrence plots and diagonal segments (lines) are evidence enough of nonstationarity and chaotic dynamics respectively. However, the interpretation of these diagrams can often be very difficult and the results may be misleading or subjective.

Following Marwan [44] we can interpret recurrence plots via large scale (*typology*) and small scale patterns (*texture*). The typology gives us a general concept of the involved dynamics and can be classified as homogeneous, periodic, drifting or disrupted. Homogeneity in recurrence points usually implies that the system observed is characterized by stationary and autonomous dynamics, such as the random processes. Periodic structures such as diagonal lines or patterns, appear in plots of systems that are characterized by periodic or chaotic oscillations. The more complex the periodic structures the more complex the recurrence plot will be. Drift is observed by a change in the density of the recurrent points around the main diagonal. The upper left and lower right corners of the plots are less dense in points for systems with slowly varying dynamics. Finally, sudden changes of dynamics and extreme events can cause large areas of the plots to be vacant.

Small scale structures (texture) can be defined on the basis of recurrence point formations. Isolated recurrences can be observed for rare states or heavy fluctuations, though they are not unique indications of noise or randomness (Marwan [44]). Strongly chaotic systems will be replete with parallel line segments. This simply indicates that trajectories visit the same regions of phase space at different times. The length of these segments are an indication of the duration of these "visits" and is related to the Lyapunov exponents of the system. Line segments sometimes appear to be perpendicular to the main diagonal (45 degrees). These can often be a good indication of an unfortunate selection of embedding parameters (Marwan [44]). Sometimes strong vertical (and horizontal due to the symmetry of recurrence plots) lines will appear. These are typical in systems that exhibit intermittent dynamics (such as atmospheric turbulence) and their length is an indication of the time for which the system remains in a stable state or exhibits very slow dynamics, referred to as laminar states.

The reader can observe several of the typology and texture classification criteria in both unthresholded (Figure 1) and thresholded recurrence plots (Figure 2). However it becomes apparent that an unfortunate selection of either the graphical resolution or the size of the recurrence plot, can severely distort our view of the dynamics and introduce bias in interpretation. One obvious way to improve the informational content of recurrence plots is to focus on magnified portions of the matrices and inspect these for line segments and other indications of nonlinear and complex dynamics (see Figure 3). However, this achieves still a rather subjective and qualitative view of the phase space dynamics. To overcome the above limitations of the simple visual inspection of recurrence plots, Zbilut and Webber [69] have introduced (RQA) methodology, based on the information contained in recurrence matrices. RQA allows for the determination of an array of measures that can indicate even more precisely whether the dynamics of the system are governed by randomness or complexity and deterministic chaos. The RQA measurement set has been enriched by the work of Marwan [44] and for our analysis here, we will be utilizing the following subset of available RQA metrics:

1. Recurrence (REC) is defined as the percentage of recurrent points in an RP:

$$\text{REC} = \frac{1}{m^2} \sum_{i,j=1}^{m} \mathbf{R}_{i,j}. \tag{6}$$

   Usually, when the threshold level ε increases, the percentage level of recurrent points in the recurrence matrix is expected to increase.

2. Determinism (DET) is defined as the percentage of recurrence points which form diagonal lines (segments) parallel to the main diagonal:

$$\text{DET} = \frac{\sum_{l=l_{min}}^{m} lP(l)}{\sum_{i,j}^{m} \mathbf{R}_{i,j}}, \tag{7}$$

   where l denotes length of diagonal line and $P(l)$ denotes the frequency (distribution) of l length parallel to the main diagonal segments in the RP. In the case of a deterministic-chaotic system, these parallel line segments are an indication of the trajectories being close in phase space for time scales that are equal to the length of the segments. However, very long lines should be regarded as an indication of non-chaotic periodicity.

3. The longest diagonal line is defined as:

$$\text{L}_{max} = \max(\{l_i; i = 1, 2, \cdots, N_l\}), \tag{8}$$

   where N_l denotes the number of lines that appear in the plot. L_{max} is inversely proportional to the maximal (positive) Lyapunov exponent of the sequence and is also referred to as "divergence".

4. Entropy:

$$\text{ENT} = - \sum_{l=l_{min}}^{m} p(l) \ln p(l). \tag{9}$$

This does not refer to the entropy of the sequence or the system but the entropy of the distribution of the lines in the recurrence plot. It is a good indicator of the structure of the overall plot and the complex deterministic character of the underlying dynamics.

5. Trend:

$$\text{TREND} = \frac{\sum_{i=1}^{\bar{m}} (i - \bar{m}/2)(\text{REC}_i - \langle \text{REC}_i \rangle)}{\sum_{i=1}^{\bar{m}} (i - \bar{m}/2)^2}. \tag{10}$$

This measures the paling of the plot towards the edges. It is estimated as the slope of the linear regression line of REC on the displacement from the main diagonal (excluding the last 10% of the total range) and is expressed in units of the percentage of local recurrence per 1000 points. It provides information on the stationarity of the process and the presence of any trend or drift.

6. Laminarity is an analogous definition to that of determinism (DET in eq. 7) and is defined as:

$$\text{LAM} = \frac{\sum_{v=v_{min}}^{m} v P(v)}{\sum_{v=1}^{m} v P(v)}, \tag{11}$$

where v denotes the length of the vertical line structure. The LAM measure shows the amount of vertical sections in the recurrence plot and indicates the occurrence of laminar states. It does not though provide any information on the duration of these states. LAM is low when there are more single recurrence points than vertical sections.

7. The average length of all laminar states (from eq. 11) is called "Trapping Time" and is defined as:

$$\text{TT} = \frac{\sum_{v=v_{min}}^{m} v P(v)}{\sum_{v=v_{min}}^{m} P(v)}. \tag{12}$$

This measures the average time the system spends "trapped" in a "laminar" state. It also provides an indication for the amount of laminar phases.

The RQA measures based on vertical structures are the contribution of Marwan [44] over the original work of Zbilut and Webber [69]. The main functionality of measures such as LAM and TT is that they allow us to determine chaos to chaos transitions, such as the ones that can be found in the logistic map ($x_{n+1} = a x_n (1 - x_n)$). Applications on physiological time series have proven that RQA can detect, quantify and forecast states that lead to catastrophic events (e.g. life-threatening cardiac arrhythmia).

2.1 Embedding Considerations

From the presentation of RQA so far, it becomes clear that the embedding dimension d_E, time delay τ and resolution ε parameters are of crucial importance to the generation of an "accurate" recurrence plot. As mentioned earlier, unfortunate choices can either hinder the discovery of low-dimensional dynamics or produce false positive indications of chaotic structure. However, Iwanski and Bradley [35] relaxed the necessity for accurate embedding whereas more recently Thiel et al. [66] show that with no embedding in recurrence plots, we can actually receive accurate and unbiased information on the complexity of the sequence under examination. In Atay and Altıntaş [5] it is also shown that the time delay τ may be more crucial than the embedding dimension d_E as the average length of line segments parallel to the main diagonal can be insensitive to the choice of the latter. Moreover, according to Thiel et al. [64], the most crucial statistic to quantify the predictability of the system via RQA, is the distribution of the diagonal line segments. It is also suggested that the topological reconstruction of an attractor from the thresholded recurrence plot is possible, whether the series exhibit deterministic or stochastic dynamics or a mixtures of those (see also Balakrishnan et al. [6]; Gao and Cai [26]). Thus recent research suggests that accurate embedding in the case of RQA may not be a crucial issue and this simplifies procedures considerably. In our analysis, following Iwanski and Bradley [35] and Thiel et al. [66], we adopt the strategy of $d_E = \tau = 1$ in all recurrence plots and quantification analysis of macroeconomic time series. Regarding the level of resolution ε, we follow Webber and Zbilut [67] who suggest a threshold level of the lower 10% of the maximum rescaled distance between all embedded vectors, using a maximum norm in equation (4). However, when the noise component is known, threshold levels up to five times its standard deviation may be appropriate as suggested in Thiel et al. [65] and Matassini et la. [45]. Although the noise content may be unknown in many economic and financial time series, existing techniques such as wavelets, can be used to preprocess the data before RQA and provide stronger evidence of recurrent dynamics (Antoniou and Volrow [3]). Recurrence plots and RQA have been used in the past in economics to analyze mainly financial time series and exchange rate sequences, however the methodology has still not enjoyed the same popularity as in the physical sciences (Antoniou and Volrow [2, 3]; Gilmore [27]; Holyst et al. [33]; McKenzie [48]; Belaire-Franch et al. [10]; Ferreira et al. [22]). This work can be regarded as a "pilot" application of RQA in macroeconomic time series analysis.

3 RQA Results

We applied RQA on a set of macroeconomic time series from the US economy as well as on some simulations of popular stochastic and chaotic processes. The macroeconomic data are monthly time series that span the period 1960 to 2002. We analyzed the growth rates (logarithmic differences) of five US macroeconomic time series: Interest Rates (NBER series 13002), the Consumer's Price Index (CPI all urban consumers, Bureau of Labor Statistics, series CUUROOOOAA0), the Industrial Production Index (NBER series 01001), the Dow Jones stock price index (NBER series 11009) and the Unemployment level (Bureau of Labor Statistics, series LNS13000000). The results of the RQA on the rates of these sequences are listed in Table 1. Some of the unthresholded recurrence plots are depicted in Figure 1, whereas thresholded recurrence plots are depicted in Figure 2.

An immediate observation from the tabulated results is that the recurrence plots of the macroeconomic data suggest a very strong nonstochastic nature for the underlying dynamics. The level of DET ranges between 16% (Industrial Production Index) to 70% (Interest Rate), which shows that the recurrence plots are replete with parallel line segments to the main diagonal. This has a serious implication on the predictability of the sequences as the low entropies of the distributions of these lines

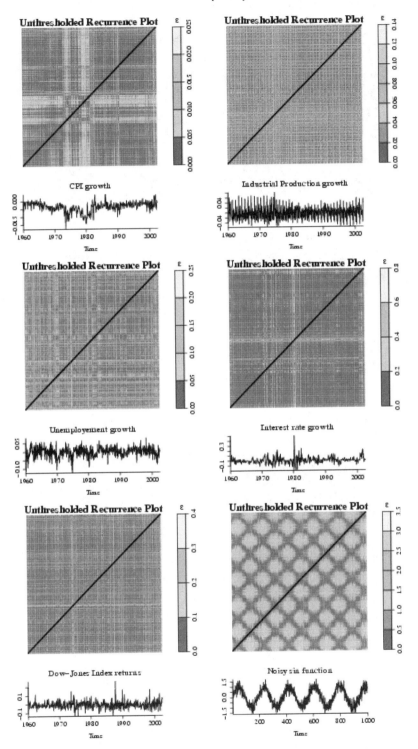

Fig. 1. Unthresholded Recurrence Plots. From left to right, top to bottom: CPI, Industrial Production, Unemployment, Interest Rate, Dow Jones Stock Index, Sine with noise.

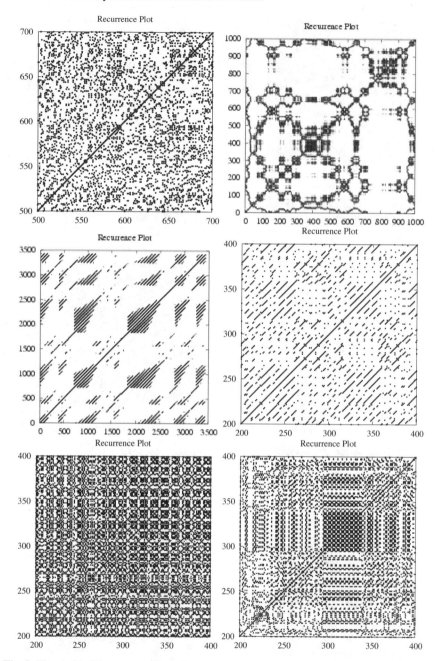

Fig. 2. Thresholded Recurrence Plots. From left to right, top to bottom: White Noise, Brownian Motion, Lorenz attractor, Hénon attractor, Industrial Production index growth (detail), and detail of Mackey-Glass process from equation (13).

	REC	DET	ML	ENT	TREND	LAM	TT
CPI	43.967%	43.503%	30	2.417	27.629	59.523%	6.760
Ind. Prod.	30.842%	16.020%	36	2.095	-5.406	16.497%	4.471
Int. Rate	66.346%	70.165%	91	3.494	33.115	79.543%	11.253
DJ Returns	53.168%	38.000%	26	2.224	1.503	45.431%	5.928
Unemployment	39.002%	20.215%	13	1.755	-11.743	30.670%	5.382
Hénon	6.364%	81.229%	33	2.697	-0.029	5.194%	2.568
Lorenz	29.266%	96.398%	3496	4.908	-0.396	99.470%	22.327
ARIMA(1,1,1)	2.493%	2.801%	7	1.086	-4.599	1.262%	5.125
white noise	3.965%	0.006%	5	0.000	0.097	0.000%	N/A
MG	34.153%	19.738%	167	4.084	-0.055	0.006%	10.000
noisyMG	50.246%	2.110%	25	2.197	-0.154	9.616%	12.444
s-noisyMG	49.054%	20.050%	28	2.073	-0.276	35.091%	6.866

Table 1. RQA results.

(ENT) also suggest very strong non-random dynamics. When these results are compared to those of random or chaotic sequences, we see that the recurrence plots of the macroeconomic data reveal similar dynamics to those of the Hénon and Lorenz attractors (for details for the chaotic processes and their phase space reconstruction parameters refer to Sprott [60]). These attractors reveal the highest level of DET as expected. On the other side, simulated normal noise and ARIMA processes (the AR and MA coefficients are 0.5), exhibit very low levels of deterministic structures and recurrent points in their recurrence plots. The laminar states (LAM) are also lower for these processes than the rest of the data with the random sequence having the lowest measurements. The trapping time (TT) statistic shows that the periods of slowly drifting dynamics or stable states range between 4 (Industrial Production Index) and 11 months (Interest Rate). In a nutshell, the macroeconomic data reveal dynamics in the recurrence plots that can be characterized as complex-deterministic as opposed to the random-stochastic ones of the autoregressive and random processes. For all the macroeconomic sequences we used an embedding dimension $D_E=1$, a time delay $\tau=1$ and a threshold level of $\varepsilon=10\%$ of the maximum rescaled distance between embedded vectors of each sequence. The rest of the sequences where embedded according to the stylized facts on the reconstruction of their phase space dynamics (Zbilut and Webber [69]; Sprott [60]; Webber and Zbilut [67]; Marwan [44]). The above results agree with the typology and texture classification criteria as outlined in Section 2. In Figure 2 we can also see very clearly the differences between the recurrence plots of the simulated processes and the Industrial Production Index, which exhibits a high level of deterministic dynamics.

Visual inspection of all recurrence plots confirms the story of the RQA results as discussed in the previous paragraph and tabulated in Table 1. In Figure 1, the unthresholded plots show a wealth of complexity of dynamics in all macroeconomic sequences. Detailed examination of the plots revealed that outliers were reported by the recurrence plots in all macroeconomic sequences with similar time signatures.

These refer mainly to the financial oil crises of the 70's, strongly evident in the CPI recurrence plot as light colored vertical and horizontal segments. The unthresholded recurrence plots are more informative. A comparison of known chaotic processes, such as the Hénon and Lorenz sequences, with details of the plot for the Industrial Production index, show that the latter exhibits more the characteristics of the former than those of random sequences. Careful examination of the recurrence plots of the macroeconomic sequences revealed that they were replete with small diagonal segments which could imply the presence of strong quasi-periodic components in their data generating processes. However, we should point out that the macroeconomic sequences we examine are monthly time series, thus even small parallel segments to the main diagonal are of crucial importance for the classification of the observed dynamics. Series with a finer resolution, such as daily stock index returns, reveal more details as we can see in Figure 3. There we can easily discern the diagonal lines of some length, which may imply strong non-linear determinism present in the FTSE index returns.

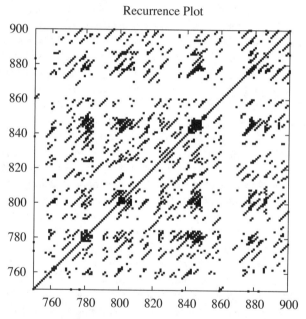

Fig. 3. A detail of a thresholded recurrence plot for daily FTSE all share returns since 1/1/1970 (8192 daily observations).

Interesting features presents the high-dimensional Mackey-Glass (MG) equation as studied in Kyrtsou and Terraza [40]. In our simulation the following discrete form is used:

$$x_t = 2.1 \frac{x_{t-1}}{1 + x_{t-1}^{30}} - 0.05 x_{t-1}. \tag{13}$$

As it can be seen in Table 1, for a MG simulated process as in equation (13), we obtain high levels for determinism and entropy. The addition of noise to the deterministic sequence perturbs the initial results. Adding a heteroskedastic stochastic part in the first equation we get the noisy Mackey-Glass model (noisyMG), originally proposed by Kyrtsou and Terraza [40]. The radical change in the empirical findings, when heteroskedastic noise is present in process MG, could mean that in reality the underlying deterministic structure is more complex. As a first attempt to identify such structures, we simulate a heteroskedastic MG with additive seasonality (s-noisyMG). Looking again at Table 1 we observe that the RQA measures for s-noisyMG take values which are closer to those obtained for the US macroeconomic series. This may imply some qualitative resemblance in the gata generating processes of our simulated time series and the original macroeconomic sequences.

The message that recurrence plots deliver is that the sequences are characterized by complex dynamics. The extent to which this complexity may imply chaos can be assessed by the RQA results of Table 1 which suggest the presence of strong nonlinear determinism. However to maintain the hypothesis of chaos, while our results do not refute it, a more rigorous empirical framework is suggested (Kantz and Schreiber [36]; Abarbanel [1]; Kyrtsou [39]; Antoniou and Vorlow [4]), combining RQA with statistics based on invariant measures and a statistical hypothesis testing framework (Theiler et al. [63]).

4 Conclusions and Future Research

In the previous section we presented RQA results on a set of macroeconomic time series from the US economy. As the RQA measures suggest,the macroeconomic sequences are characterized by a nonlinear dynamic structure that could even be considered to be chaotic. The significant levels of determinism imply nonlinear predictability whereas there is also a strong indication of the presence of complex cycles and laminar states. The existence also of high-dimensional underlying dynamics cannot be excluded. The comparison of the results on real data and simulations reveals that macroeconomic variables behave more complexly, rather like either chaotic or noisy chaotic sequences than pure random signals. This is also corroborated by the visual information provided by the recurrence plots. The above results can be regarded a step bringing us closer to understanding economic dynamics as highly complex and possibly chaotic. While we do not exclude the existence of chaos, its verification in our case should involve a more rigorous investigation, possibly utilizing a Monte-Carlo statistical hypothesis testing framework. Such an exercise could be realized by employing *Surrogate Data Analysis* (Theiler et al. [63]) which allows to test for the presence of "weak" chaos and the absence of linear stochastic dynamics.

References

1. Abarbanel HDI (1995) Analysis of observed ohaotic data. New York: Springer-Verlag

2. Antoniou A, Vorlow CE (2000) Recurrence plots and financial time series analysis. Neural Network World 10: 131-146
3. Antoniou A, Volrow CE (2004) Recurrence quantification analysis of wavelet pre-filtered index returns. Physica A: Statistical Mechanics and its Applications 334: 257-262
4. Antoniou A, Volrow CE (2005) Price clustering and discreteness: Is there chaos behind the noise? Physica A: Statistical Mechanics and its Applications 348: 389-403
5. Atay FM, Altıntaş Y (1999) Recovering smooth dynamics from time series with the aid of recurrence plots. Physical Review E 59: 6593-6598
6. Balakrishnan V, Nicolis G, Nicolis C (2000) Recurrence time statistics in deterministic and stochastic dynamical systems in continuous time: A comparison. Physical Review E 61: 2490-2499
7. Barnett WA, Chen P (1988) The aggregation-theoretic monetary aggregates are chaotic and have strange attractors: An econometric application of mathematical chaos. In Barnett WA, Berndt ER, White H (eds), Dynamic econometric modeling: Proceedings of the third international symposium in economic theory and econometrics, Cambridge University Press
8. Barnett W, Hinich H (1993) Has chaos been discovered with economic data? In Ping C, Richard D (eds) Evolutionary dynamics and nonlinear economics, Oxford University Press
9. Baumol W, Benhabib J (1989) Chaos: Significance, mechanism, and economic applications. Journal of Economic Prespectives 3: 77-105
10. Belaire-Franch J, Contreras D, Tordera-Lledo L (2002) Assessing nonlinear structures in real exchange rates using recurrence plot strategies. Physica D: Nonlinear Phenomena 171: 249-264
11. Boldrin M, Woodford M (1990) Equilibrium models displaying endogenous fluctuations and chaos: A survey. Journal of Monetary Economics 25: 189-222
12. Bordignon S, Lisi F (2001) Predictive accuracy for chaotic economic models. Econonomics Letters 70: 51-58
13. Brock W (1990) Chaos and complexity in economics and financial science. In von Furtenberg G (ed) Acting under uncertainty: Multidisciplinary conceptions, Kluwer
14. Brock WA (1991) Causality, chaos, explanation and prediction in economics and finance. In Casti JL and Karlqvist A (eds) Beyond belief: Randomness, prediction and explanation in science, CRC Press
15. Brock WA, Dechert WD (1991) Non-linear dynamical systems: Instability and chaos in economics. In Hildenbrand W and Sonnenschein H (eds) Handbook of mathematical economics, Amsterdam: North-Holland
16. Brock WA, Hsieh DA, LeBaron B (1991) Nonlinear dynamics, chaos, and instability: Statistical theory and economic evidence. MIT Press
17. Brock WA, Sayers CL (1988) Is the business cycle characterized by deterministic chaos? Journal of Monetary Economics 22: 71-90
18. Bullard JB, Butler A (1993) Nonlinearity and chaos in economic models: Implications for policy decisions. Economic Journal 103: 849-867
19. Butler A (1990) A methodological approach to chaos: Are economists missing the point? Federal Reserve Bank of St. Louis Review 72: 36-48
20. Casdagli MC (1997) Recurrence plots revisited. Physica D: Nonlinear Phenomena 108: 12-44
21. Eckmann JP, Oliffson KS, Ruelle D (1987) Recurrence plots of dynamical systems. Europhysics Letters 4: 973-977

22. Ferreira FF, Francisco G, Machado BS, Muruganandam P (2003) Time series analysis for minority game simulations of financial markets. Physica A: Statistical Mechanics and its Applications 321: 619-632

23. Frank MZ, Gencay R, Stengos T (1988) International chaos? European Economic Review 32: 1569-1584

24. Frank MZ, Stengos T (1988) Some evidence concerning macroeconomic chaos. Journal of Monetary Economics 22: 423-438

25. Frank MZ, Stengos T (1988) Chaotic dynamics in economic time-series. Journal of Economic Surveys 2: 103-133

26. Gao JB, Cai HQ (2000) On the structures and quantification of recurrence plots. Physics Letters A 270: 75-87

27. Gilmore CG (2001) An examination of nonlinear dependence in exchange rates, using recent methods from chaos theory. Global Finance Journal 12: 139-151

28. Grandmont J-M (1985) Endoggenous competitive business cycles. Econometrica 53: 995-1045

29. Grandmont J-M (1987) Nonlinear economic dynamics. Academic Press

30. Grandmont J-M (1987) Stabilizing competitive business cycles. In Grandmont J-M (ed) Nonlinear economic dynamics, Academic Press

31. Granger CWJ (1994) Is chaotic economic theory relevant for economics? Journal of International and Comparative Economics 3: 139-145

32. Hommes CH (2001) Fianncail markets as non-linear adaptive evolutionary systems. Quantitative Finance 1: 149-167

33. Holyst J, Zebrowska M, Urbanowicz K (2001) Observations of deterministic chaos in financial time series by recurrence plots, can one control chaotic economy? The European Physical Journal B 20: 531-535

34. Hsieh DA (1991) Chaos and nonlinear dynamics: Application to financial markets. Journal of Finance 46: 1839-1877

35. Iwanski JS, Bradley E (1998) Recurrence plots of experimental data: To embed or not to embed? Chaos 8: 861-871

36. Kantz H, Schreiber T (1997) Nonlinear time series analysis. Cambridge University Press

37. Kellert SH (1994) In the wake of chaos: Unpredictable order in dynamical systems. University of Chicago Press.

38. Kesley D (1988) The economics of chaos or the chaos of economics. Oxford Economic Papers 40: 1-31

39. Kyrtsou C (2005) Evidence for neglected non-linearity in noisy chaotic models. International Journal of Bifurcation and Chaos, in press

40. Kyrtsou C, Terraza M (2003) Is it possible to study chaotic and ARCH behaviour jointly? Application of a noisy Mackey-Glass equation with heteroskedastic errors to the Paris Stock Exchange returns series. Computational Economics 21: 257-276

41. Liu T, Granger CWJ, Heller W (1992) Using the correlation exponent to decide if an economic series is chaotic. Journal of Applied Econometrics 7: 25-39

42. Mandelbrot BB (1982) The fractal geometry of nature. San Francisco: WH Freeman

43. Mandelbrot BB, Hudson RL (2004) The (mis)behavior of markets: A fractal view of risk, ruin, and reward. Profile Business

44. Marwan N (2003) Encounters with neighbours: Currenrt developments of concepts based on recurrence plots and their applications. PhD thesis, Institute of Physics, Potsdam University

45. Matassini L, Kantz H, Holyst J, Hegger R (2002) Optimizing of recurrence plots for noise reduction. Physical Review E 65:021-102

46. Mayer-Kress G (1996) Messy futures and global brains. In Kravtsov YA and Kadtke JB (eds) Predictability of complex dynamical systems, Springer Verlag
47. Mayfield ES, Mizrach B (1992) On determining the dimension of real-time stock-price data. Journal of Business and Economic Statistics 10: 367-374
48. McKenzie MD (2001) Chaotic behavior in national stock market indices: New evidence from the close returns test. Global Finance Journal 12: 35-53
49. Mirowski P (1989) 'tis a pity econometrics isn't an empirical endeavor: Mandelbrot, chaos, and the Noah and Joseph effects. Ricerche Economiche 43: 76-99
50. Mirowski P (1990) From Mandelbrot to chaos in economic theory. Southern Economic Journal 57: 289-307
51. Osborne AR, Provenzale A (1989) Finite correlation dimension for stochastic systems with power-law spectra. Physica D 35: 357-381
52. Ott E, Grebogi C, Yorke JA (1990) Controlling chaos. Physical Review Letters 64: 1196-1199
53. Peters EE (1991) Chaos and order in the capital markets. New York: Wiley
54. Ramsey JB (1996) If nonlinear models cannot forecast, what use are they? Studies in Nonlinear Dynamics and Econometrics 1: 65-86
55. Ramsey JB, Sayers CL, Rothman P (1990) The statistical properties of dimension calculations using small data sets: Some economic applications. International Economic Review 31: 991-1020
56. Sauer T, Yorke JA, Casdagli M (1991) Embedology. Journal of Statistical Physics 65: 579-616
57. Scheinkman J (1990) Nonlinearities in economic dynamics. Economic Journal 100: 33-48
58. Scheinkman JA, LeBaron B (1989) Nonlinear dynamics and stock returns. Journal of Business 62: 311-337
59. Scheinkman JA, LeBaron B (1989) Nonlinear dynamics and GNP data. In Barnett WA, Geweke J, Shell K (eds) Economic complexity: Chaos, sunspots, bubbles, and nonlinearity, Proceedings of the fourth international symposium in economic theory and econometrics, Cambridge University Press
60. Sprott C (2003) Chaos and time-series analysis. Oxford University Press
61. Takens F (1980) Detecting strange attractors in turbulence. In Rand DA, Young L (eds) Dynamical systems and turbulence, Lecture notes in mathematics, Springer-Verlag
62. Theiler J (1986) Spurious dimensions from correlation algorithms applied to limited time-series data. Physical Review A 34: 2427-2432
63. Theiler J, Eubank S, Longtin A, Galdrikian B, Farmer JD (1992) Testing for nonlinearity in time series: the method of surrogate data. Physica D 58: 77-94
64. Thiel M, Romano MC, Kurths J (2004) How much information is contained in a recurrence plot? Physics Letters A, forthcoming.
65. Thiel M, Romano MC, Kurths J, Meucci R, Allaria E, Arecchi FT (2002) Influence of observational noise on the recurrence quantification analysis. Physica D: Nonlinear Phenomena 171: 138-152
66. Thiel M, Romano MC, Read PL, Kurths J (2004) Estimation of dynamical invariants without embedding by recurrence plots. Chaos 14(2)
67. Webber CL, Zbilut JP (1994) Dynamical assessment of physiological systems and states using recurrence plot strategies. Journal of Applied Physiology 76: 965-973
68. Wolff R (1990) A note on the behaviour of the correlation integral in the presence of a time series. Biometrika 77: 689-697
69. Zbilut JP, Webber CL (1992) Embeddings and delays as derived from quantification of recurrence plots. Physics letters A 171: 1991-214